PIETY AND POWER

PIETY AND POWER

THE ROLE OF THE
ITALIAN PARISHES IN THE
NEW YORK METROPOLITAN AREA,
1880-1930

by

SILVANO M. TOMASI

CENTER FOR MIGRATION STUDIES
1975

Piety and Power:
The Role of the Italian Parishes
in the New York Metropolitan Area,
1880-1930

First Edition

Copyright © 1975 by
The Center for Migration Studies of New York, Inc.

Center for Migration Studies
209 Flagg Place
Staten Island, New York 10304

ISBN 0-913256-16-1
Library of Congress Catalog Card Number: 74-79913
Printed in the United States of America

CONTENTS

PREFACE

The American Catholic Church, viewed from within, is neither monolithic nor homogeneous. The immigrant groups, which provided the amazing growth and vitality of American Catholicism, created parishes, schools, orphanages, hospitals and other institutions which reflected the new environment and the many cultural traditions and life-styles of their countries of origin. The variety of ethnic congregations within American Catholicism, however, was seen as a threat to its unity, as an anti-American label or as a useless complication.

This book looks at the experience of Italian immigrants within American Catholicism in order to understand the process of adaptation of immigrants in a new society and the use they made of religious institutions.

Limited to the study of the national parish and to the New York Metropolitan Area, this research was initially undertaken as a doctoral dissertation at Fordham University. Italian Americans, a major ethnic group in the population of the United States and a major component of the American Catholic population, were seen by writers of American church history simply as a 'problem'. Catholics of southern and eastern European, Mexican and French-Canadian origin, although forming the majority of American Catholics, were relegated to a few paragraphs in standard manuals of history and sociology. They constitute a flagrant case of ecclesiastical colonialism, which has distorted the interpretation of the social experience of American Catholicism.

The experience of Italian Americans provides a clear example of the need to re-write American church history by highlighting the people's expectations and values, rather than only hierarchical biographies. Along with these, the many documentary sources not written in English should be utilized.

First, this study outlines a concept of assimilation which rejects the traditional views of total conformity to Anglo-Protestant society and of the melting of cultures into some super-homogenized new one in which ethnic variations would no longer be visible. Assimilation is defined as a process of emergence of marginal immigrant groups into the power-plays of all the subgroups forming American society (Chapter I). Chapter II presents facts and figures on Italian immigrants and their social and religious background. The interpretations given to the arrival of Italian immigrants and the growth and activities of the Italian parishes constitute the central contribution of this work (Chapters III-V). The implication of the Italian experience for the role of pluralism in the American Catholic Church is briefly discussed in the conclusion (Chapter VI). Reference to pertinent books, pamphlets and articles is made in the bibliography, which completes the documentation cited in the footnotes following the various chapters.

Without the constant encouragement and guidance of many persons, this research would probably have never been completed. First are Joseph P. Fitzpatrick of Fordham University, under whose guidance I embarked on this research, and my brother Lidio, who daily reminded me of the unfinished task. Dr. Henry Browne, now of Rutgers University, made available to me the Archives of the Archdiocese of New York. Msgr. James King and Father Anthony Bevilacqua opened the archives of the Diocese of Brooklyn for me and Father Francis R. Seymour allowed me to use the archives of the Archdiocese of Newark. To all of them and to Father Mario Francesconi, the archivist of the Scalabrinian Congregation in Rome, I am deeply indebted.

Archival sources consulted extend from the archives of the Foreign Ministry of Italy to those of the Congregation for the Propagation of the Faith at the Vatican; of the Archdioceses of Boston and Baltimore; of the Diocese of Providence, R.I., and of scattered individual parishes. Particularly useful were the archives of the Centro Studi Emigrazione of Rome and of the Center for Migration Studies of New York. Although I touched many bases in the search for documents and found strong evidence to support my conclusions, it became apparent that a vast and unexplored field remains open to scholarly investigation. This first step will hopefully encourage others to analyze the experience of all immigrants and their children in the American pluralistic context of piety and power.

SILVANO M. TOMASI, C. S.

LIST OF TABLES

FIGURES

ABBREVIATIONS

AAB—Archives Archdiocese of Baltimore
AAN—Archives Archdiocese of Newark
AANY—Archives Archdiocese of New York
ACSC—Archives Congregation of Saint Charles (Rome)
ADB—Archives Diocese of Brooklyn
NTP—Norman Thomas Papers, New York Public Library
PFC—Propaganda Fide Calendar, Propaganda Fide Archives (Rome)

CHAPTER I

Americanization and Religion

Laborers and peasants arriving from southern and eastern Europe at the end of the nineteenth century soon discovered that in America they were a class of underdogs suitable for low paid and low prestige jobs. From the tenement house, the factory plant and the church basement, the promised land of the United States looked like a mixed blessing.

The dream of liberation from oppressive economic conditions and political systems had pushed the immigrants out of the villages of southern Italy and the plains of central Europe. The dream was now relegated to a distant future, after years of hard work, disappointments and humiliations. Before the fruits of the American promise could be reaped, the immigrants were confronted with the struggle of their affirmation in the new society. The process of learning a new language and a new life-style in the screeching noise of city subways and cars, so far removed from the sound of the church bell in the Old Country, was the complicated and overwhelming experience which formed today's America.

In this historical process of adjustment of the immigrants, religion played an important part. This study attempts to capture the role of religion in the americanization of the Italian immigrants.

Religion is seen as a combination of traditions, values and beliefs which shape a specific outlook on life and lead to the establishment of institutions for their preservation. Italian, German, Polish and other Catholic immigrants created for their own use a religious institution they did not share with the rest of America: the national parish. Unable

1

to participate on an equal footing in the existing English-language parishes and other religious structures of American society, the immigrants rallied around their own saints and priests to protect their self-respect and their piety. Thus, the history and the function of the ethnic parish for Italian immigrants was chosen as a specific field of research.

Political, economic and religious institutions, however, lead to integration to the extent that they are functional for the groups which form society, but generate conflict to the extent that these groups participate in them without equal opportunity. Immigrants, settling in a new environment, disturb the established ways of the host society. Their interests and customs are in conflict with those of the people receiving them. Work conditions, political power, housing, family style and religious preference are subjected to contrasting interpretations and play different functions for the newcomers than they do for their hosts.

The ethnic parish was born as a compromise between the demands of immediate assimilation and the resistence of immigrants to abandon their traditional religiosity. It was not accepted as equal to the territorial parish, established for all people within clearly defined boundaries rather than for people of a specific language, and it became a base for both integration and conflict.

In the system of government of the American Catholic dioceses, the ethnic parishes brought about structural pluralism. Their different cultural manifestations and their subordinate political position gave origin to a new network of churches for the exclusive service of the immigrants, but under the accepted control of the bishops. The American Catholic bishops came to preside in this way over two or more networks of Irish, Italian, Polish and German parishes and charitable institutions.

The point of view adopted in this study is, in fact, that pluralism in American society derives from the different cultures of the immigrant groups and their different position in the control of the levers of power. This pluralism was present and still persists as a major social dimension of the Church.

Two lines of analysis, therefore, are pursued in order to outline an adequate theoretical framework: the social function of the ethnic parish and the process of assimilation of immigrant groups in the American context of pluralism.[1]

The Ethnic Parish and Assimilation.

Warner and Srole found the national church in Yankee City to be a subsystem within two different systems: the national social system of the country in which it appears, and the extended church system. The church was the first line of defense behind which the immigrants could organize themselves and preserve their group identity. Not only was the church the first formally organized structure of the ethnic community system in Yankee City, it was the only structure that, at least initially, was a close reproduction of a structural type characteristic of the national society of origin. After analyzing the different cases of the Irish, the Jews, the Italians, the Greeks and the French-Canadians, the writers conclude: "The church structure of an ethnic group threatened with loss of identity serves more than any other structure to organize the group as a community system." [2] The church structures functioned to maintain the ethnic personality type by organizing the group around religious and cultural symbols and the behavioral modes of the country of origin. This role of social integration was reconfirmed by Nahirny and Fishman, who also responded to the criticism that attempts of ethnic minorities to maintain the integrity of their group tend to reinforce the already existing system of stratification. They noted how mass immigration from Eastern and Southern Europe, and possibly from Ireland as well, came from primordial collectivities. The immigrants conceived their ethnic identity in terms of concrete and particular symbols. For them religion was fused with all the institutions and roles of society. It was more a way of life than a prescribed set of beliefs and practices. In America, the peasant way of life had to be consciously reconstituted as well as readjusted to the conditions of the city.[3] The fact that the immigrants most successfully transplanted their religion, an aspect of their old way of life which had been institutionally sustained in the old country, is significant. Religious organizations "became, in fact, the focal point of the immigrants' communal life as well as the mainstay of their ethnicity." [4]

The ethnic parish, was not only an efficient instrument of social control; it even sanctioned, to a degree, the cultural change in the ethnic community. This was an indispensable condition for its proper functioning as a subsystem of the national society. If ethnic stratification is viewed as an on-going process rather than as a structure, then we may say that the ethnic parish presided over the change from a communal to an associational society, a transition necessary for the social mobility and the integration of the immigrants.

In discussing the institutions and patterns of communication of the Addams area in Chicago, Suttles shows how there also the "church (for the ethnic groups) provides a common establishment where a continuing group of people waive their individuality in favor of their common welfare." [5] He points out the distinction between being 'moral,' or practicing religion, and being 'religious,' or having a world view and attitude shaped by religion. This distinction helps to understand why the Italian church in that neighborhood is considered the most powerful single institution and is often the scene of informal arrangements between the Italians and the other ethnic groups. Mexicans, Negroes and Puerto Rican groups in the area are at a disadvantage in comparison with the Italians, whose church united them as a residential and ethnic congregation. Since most other bodies of social control refuse to acknowledge the ethnic sections in the Addams area, the church is virtually the only one that local residents can potentially make their own and whose services they can freely claim as their right.[6]

The Greek Orthodox church played a similar role in the assimilation process of Greek Americans. It has been among the main unifying structures in the community. Vlachos, for example, concludes that Greek Americans were held together psychologically by the church, which embodied the ethics and ideals they believed and the socio-religious rituals they cherished.[7]

The key role of institutionalized religion among the Irish has been discussed many times, more recently by Herberg and Shannon, who emphasized the key function of the local church in the political and social life of the ethnic community.[8]

For the Polish immigrants, the parish became the "old primary community, reorganized and concentrated." W. I. Thomas and F. Znaniecki describe the new immigrant parish in *The Polish Peasant* as a reconstruction of the parish and the commune of the old country which served as a "framework for the permanent organization of the community." In the American Polonia, to use Thomas and Znaniecki's words, "the church organization was familiar to every member of the community; it had firmly established forms and well trained professional leaders; it introduced at once a contact between the activities of the community and a world-wide system of activities."[9]

In England, as in the American experience, immigrants and other marginal and minority groups of society have often resorted to religious forms to find refuge against the stresses and strains of settling down in a new country. Reporting on West Indian immigrants, Calley found that sects and sect-like religious institutions "form a buffer between the immigrant group and society. They cushion the impact on the individual of a new way of life in a new type of society having unfamiliar values."[10]

The absorption of immigrants into a new society is a process requiring acquisition of new skills, performance of new roles and the reformation of a self-image. This process of resocialization brings about rapid social change with consequent insecurity and disorganization for the individual and the group. Anomie and alienation are also felt toward the established religious institutions of the new society. Thus, alternate social forms are developed. Sociologists like Max Weber, Ernst Troeltsch, and Richard H. Niebuhr have shown, in fact, that the normal religious institutional response to a position of deprivation in society has been a sectarian one. The sect, as opposed to the church, is a vehicle for the marginal group to elaborate their own social solidarity, to enjoy group rituals, to participate in group life with a feeling of worthwhileness. It is also characterized by separatism and defiance of, or withdrawal from, the demands of the secular sphere; by preference of isolation to compromise; by exclusiveness expressed in attitude and social structure; by conversion and voluntary joining.[11] But a strictly sectarian response would certainly block the process of assimilation. To this effect, Eisenstadt has pointed out that the immigrant process of re-socialization starts from an already given social basis: the groups within which the immigration process took place. Primary groups are transformed by developing group values and aspirations compatible with the values and roles of the absorbing society and capable of being realized within it. The formation of new channels of communications with the wider society and the extension of activities beyond the primary group are also vehicles for its transformation. Between the immigrants and the absorbing society there is, in general, some incompatibility in role expectations and in role demands. A full analysis of the absorbing society is necessary. "If the ultimate success of institutionalization," continues Eisenstadt, "from the immigrants point of view, is the attainment of a new stable status and status-image, then clearly it entails full acceptance by and participation in the absorbing society."[12] The change brought about in the adoptive society results in a pluralistic structure. Here the immigrant accepts and performs the universal roles of the host society, while preserving some specific values and adapting them to the new country.

The immigrants were caught between the tendency toward sectarian separatism and the process of re-socialization leading to institutionalization and pluralization. The existing literature of the sociology of religion gives strong indications that the ethnic parish played a role of mediation. To the extent that the ethnic parish was a *religious organization,* its mediating role affected the universal church. To the extent that it was a strong *social organization* of the immigrant community, it affected society at large.

Group Assimilation in America.

A model of cultural and social assimilation of immigrant groups in American society can be built by taking into consideration the independent variables of time, position of the immigrant groups in society and reduplication of institutions. The dynamics of interaction of an immigrant group with the host-society depend on the historical moment of immigration and insertion into a new political and economic system; on the structural position of the immigrant group within this system; and on the structurally derived type of social relationship. The immigrant group acts as a new subsystem versus the original establishment as the total system. The area of contact of the two systems, analyzed from the viewpoint of institutional linkage, offers the social space where functionality and conflict play the role of mutual checks. The emerging equilibrium is situated at constantly different levels due to the evolution of the time variable affecting the interacting systems.

Stage I: Marginality, Conflict and Discrimination.

The legal and ideological premises of American society[13] are such that assimilation and pluralization are not mutually exclusive. New immigrant groups, the Italian in particular, began at the bottom of the social scale. As a consequence of their poverty and marginality they had no control over the institutions on which they depended for employment, politics, education, health, and justice. Geographically and socially isolated, they began to perceive themselves as separate. The awareness of the immigrants' separateness was brought about by their cultural diversity and by the institutions which emerged from their culture. On the other hand, the awareness of a frustration of expectations set the conditions for conflict outside, and solidarity inside, the ethnic group. External and subconscious cultural traits and discrimination impeded immediate cultural assimilation and participation in the institutional system of the host society.

At this stage there is acceptance of cultural pluralism in the receiving society. Social pluralism, however, defined as "the segmentation of a society into groups and sets of institutions on a basis other than functional differentiation or pure duplication of culturally identical, undifferentiated units (such as lineage or clans)," is rejected.[14]

There is a minimum of institutional contact between the ethnic groups and the rest of society. There exists also a potential for primitive and violent manifestations of conflict, a situation favored by the psychological condition of anomie of the immigrants in the process of building a new image of themselves.[15]

Conflict, on the other hand, plays a significant and positive role. It forces the immigrants to perceive themselves as the receiving society does (as Italians, for example) rather than as an assemblage of small clans from the various villages of southern Italy. Thus, the immigrants

Figure I, 1. *A Model of Cultural and Social Assimilation*

	Historical Moment	Structural Position	Structurally derived type of social relations vs. the established social system	Assimilation
Stage I	of poverty and/or marginality	institutional dis-establishment vs. institutional establishment	separateness and de-socialization—violence and conflict	low cultural and social assimilation
Stage II	of transition or compromise	linkage between the two institutional systems	bargaining	begins cultural assimilation—low social assimilation
Stage III	of sufficient achievement and full citizenship	acceptance; outsiders become insiders and block other groups	collaboration	cultural assimilation—begins social assimilation

derive from their conflict with other ethnic groups already established
on the American scene a new social identity more universal and effective.

Both cultural and social assimilation are low. The host society's
process of pluralization is ambiguous. On an ideological level, the
receiving country (in this instance the United States) admits pluralism
legally but does not implement it socially.[16]

*Stage II: Transition, Ethnic Institutional Strength and
Bargaining.*

The economic and social marginality of the immigrant groups begins
to be remedied through the opportunities offered by the receiving society. These opportunities are found in the process of labor demand
and supply; the incipient process of resocialization in the educational
system; the individual mobility of the immigrants; and their ability to
form organized structures to serve their interest. The rise and growth of
ethnic labor unions, ethnic churches, hospitals, and social agencies,
took place immediately after the first impact of the adoptive country on
the immigrants and the consequent cultural shock, economic insecurity and psychological anomie. The institutional completeness of the
ethnic community[17] is correlated to its degree of ability to perform all
the services requested by its members. Breton writes that in contemporary North American cities very few, if any, ethnic communities can
be found showing full institutional completeness. It seems possible,
nonetheless, to state in historical perspective that most immigrant
groups to the United States passed through an experience revealing a
very high degree of institutional completeness. This transitional stage
applies well to "new immigration" groups.

Therefore, the Italian immigrants built a network of clubs, unions,
churches and newspapers, which brought about a "we-feeling" or con-
sciousness of ethnicity and community. This newly formed solidarity
absorbed many internal conflicts, developed ethnic leadership and an
institutional network which the established social system had to take
into account. Of the several institutions developed within the Italian
ethnic community, the church had a unique double function of
linkage with the past, where the immigrants' *weltanschauung* was
formed, and with the present, where new social and cultural roles were
learned. In this connection, Parsons regards the ethnic factor as a
secondary basis of stratification. It modifies the system in two ways: the
degree of accordance or variance of the subgroup's value system, and
the degree of accommodation or social integration of the group within
the larger culture.[18] Since he sees the systematic character of a social

system as given by the two characteristics of boundary maintenance and the tendency toward equilibrium, a new subsystem like the ethnic parish could modify the existing stratification lines only by accepting the standards already set up. But organizations may be viewed also as interacting social units, which are deliberately constructed toward the achievement of specific objectives.[19] This view tends to be confirmed by the available empirical evidence, scarce as it is, on the social role of the ethnic parish in the process of the immigrants' integration.

At this second stage of the paradigm a beginning of cultural assimilation is unavoidable, even though social assimilation is low, since the two institutional systems persist as indicators of differently structured groups.

Stage III: Achievement, Inclusion and Collaboration.

To understand the degree of assimilation and the dynamics of conflict and cooperation moving the immigrant group from a stage of separateness to one of collaboration, it is essential to focus on the linkage system between ethnic and national institutions. Once the internal cohesiveness of the ethnic groups is reached and the ability of bargaining in political and economic competitive situations is exercised, participation in the power structures and in the rewards of the larger society is unavoidable. The achievement of what has been defined as full citizenship[20] causes the initial outsiders to become insiders. The receiving society incorporates the new subgroup, thus increasing its own process of pluralization. The ethnic group, on the other hand, assumes the behavioral patterns of the national society. It collaborates within the total national system because of interdependence of political and economic interests, without necessarily losing its cultural identity.

The cycle of conflict, compromise and cooperation leads to a relationship of checks and balances for the interacting systems. It leads, also, to a new cycle of conflict, compromise and cooperation in relation to the newer marginal groups of recently arriving immigrants and to other economically and politically deprived groups. But the succession of structurally derived types of social interaction is not a mechanical process. Intervening variables may change the transition of the ethnic group from one stage to the next.

Formulation of Hypotheses.

The thrust of this research is directed mainly to the study of the second stage of the theoretical model. The ethnic parish is identified as a religious and social institution, emerging and operating in the Italian immigrant community and playing a relevant role in the process of linkage between the national and the ethnic social systems.

As a direction for research the following hypotheses are used:

1. The Italian immigrant community built the ethnic parish as a religious institution to meet the particularistic demands and expectations of a deprived group. The ethnic parish therefore assumed the character of a quasi-sect.

2. The ethnic parish also played a relevant role as a social institution in the process of the immigrants' assimilation as a symbol and an agent of group solidarity.

3. As a latent consequence of 1 and 2, the ethnic parish served as a system of universal mediation and linkage across ethnic boundaries. It served as one of the bases of power in the assimilation of the Italian immigrant group into the pluralistic structure of American society.

An exploratory study such as this, based on available materials, seeks first of all an insight into the total situation and aims at suggesting explanations. But an investigator may have one or two hypotheses deduced from sociological or psychological theory.[21] The latter approach helps in defining the field of research, increases its validity and establishes a more reliable base for the formulation of further hypotheses.

Conclusion.

The integration of new groups into American society cannot be understood without a total study of the patterns of intergroup relations and conflict typical of pluralistic societies. Marginal and immigrant groups, given certain conditions, can insert themselves into a pluralistic social context, following a process of interaction that reflects variables of time and social stratification. In this process, religious institutions can play a crucial role in terms of social solidarity, linkage and religious identification.

It is against this background of group assimilation that the religious experience of Italian immigrants arriving in the United States assumes an adequate perspective.

NOTES

1. An extensive discussion of the various theories of assimilation and pluralism is found in S. M. Tomasi, "Assimilation and Religion: The Role of the Italian Ethnic Church in the New York Metropolitan Area, 1880-1930," Ph. D. Thesis, Department of Sociology, Fordham University, 1972. Pp. 413. The methodology of this research is derived from historical sociology. (cf. ch. III of "Assimilation and Religon. . . ," op. cit.)

Since no systematic study of the significance of the Italian ethnic church has been done so far, the only present possibility of learning about its emergence, development and function is through the available documents. These are the documents that preserve the content of communication between the immigrants, their lay and ecclesiastical leadership, and the representatives of the host society.

There are three classes of extant documentary sources on the Italian ethnic church on which this research is based: (a) personal (b) publicly produced documents and (c) interviews.

a) *Personal documents* include letters of immigrants, unpublished diaries, memoranda, confidential ecclesiastical reports of official character, privately printed pamphlets and manifestos. But there is no systematic collection of materials pertaining to the Italians in America and the research for personal documents had to extend to several cities. In particular, the Archives of the Archdiocese of New York at Dunwoodie, of the Archdiocese of Newark, the Diocese of Brooklyn, the Archdioceses of Baltimore and Boston, have been useful for the many letters of Italian priests and of priests who served in Italian parishes. The archives preserve also many petitions and protests of immigrants and annual reports of ethnic parishes. The Archives of Propaganda Fide in Rome preserve the official letters of the American Catholic Hierarchy for the period under study, including special reports on national churches and Italian immigration.

The General Archives of the Congregation of St. Charles in Rome contain thousands of letters from Italian parishes in the United States and memoirs of priests who served Italian immigrant communities. The vast majority of these first-hand documents are in Italian, including the pertinent correspondence of the bishops of the New York Metropolitan Area. Occasionally, letters in Latin and French have been found. The documents mentioned have been utilized as primary sources. They have been selected on the basis of direct reference to the geographical area to which the research is limited. They are generally the product of first generation immigrants and reflect their world. Their translation into English, as used in the text, has been supplied by the writer.

b) *Publicly produced documents* include newspapers, population censuses, statistics and previous surveys by social scientists, magazine reports and books. The ethnic press of the Italian immigrants pays constant attention to the role of the ethnic church even if this attention is in the form of polemical controversies. Two Italian-language publications were found especially valuable for this study: *Il Carroccio* and *Il Crociato*, both of New York. *Il Bollettino dell'Emigrazione*, a bulletin of the Italian Foreign Ministry, has yielded important information from the consular reports from the United States. *L'Emigrato Italiano*, a monthly published in Italy since 1903, and *Italica Gens* (1910-1916), report regularly on Italian parishes in the United States. *The Assembly Herald, The Missionary Review of the World* and *La Rivista Evangelica del Nord America* (1899-1908), give, instead, extensive coverage to Protestant activities among Italian immigrants.

c) *Interviews.* To the written materials were added some, in depth, open-ended interviews held with people active in the first part of the century in the Italian communities. These interviews were given by the late Father Pio Parolin, C. S., the late Msgr. Nicholas Fusco, the late Dr. Carlo de Biasi, Msgr. Santi Privitera, Dr. Leonard Covello, Dr. Peter Riccio and a dozen first generation Italian men and women from the New York-Brooklyn area who were in the United States at least at the time of World War I. These interviews confirmed the general experience emerging from the personal documents and their testimony has been used as supportive evidence. The collection of data has followed a time-sequence and it reflects the trends of Italian immigration. The span of time within which the research is placed ranges from 1880 to 1930.

The analysis of this research is based on all available documentation on the Italian ethnic church. It is limited by the already established historical and geographical qualifications and by the medium of communication, the written personal and publicly produced documents. Three major themes were pursued as qualitative units of analysis: The Italian ethnic church 1) as a quasi-sect; 2) as an agent of social solidarity; 3) as a linkage system in a pluralistic society.

2. Lloyd W. Warner and Leo Srole, *The Social Systems of American Ethnic Groups.* New Haven: Yale University Press, 1949, p. 218.

3. Vladimir C. Nahirny, Joshua A. Fishman, "Ukrainian Language Maintenance Efforts in the United States," in Joshua Fishman, ed., *Language Loyalty in the United States.* The Hague: Mouton & Co., 1966. Pp. 318-357.

4. Ibid., op cit., pp. 330. For further discussion on the interplay of ethnicity and religion, see; "Religious Groups and Ethnic Group Identification or Withdrawal" in J. Milton Yinger. *Sociology Looks at Religion.* New York: The Macmillan Co., 1961. Pp. 89-113.

5. Gerald D. Suttles, *The Social Order of the Slum. Ethnicity and Territory in the Inner City.* Chicago: The University of Chicago Press, 1968, p. 42.

6. Ibid., op. cit., pp. 45.

7. Evangelos C. Vlachos, *The Assimilation of Greeks in the United States.* Athens: National Center for Social Researches, 1968, p. 105. cf. also: Theodore Saloutos, "The Greek Orthodox Church in the United States and Assimilation," *International Migration Review,* VII, 4 (Winter, 1973), 395-407; Philip, Kayal, "Religion and Assimilation: Catholic "Syrians" in America," Ibid., 409-425.

8. Will Herberg, *Protestant, Catholic, Jew.* New York: Doubleday, 1960. William Shannon, *The American Irish.* New York: Macmillan, 1966.

9. William I. Thomas and Florian Znaniecki, *The Polish Peasant in Europe and America.* New York: Dover Publications, 1958. Vol. II, p. 1525.

10. Malcom J. C. Calley, *God's People. West Indian Pentecostal Sects in England.* Issued under the auspices of the Institute of Race Relations. London: Oxford University Press, London, New York, 1965. Pp. 144-145. Anne Parsons, "The Pentecostal Immigrants: A Study of Ethnic Central City Church." *Journal for the Scientific Study of Religion,* Vol. 4, no. 2 (Spring, 1965), pp. 183-197.

Also Thomas F. Odea and Renato Poblete, S. J., "Anomie and the 'Quest for Community': The Formation of Sects Among the Puerto Ricans of New York," *The American Catholic Sociological Review,* vol. XXI, I(Spring, 1960), pp. 18-36.

11. Thomas F. O'Dea, "Mormonism and the Avoidance of Sectarian Stagnation: A Study of Church, Sect, and Incipient Nationality," *The American Journal of Sociology,* LX, (November 1954), p. 286.

12. S. N. Eisenstadt, *The Absorption of Immigrants. A Comparative Study Based Mainly on the Jewish Community in Palestine and the State of Israel.* Glencoe, Ill: The Free Press, 1955, p. 2 and Passim. Also, S. N. Eisenstadt, "The Process of Absorption of New Immigrants in Israel," *Human Relations,* Vol. V, 1952, pp. 223-246.

13. Talcott Parsons, "Full Citizenship for the Negro American? A Sociological Problem," in Talcott Parsons and Kenneth B. Clark, eds., *The Negro American.* Boston: Houghton, Mifflin, 1966, pp. 709-754.

14. Benjamin N. Colby and Pierre L. van den Berghe, *Ixil Country. A Plural Society in Highland Guatemala.* Berkeley: University of California Press, 1969. pp. VII and 7.

15. cf. Rivke Weiss Bar-Yosef, "Desocialization and Resocialization: The Adjustment Process of Immigrants," *The International Migration Review,* II, n. 3. (Summer, 1968), pp. 27-43.

16. Talcott Parsons, op. cit., pp. 29-46.

17. Raymond Breton, "Institutional Completeness of Ethnic Communities and the Personal Relations of Immigrants," *The American Journal of Sociology,* LXX, n. 2 (September, 1964), pp. 193-205.

18. Talcott Parsons, "A Revised Analytical Approach to the Theory of Social Stratification," in R. Bendix and S. M. Lipset, eds., *Class, Status and Power.* Glencoe: Free Press, 1953. Pp. 116 f. Talcott Parsons, *The Social System.* New York: Free Press, 1951. Pp. 6 and passim: pp. 481.

Talcott Parsons, "Some Considerations on the Theory of Social Change," *Rural Sociology,* v. XXVI, n. 3, 1961.

19. Talcott Parsons, *Structure and Processes in Modern Societies.* Glencoe: The Free Press, 1960. Pp. 17 f.

cf. also, Barry Young and John E. Hughes, "Organizational Theory and the Canonical Parish," *Sociological Analysis,* v. 26, n. 2, Summer 1965. Pp. 57-71.

20. Talcott Parsons, "Full Citizenship, etc.," op. cit. The model described takes into account both the order and conflict perspectives that are found in sociological theory. cf. Gerald M. Shattuck, "Structural Change and Social Work Intervention: Relationships Between Policy and Theory," Fordham University, 1969 (mimeo), pp. 16.

21. Fred N. Kerlinger, *Foundations of Behavioral Research.* New York: Holt, Rinehart & Winston, 1964, pp. 539 and following.

CHAPTER II

They Came from Italy

Emigration from Italy.

The Italians were the largest foreign-born group in the United States in 1930 and the most numerous of the "new immigrants" from southern and eastern Europe. (Table 1) Small colonies of northern Italian merchants and political refugees had been present in the port cities of the eastern United States since the time of the Civil War. In 1850, the Census had registered 3,697 foreign-born Italians, 915 of them in Louisiana and 833 in New York. By 1890, the foreign-born Italian population of the United States numbered 182,580 and it constantly increased until 1930,

Table 1. *Foreign-born Italians in the United States, 1850-1970*

Year	Number	Year	Number
1850	3,679	1920	1,610,113
1860	11,677	1930	1,790,429
1870	17,157	1940	1,623,580
1880	44,230	1950	1,427,145
1890	182,580	1960	1,255,812
1900	484,027	1970	1,008,533
1910	1,343,125		

Source: U.S. Bureau of the Census. *Historical Statistics of the United States, Colonial Times to 1957.* Washington, D.C. 1960, p. 66. Also, *Historical Statistics of the United States, Colonial Times to 1957; Continuation to 1962 and Revisions.* U.S. Government Printing Office, Washington, D.C. 1965. Also, *1970 Census of Population,* Supplementary Report PC (S1)-35, April 1973.

when it reached a peak of 1,790,429. New York City alone counted half
a million first-generation Italians and 630,105 second generation over a
fifth of the total population of Italian origin in the United States estimated at five million in 1930.[1] The large contingent of foreign-born
Italians had accrued from the steady and rapidly increasing flow of immigration. Between 1876 and 1878 the average number of immigrants
coming from the former states of the Italian peninsula was 1,470 a year.
The number of arrivals for the year 1907 was 285,731. (Table 2)

This immigration flow was altered only by the intervention of special
Immigration Acts and by the economic conditions prevailing in the
United States job market.[2]

The Italians migrating to the United States came mostly from
Southern Italy and Sicily. (Tables 3 and 4) The official Italian statistics
report that 5,058,776 Italians migrated to the United States in the 1876-
1930 period: 4,034,204, or 80 percent of the total, were southerners, and

Table 2. *Total Immigration Compared to
Italian Immigration to the United States, 1881-1930
(Fiscal year ending on June 30)*

Year	Total Immigration	Italian Immigration	
		Number	% of Total Im.
1881	669,431	15,401	2.3
1882	788,992	32,160	4.1
1883	603,322	31,792	5.3
1884	518,592	16,510	3.2
1885	395,346	13,642	3.5
1886	334,203	21,315	6.4
1887	490,109	47,622	9.7
1888	546,889	51,558	9.4
1889	444,427	25,307	5.7
1890	455,302	52,003	11,4
1881-90	5,246,613	307,309	5.9
1891	560,319	76,055	13.6
1892	579,633	61,631	10.6
1893	439,730	72,145	16.4
1894	285,631	42,977	15.0
1895	258,536	35,427	13.7
1896	343,267	68,060	19.8
1897	230,832	59,431	25.7
1898	229,299	58,613	25.6
1899	311,715	77,419	24.8
1900	448,572	100,135	22.3
1891-00	3,687,564	651,893	17.7

Table 2 (Continued)

Year	Total Immigration	Italian Immigration	
		Number	% of Total Im.
1901	487,418	135,996	27.9
1902	648,743	178,375	27.5
1903	857,046	230,622	26.9
1904	812,870	193,296	23.8
1905	1,026,499	221,479	21.6
1906	1,100,735	273,120	24.8
1907	1,285,349	285,731	22.2
1908	782,870	128,503	16.4
1909	751,786	183,218	24.4
1910	1,041,570	215,537	20.7
1901-10	8,795,386	2,135,877	24.3
1911	878,587	182.882	20.8
1912	838,172	157,134	18.7
1913	1,197,892	265,542	22.2
1914	1,218,480	283,738	23.3
1915	326,700	49,688	15.2
1916	298,826	33,625	11.3
1917	295,403	34,596	11.7
1918	110,618	5,250	4.7
1919	141,132	1,884	1.3
1920	430,001	95,145	22.1
1911-20	5,735,811	1,109,484	19.3
1921	805,228	222,260	27.6
1922	309,556	40,319	13.0
1923	522,919	46,674	8.9
1924 n	706,896	56,246	8.0
1925	294,314	66,203	2.1
1926	304,488	8,253	2.7
1927	335,175	17,297	5.2
1928	307,255	17,728	5.8
1929	276,678	18,008	6.5
1930	241,700	22,327	9.2
1921-30	4,107,209	455,315	11.1

Source: U.S. Bureau of the Census, Historical Statistics of the United States, Colonial Times to 1957. Washington, 1960, pp. 56 and f.

only 1,024,572, or 20 percent, were from the central and northern regions. The regional origin of southern immigrants indicates the predominance of Sicilians. In fact, 1,105,802 or 27.4 percent of the immigrants came from Campania, the area around Naples; 652,972 (16.2 percent) from Abruzzi and Molise; 300,152 (7.4 percent) from Apulia;

232,389 (5.8 percent) from Basilicata; 522,442 (13 percent) from Calabria; 1,205,788 (29.9 percent) from Sicily; and 14,669 (0.4 percent) from Sardinia.[3]

The emigration movement toward the United States has been the most consistent ever to take place from Italy to any country. From 1881 to 1890 the annual emigration average was about 37,000 persons; from 1901 to 1910, 233,000; and from 1911 to 1920, .157,000. This human avalanche of immigrants into the cities of the eastern seaboard of the country created critical conditions in housing, health, schools and churches. At the same time the newcomer became the worker in an unprecedented industrial development. If the immigration figures were high, those of repatriating Italians were also impressive. As Italian immigration increased in absolute numbers and percentages, so did the percentage of those going back to Italy. The *Reports* of the Immigration Commission and of the Commissioner General of Immigration show that from 1887 to 1890 the percentage of people returning to Italy was only 10 percent of those who came. This statistic, however, climbed to 34

Table 3. *Immigration to the United States from*
North and South Italy,
fiscal years 1899 to 1910, inclusive

Fiscal years—	Number				Percent	
	North Italian	South Italian	All Others	Total	North Italian	South Italian
1899	11,821	65,587	11	77,419	15.3	84.7
1900	15,799	84,329	7	100,135	15.8	84.2
1901	20,324	115,659	13	135,996	14.9	85.0
1902	25,485	152,883	7	178,375	14.3	85.7
1903	34,571	195,993	58	230,622	15.0	85.0
1904	34,056	159,127	113	193,296	17.6	82.3
1905	35,802	185,445	232	221,479	16.2	83.7
1906	40,940	231,921	259	273,120	15.0	84.9
1907	47,814	237,680	237	285,731	16.7	83.2
1908	21,494	106,824	185	138,503	16.7	83.1
1909	22,220	160,800	198	183,218	12.1	87.8
1910	26,699	188,616	222	215,537	12.4	87.5
Total	337,025	1,884,864	1,542	2,223,431	15.2	84.8

Source: Reports of the Immigration Commission, III, p. 141. The Bureau of Immigration, following the general practice of ethnologists, divides the people of Italy into two races—North Italians and South Italians, the former being natives of the compartimenti of Piedmont, Lombardy, Venetia, and Emilia, and the latter natives of the remainder of continental Italy and the islands of Sicily and Sardinia.

Table 4. *Italian Emigration in 1909
to the United States by region of origin*

Regions	Number of Migrants	% of all Migrants from the region	% of all Italians to the U.S.
Piemonte	8,491	15.08	3.03
Liguria	1,716	22.53	0.61
Lombardia	4,603	9.17	1.64
Veneto	4,694	5.62	1.67
Emilia	5,538	18.17	1.98
Toscana	8,005	25.76	2.86
Marche	6,172	26.91	2.20
Umbria	2,773	25.98	0.99
Lazio	14,603	86.20	5.21
Abruzzi	39,440	73.80	14.07
Campania	53,511	78.61	19.09
Puglie	17,069	62.09	6.09
Basilicata	8,354	60.20	2.98
Calabria	32,247	61.40	11.50
Sicilia	72,429	76.38	25.83
Sardegna	706	12.54	0.25

Source: Coletti, Francesco. Dell'emigrazione italiana, op. cit. p. 65.

percent from 1891 to 1900; to 57 percent from 1901 to 1910; and 82 percent from 1911 to 1920. A consequence of permanent or temporary returns to Italy was confusion in the collection of statistics and in the assessment of the total Italian population in the United States. In 1896, for example, the Immigration Service registered 14,236 Italian arrivals who had been in the United States before and were now returning; 20,248 who were entering the country for the first time to join their immediate family, and 31,961 other new immigrants. In 1887, 59,431 immigrants came from Italy, but 10,913 had been in the United States before and were returning. The *Report* commented "that a very large proportion of the immigrants, arrived from the countries (like Italy) which as a rule do not furnish the most desirable immigration . . . could not properly be regarded as new immigrants, since they had either been in this country at least once before, or came here for the purpose of being reunited with their immediate families."[4] About 15 percent of all immigrants arriving

from Italy between 1899 and 1910 had been in the United States previously. The unique traits of Italian emigration were soon observed. In
1892 one of the United States Commissioners of Immigration wrote:

> The return movement, singularly enough, in Italy I found to be entirely
> unlike that of to Scotland and other portions of Great Britain and
> Ireland, as the Italians commenced to come back from the United States
> in August, and this back movement continues pretty strongly until
> November, when it commences to go the other way, from Italy to the
> United States. . . . Probably until quite recently, nearly every man who
> left Italy for the United States was contracted for, as they greatly
> preferred an assured place, even at small wages, in a foreign country.
> The great majority going to the United States do well—quite well for
> Italy. There is an endless stream of letters going from the United States
> to their friends in Italy—those who can not write get friends to write for
> them—and these letters nearly always tell of the well doing of the
> emigrants. There is a continual stream of men coming back through
> every port of Italy and through every mountain tunnel into Italy from
> the northern ports of Europe, in the fall time, who all incite others to
> also go to the United States. . . . Those who return, are constantly
> bestirring others to go. Each Italian in the United States can easily
> secure a place for a friend, and the process is ever being repeated.[5]

In this way, the Italians became known as 'birds of passage' in the
New World. They were slow to sink their roots in a foreign soil and to
convince themselves that returning to Italy was a dream they simply
did not want to fulfill.[6] The process of transition from immigration to
the formation of another American community was inevitable. The Industrial Commission on Immigration reported:

> By 1880 . . . a large proportion of these early Italian immigrants were
> men without their families. . . . During these years the itinerant class—
> ragpickers, organ grinders and the like—which predominated in the
> earliest Italian immigration, was being replaced by another class—the
> stable element of the population in the home country—the steady, in-
> dustrious peasantry whom only extreme poverty induced to break the
> bonds attaching them to their native land. Called here by the industrial
> expansion of the country after the civil war, this class came as unskilled
> day laborers, were taken charge of in masses by Italian bankers and
> padroni, and sent hither and thither as occasion was found for their
> labor. New York City has been and is the headquarters of this class. As
> has been remarked, 97 percent of all Italian Immigrants to this country
> now land at the port of New York. Some proceed directly to other parts
> of the country and return to the city in dull seasons, to be maintained,
> perhaps, by the contractor until other employment can be found, or at
> any rate to be on the spot when employment is offered.
> The newer immigrants of this class are mainly men without families,
> either unmarried or having left their families at home, and many of

them return year by year to Italy in the dull season with the money they have earned here. But after a few years of this the family is either brought over or the "cafone" marries and settles down here, becoming a permanent member of the community.[7]

The indecision to settle permanently affected the development of organized life in the immigrant community. If America was only a temporary place of work and quick enrichment, it was perfectly normal for the immigrant to concentrate on economic profits rather than on his future place in the adoptive country. Italian priests who were beginning a systematic religious assistance to the immigrants confirmed their unsettled condition. In 1888, Father Felice Morelli wrote from New York City to Bishop Scalabrini of Piacenza:

> Last week we received a visit from the Bishop of Providence. He has 1500 Italians in his city and would like to have a missionary to stay in his episcopal residence. If Your Excellency would send me two priests as I asked in my last letter, one could be sent there. . . . Besides, with two other priests, we could create a *missione ambulante* (flying missionary band), i.e. reach the Italians scattered here and there for their work without fixed abode. Saturday I paid a visit to the Italians who work on the railroads leading from Brooklyn to the West of America. In less than five kilometers I found about 2000 Italians who had not seen a church in a long time! I spoke with them, especially with the leaders, and I could find out they would be very much disposed to hear the word of God. I have promised that next November we will give them a mission. They have promised that they will build a large wooden *capanna* (barn) and will come to hear us in large numbers. With these people there is no way one can do better since they change site every month and move forward as the work progresses. The same could be done in Paterson and in various other places of Vineland. . . .[8]

The immigrants' expectation to return is also manifested by the demographic imbalance of the immigrant group. Young men were the typical immigrants, while older people and women remained in Italy. Between 69 and 83 percent of all arrivals were people in the 14-44 year age bracket. (Table 5)

From 1869 to 1910 male immigrants constituted seventy-eight percent of all immigrants from Italy to the United States. In this respect immigration from Italy was different. The sex ratio among immigrants was more evenly distributed in the case of Germans, Irish and Jews. The number of male Italian migrants remained at three times that of female ones until 1924. To complicate the social significance of this data, the familial conditions of the immigrants were aggravated by the fact that many men were separated from their families, which would join them at a later date.[9]

Table 5. *Age and Sex Composition of Italian Immigrants*
to the United States, 1881-1930 (Percentages)

YEAR*	Age			TOTAL	Sex	
	0-13	14-44	45 & Over		M	F
1881-1890	15.3	69.2	15.5	100.0	78.9	21.1
1890-1900	16.9	71.3	11.8	100.0	77.2	22.8
1901-1910	10.8	83.5	5.4	100.0	77.1	22.9
1911-1920	14.5	76.9	8.6	100.0	69.4	30.6
1921-1930	18.1	73.3	8.6	100.0	60.6	39.4

*Years ended on June 30.
Source: Commissioner General of Immigration. Annual Reports—1892-1930, passim.

In fact, during the years immigration decreased, in comparison to the preceding year, the proportion of women and children below 14 years of age, increased in comparison to the total number of arrivals.

The demographic profile of the Italian immigrants reveals the inevitable difficulties for communal action in a transplanted community fragmented by instability of family life, psychologically commited to return to Italy and suddenly relegated to the lowest rung of the host-society. The picture of the marginality and uprootedness of Italian immigrants would not be complete, however, without adding to their disadvantages the lack of essential instruments of social mobility in an urban industrial environment, lack of education and of professional training.

The illiteracy of the immigrants was universal in terms of knowledge of the English language and it was extremely high with regard to the Italian language. The local dialect, in most cases, was the only linguistic equipment of the immigrant and it confined his culture to the isolated *paese* from which he had come. (Table 6 and 7) The unification of Italy had contributed to the educational betterment of the population of the peninsula, but in southern Italy and Sicily (the regions which supplied most of the immigrants), illiteracy ranged between 66.9 to 78.7 percent. In 1907 these figures dropped to a range from 40.4 to 50.1 percent. In 1910, the percentage of illiterates in the total Italian adult population over 14 years of age in the United States was still at 41.03.[10] Mostly laborers, servants and farmers, these illiterate immigrants made up the bulk of Italian immigration—the transplanted peasant mass of the poorest regions of Italy. They formed an army of unskilled workers with few technicians and almost no professionals among them.

G. E. Palma di Castiglione, Director of the Italian Labor Bureau in New York, rightly stated in 1913:

In this mass, therefore, are absent those elements of leadership which could have given it an awareness of its strength, set out well defined goals and, at the same time, established the norms of discipline and organization necessary to reach them. The professional composition of Italian emigration explains the social physiognomy that our colonies in the United States present to the eyes of observers. It furnishes the major explanation of the deficiencies of social development of these colonies.[11] (Table 8)

Between 1871 and 1910 the percentage of unskilled laborers in the total active immigrant population from Italy ranged from a minimum of 74.3 to a maximum of 90.1. Even allowing for the uncertainty of immigration statistics, there can be no doubt on the absolute lack of technical preparation of the immigrants for their new social environment.[12]

In a series of diplomatic and consular reports from Italy, American officials largely confirmed the above picture of destitution and ignorance. In 1888 the American Consul General from Rome and the other consuls from Palermo, Messina, Catania, Naples and Venice (the regions of highest emigration) described the migrants directed to the United States either with utter contempt or with the compassion aroused by a desperate situation. They rarely expressed an occasional note of hope.

Table 6. *Number and percent of North and South Italian Immigrants to the United States who were 14 years of age or over and were illiterate, 1900-1908*

Fiscal Years	Illiterates Over 14 Years of Age			Percentage of Illiterates Among Immigrants Over 14 Years		
	North	South	Total	North	South	Total
1900-1901	3,122	58,493	61,615	15.40	58.54	51.27
1901-1902	3,556	76,529	80,085	14.00	56.29	49.63
1902-1903	4,283	84,512	88,795	12.59	48.43	42.68
1903-1904	4,150	74,889	79,039	12.55	54.10	16.09
1904-1905	5,058	95,407	100,465	13.91	56.35	48.81
1905-1906	5,042	114,957	119,999	11.92	53.72	46.82
1906-1907	4,741	115,803	120,544	9.97	53.22	45.46
1907-1908	1,885	46,654	48,539	8.60	59.67	42.58

Source: Ministero degli Affari Esteri. Commissionato dell' Emigrazione. *Emigrazione e Colonie.* Raccolta da Rapporti dei R. R. Agenti Diplomatici, Consolari, Vol. III, America. Rome. Tipografia dell' Unione Editrice, 1909, p. 49.

Table 7. *Illiteracy of recruits into the
Italian Army (in percentages), 1872, 1901, 1907*

Region	1872	1901	1907
Abruzzi e Molise	66.9	44.2	40.43
Campania	71.3	44.2	42.72
Puglie	71.2	53.1	51.40
Basilicata	75.0	49.2	52.54
Calabria	77.1	54.1	49.91
Sicilia	78.7	53.3	50.12
Italy	56.5	32.6	31.09

Source: Coletti, op. cit. p. 259.

The potential immigrants were described as intensely ignorant, with an intelligence of such low order to do more harm than good to the United States. In fact, they were looked upon as being of such a "stupendous ignorance unequaled by any other class of people found in the civilized world."[13] Migrants to the United States from the consular district of Palermo came generally from the surrounding countryside and the adjacent cities and towns. Consul Caroll reported in 1888:

> They are ignorant in the truest sense and are unable to either read or write; yet they are able bodied and hard working people as a rule, but they are dirty, and often filthy, and would be out of their element in any other condition. Generally they have no intention of becoming citizens, nor would they be desirable as such. Their sole ambition is to make a little money and return to their own country and exist thereon by one venture or another for the balance of their days. At their own homes they can subsist on almost nothing.[14]

The American official in the southern consular district of Messina, which comprised also the provinces of Reggio and Catanzaro, noticed that, as a rule, those emigrants expected to return to Sicily as soon as they had accumulated $800 or $1,000 with which to purchase a plot of land or open a small oil or wine shop. It was believed, however, that nine-tenths of these emigrants changed their minds, sent for their children and settled permanently. Five percent of the emigrants to the United States from the province of Messina were barbers, tailors, carpenters; the balance, field laborers. The emigrants from Calabria were shepherds and field laborers and a few, masons and shoemakers.[15]

Table 8. *Distribution by profession of Italian immigrants to the United States, 1871-1910 (in percentages)*

Years	% of all Italian immigrants			% of all active Italian immigrants			
	Non-active Population	Active Population	Total	Profes- sionals	Skilled Workers	Unskilled Workers	Total
1871-75	28,88	70,12	100,00	3,73	10,62	85,75	100,00
1876-80	40,57	59,43	100,00	5,11	11,80	83,09	100,00
1881-85	28,84	71,16	100,00	1,53	12,76	85,71	100,00
1886-90	33,80	66,20	100,00	0,80	9,09	90,11	100,00
1891-95	36,26	63,74	100,00	0,60	13,26	86,14	100,00
1896*	—	—	—	—	—	—	—
1897	38,85	63,15	100,00	0,64	23,84	75,52	100,00
1898	42,20	37,80	100,00	0,77	24,86	74,37	100,00
1899	39,00	61,00	100,00	0,65	24,25	75,10	100,00
1900	26,08	73,92	100,00	0,48	18,35	81,17	100,00
1901-05	20,66	79,34	100,00	0,54	16,59	82,87	100,00
1906-10	22,82	77,18	100,00	0,51	14,01	85,68	100,00

*Data for 1896 not available.

Source: G. F. Di Palma di Castiglione, "L'immigrazione italiana negli Stati Uniti dell'America del Nord dal 1820 al 30 giugno 1910,"*Bollettino dell'Emigrazione*, XII, 2 (1913), pp. 98-112.

Of the persons emigrating from Naples, that Consul reported, 85 to 90 percent were farm hands, and the balance, journeymen mechanics, mainly tailors, shoe-makers, and carpenters. They were not as a rule first class mechanics or artisans.[16] It is no surprise that Italian emigrants could be seen by some as a threat to American institutions.

> The political system of our country, Consul Johnson wrote from Venice, is dependent upon individual independence of action of each of its citizens, which necessitates a sufficient degree of intelligence and education to insure the good results that, generally speaking, have so far been realized. It is, therefore, clearly evident that people who have been nurtured by and have lived under the influence of traditions and institutions, that have resulted in making them dependent and almost at a mercy of a class will be hardly better fitted to perform the duties required of independent citizens than slaves newly released from bondage.[17]

But ignorant and reluctant as they were to become American citizens, Italian immigrants were considered by some as a desirable addition to the American population.

> It is true that the Italian immigrant, is, as a rule, very ignorant, wrote the Consul General from Rome in 1888, but in that respect he does not greatly differ from emigrants of some other nationalities who have, nevertheless, made good citizens. If a laborer is temperate, if he is hardworking, if he is frugal, he has certainly some of the best qualities which could be sought for in any class of men. If the Italian laborer is treated with kindness he is exceptionally faithful, never shirking his work, and taking a personal interest in his employer's success. Unless the Italian emigrant changes his nature when he arrives in the United States, he is an honest, simple-minded, faithful, industrious workman.[18]

America was eager to receive the labor of arriving Italians, as it had welcomed the contribution of the waves of immigrants who preceded and followed them, but it was hesitant to accept them as people.

Distribution of the Italian Immigrants.

In 1901, the Italian Consul of New York City related to the Foreign Ministry in Rome that a significant change was taking place among the immigrants in the United States: they were coming from the Italian South.[19] The change, however, was hardly new. The predominance of southern laborers among immigrants arriving from Italy was regularly pointed out in the annual reports of the Commissioner General of Immigration for the previous fifteen years. But the consular dispatch from New York offers a contemporary insight into the immigrant community. The City was host to over 200,000 Italians who were beleaguered by illiteracy and lack of professional and technical jobs. The immigrants worked at digging the subways and the sewers of the city;

pushing carts in the streets; and taking up sanitation and other unskilled jobs where there was no great need for knowledge of the English
language and specialized training. On the other hand, the thrift and
endurance of the peasants was beginning to show. Ten thousand
Italian *botteghe* (shops) were dotting the City: 2,750 barbershops, 250
butchershops, 1,300 delicatessens, 2,300 shoe repair shops. More
than 200 Italian banking and industrial companies in the City had a
capital over $50,000.00. There were also about 200 Italian societies,
mutual aid and fraternal societies and incipient ethnic labor unions.
But only three or four of them had a treasury larger than seven or eight
thousand dollars. An attempt to federate the Italian societies had failed.
Leadership was weak due to the "absence of a class above the popular
one." The Consul injected also some comments on the presence of the
Church. He wrote:

> In the United States there are a good number of Italian Catholic priests.
> In New York and Brooklyn there are seventeen Italian parishes or
> churches with about fifty Italian priests. We can confirm that in general
> their work is efficacious, not only for the religious assistance to the im-
> migrants, but also for keeping alive our language. Many of them are oc-
> cupied in elementary schools and they preach in Italian churches mostly
> in Italian. This wave of 'italianita,' that comes from the Church, will be
> certainly revived as a consequence of the recent visit by Bishop
> Scalabrini of Piacenza to the main centers of Italian immigration in the
> United States where the illustrious prelate tried to propagate those
> highly liberal and humanitarian concepts, to which his work is in-
> spired. Very few are the Italians of Protestant cult: our immigrant is very
> little inclined to change religion. . . .[20]

Other diplomatic dispatches and newspaper articles insisted more on
the fact that New York City had the largest concentration of Italian immigrants and was the showcase of their first progress and of their
traditional shortcomings. The City was becoming the new frontier
where southern Europeans were fighting their battles in industrial
America. On a larger scale, it presented the typical evolution of the
Italian ethnic community in urban America, where most of the immigrants settled. *Il Bollettino dell'Emigrazione*, official publication of
the Italian Government, reported in 1905:

> Italians are almost always agglomerated in the large urban
> centers. . . . For example, in the State of New York, of the 273,000
> Italians that were there in 1900, 220,000 were living in the city of New
> York alone.[21] (Table 9)

At the same time there were 37,000 Italians in Illinois, 27,000 of
them residing in the city of Chicago. Boston, with 20,836 Italians, had
more than half of all the Italians in Massachusetts. The eastern cities

Table 9. *U.S. Italian Population in 1900*

	United States	N.Y. State	N.Y. City
Born in Italy of Ital. parents	484,703	182,248	145,431
Born of U.S. from Ital. parents	221,895	83,578	69,366
Ital. Father, Amer. Mother	23,076	4,203	3,126
Ital. Father, Mother of other Nationality	12,523	2,543	7,101

Source: *Bollettino del 'Emigrazione*, 11, 1905, pp. 3-14.

were the instinctive choice of the immigrants. In 1900 the six States of
Pennsylvania, New Jersey, New York, Massachusetts, Connecticut and
Rhode Island had a population of Italian residents reaching 514,931,
seventy percent of the Italians in the United States. After New York
City and Boston, the most significant urban concentration of Italians
was in Philadelphia (28,750) and Newark (13,259). By 1901 the destination of the immigrants statewise, according to the *Reports* of the
Bureau of Immigration,[22] shows an even higher concentration in the
Atlantic States: 83.5 percent of all immigrants from Italy were directed
to this region. In 1910 there is an evident decline in the percentage of
immigrants destined to the North Atlantic States, but the figure is still
very high, 74.5 percent. At this time, 16.3 percent of the destinations of
the immigrants were directed to the Central North States, especially to
the cities of Cleveland, Akron, Detroit, Chicago, St. Louis and Kansas
City. Thus, over 90 percent of all known destinations of Italian immigrants were the eastern and midwestern large cities. A few immigrants went into agriculture; about two or three percent went to the
cities of California and just as many to the cities of Louisiana and Texas.
(Table 10)

The structure of the New York Italian ethnic community, although
on a much larger scale, seems to reflect the experience of the 'urban
villagers' from Italy, or at least of the largest percentage of them, all
over America. New York City and the other ports of arrival had become
a forced choice of Italian immigrants, whose average fortune at the
time of landing did not exceed 20 lire or four dollars. The immigrants'
fare to New York had been $25.00, while the cost of the passport in Italy
had been $3.50 and the migrant's usual pay in Italy did not exceed $0.25
or $0.30 per day.[23] The arriving immigrant could ill afford the expense
of a long trip. Besides, the agent and the padrone that had arranged his

Table 10. *Distribution of North and South Italian immigrants by geographic Division, 1901-1908 (Fiscal Years) (Percentages)*

Geographic Division	1900-1903			1903-1906			1907			1908		
	North	South	Total	North	South	Total	North	South	Total	North	South	Total
North Atlantic	59.31	86.90	82.54	57.42	85.07	80.28	49.29	82.98	77.08	50.88	82.13	76.43
North Central	17.33	7.19	8.79	19.34	9.04	10.83	20.51	10.26	12.05	19.49	9.55	11.36
South Atlantic	1.20	1.54	1.49	1.78	2.59	2.45	1.37	2.62	2.40	1.38	2.69	2.45
South Central	1.69	2.79	2.62	3.02	1.78	1.99	1.95	1.52	1.59	2.53	2.31	2.35
Western	20.36	1.56	4.53	18.35	1.49	4.41	26.84	2.62	6.87	25.68	3.30	7.38
Alaska, Hawaii, Puerto Rico, Philippines	0.11	0.02	0.03	0.09	0.03	0.04	0.04	—	0.01	0.04	0.02	0.03
	100.00	100.00	100.00	100.00	100.00	100.00	100.00	100.00	100.00	100.00	100.00	100.00

Source: Ministero degli Affari Esteri Commissionato dell'Emigrazione. *Emigrazione e Colonie.* Raccolta da Rapporti dei R. R. Agenti Diplomatici, Consolari, Vol. III, America. Rome. Tipografia dell' Unione Editrici, 1909, p. 49.

trip could place the newcomer as an unskilled hand in the growing industrial and construction enterprises of the large eastern cities. Had the immigrant been able to afford to move hinterland, where the good farming land was available, he would have still remained in the city. He hated his experience as a *contadino* and eschewed agriculture wholeheartedly remembering how he was poorly fed, badly housed, illiterate and exploited by the land owners in southern Italy.[24]

A Commissioner of Immigration in New York confirmed from his experience and observation the pattern of Italian immigration. In a letter to Archbishop Corrigan inquiring about Italians, he said:

> . . . exact figures are impossible for many reasons: no attempt has been made by anyone to keep them, and the fluctuating character of the race going here and there from state to state as the demand of labor warrant it, and returning in large numbers to Italy each year, make everything estimated based on experience, impossible. . . . The total number of immigrants to the United States from Italy beginning with the end of the fiscal year 1890 which was not included in the eleventh Census is as follows:

FISCAL YEARS	TOTAL ITALIANS ARRIVED IN THE U.S.	ITALIANS WHO GAVE NEW YORK AS THEIR DESTINATION
1889-90	52,003	49,221
1890-91	76,055	73,077
1891-92	61,631	58,995
1892-93	72,145	70,178
1893-94	42,963	42,074
1894-95	35,417	33,902
1895-96	68,060	66,445
1896-97	59,431	57,775
1897-98	58,613	56,641
1898-99	78,730	76,312
1899-1900	100,000	97,514
TOTAL	705,048	682,134

*Approximated

The report of the International Steamship Conference, shows that about 25,000 Italians have returned to Italy every year, which would make the amount given above less by 250,000. Then again, the number who have been counted over two or more times in the above table of arrivals is a very appreciable factor. The tendency to give New York as their destination, regardless of where they do finally wind up is very clearly shown in the above table, all but about four percent of the total arrivals having done this. It is this unfortunate tendency which allows the *padrone* and bankers to manipulate them in the labor market.

The total number of Italians in the City of New York will be made known in a very short while from Washington as the result of the Census taken this year, but the number here at present is estimated as not less than 175,000.[25]

The archbishop of New York and his fellow bishops in the eastern and midwestern cities of the country had a vast new field of work before them.

Cultural and Religious Background of Italian Immigrants.

Summing up the conclusions of the U.S. Commissioners of Immigration on their study-visit to Italy in 1892, the Secretary of the Treasury remarked:

> . . . the great mass of the farm workers, whence come almost all of our immigrants, are poor, with poor ancestors, with no real interest in the soil, with only an interest in the climate, the legends, the patriotic songs, the flags, the religion, and the history of the country.[26]

But a vital institution—if not the most crucial to shed light on the problems the Italian immigrants had to face in the process of Americanization—was left out. The family, in fact, took precedence over every other aspect of life. At least part of the ultimate commitment demanded by religion and the world's view created by it were transferred by the southern Italian peasant to his family, rather than to the socio-institutional forms of religion. As Grasso points out, the religious and familial dimensions were blending to produce the cultural world of the *contadino*.[27] Southern Italy, at the time of the mass exodus to the United States, was (and to a certain extent still is) an underdeveloped and overpopulated region, suffering from high pressures of population of scarce land resources and from a low standard of living. But life in the South exalted the family.[28] The essential feature of the social system was the nuclear family. Family relationships gave the individual his status and guaranteed a measure of security. An individual destiny was predetermined by his birth into a family that owned land or into one that did not. A person's obligations and boundaries of social responsibility were circumscribed by the nuclear family first, and then by the persons related through marriage and godparenthood.

The southern Italian, in fact, shows concern over issues which affect him vitally, or affect the well-being of his immediate family. He shows, however, almost a pathological distrust toward persons outside the small circle of the family of procreation, distrusting least those who live within the sound of the local church bell. This *campanilismo* finds particular expression in the strong societal taboo on marrying outside the immediate community.[29] Familism, then, is the clear unifying focus characterizing southern Italian culture, a familism consecrated by traditional and devotional Catholicism.

The individual is socially and interiorly organized around the family, which determines status, roles and values for him. The dimension of kinship seems to absorb the dimension of man, with a consequent alienation of the individual. This is in contrast with the a-familistic individualism of the highly industrialized American society. The exceeding transcendence of familism was internalized in the immigrants' individual personality. Thus, immigrants could overcome their crises only by re-integrating and restructuring their personality in the direction of greater appreciation of the human person and of personal values.

As the process of emigration de-socialized the southern Italian immigrant from his familism and made him aware of his individualism, so religion progressively moved from familistic to socio-institutional manifestations and organization.[30]

Religion, in fact, was an integral part of the life of southern Italians. Just before mass migration,

> religion in Italy was all pervasive. Each locality had its periodical church festivals, devotions were carried on even in the midst of business activities, and everywhere the traveler came upon churches, shrines, and crosses. The piety of the people was not without its impressive touches. At all hours worshippers flocked to the churches. People of every age and condition had made the church an intimate part of their lives. . . . Most Italians undoubtedly know little of dogma and theology and merely worshipped as their fathers before them had done, but such worship probably was no less devout for having been handed on by custom.[31]

But American visitors and intellectuals felt an ambivalent attitude of attraction and repulsion toward Roman Catholicism in Italy. Continuity with the past, colorful ceremonies and stability could not be found in the United States as they could be found in Italy. Many of the practices seemed, however, to be an insult to reason and appeared to have been instituted to keep the people in slavish bondage of the priestly caste. "Ignorance and indolence," writes Baker, "were perhaps the worst charges that could be held against them (the clergy) as a group. Turned by their belief from modern progress, the priests neither knew how to, nor could adjust themselves, to the contemporary world. Yet the clergy commonly seemed devoted to their duties. . . ."[32] After several years of residence and travel in Italy, M. J. Spalding, Archbishop of Baltimore, could only confirm the influence of religion on the Italian character and the influence of the clergy on Italian life. He warned against judging Italian society "through a false medium or that of the peculiar political bias or religious prejudices. . . ."[33] John England, Bishop of Charleston, had also felt obliged to defend the Italian clergy from American attacks.[34] In the period of mass immigration, the polemic regarding the Italian clergy shifted from the Protestant to the Catholic Church. It was at this time that the Catholic bishops adopted as an instrument for their acceptance into American society the ideology of American nationalism. The stereotype of the Italian priest, however, remained the same.

The folk quality of southern Italian religion corresponded to its social environment. In America, instead, it became an immediate source of conflict with the more urbanized, law and organization oriented Irish Catholicism, which frequently interpreted the peasant religious behavior of Latin and Slavic immigrants as an eccletic survival of pre-christian and medieval beliefs and traditions. But the immigrants were not in a position to speculate on the type of their religious experiences with the same formal preparation of the bishops and priests they met in the new society.

In the poorest areas of the Italian South magical practices permeated the customs and activities of daily life. Neither logic nor the yardstick of the civilized conclusions of philosophers was the measuring rod of what was happening to man, says Gabriele De Rosa in his historical analysis of popular religion in southern Italy.

> Everything was working in the context of a religious mystery. Nature was not an objective reality, external, calculated, with physical and mathematical laws. It showed instead the deep marks of divine action. All the activities of man: shepherd, peasant and middle-class, converged toward this form of magic, which did not usually have in the South a demonological character, but one of primitive and naive, mysterious and human fantasy. Popular belief went so far that it was normal to register with a notary public the incantations suffered and to fulfill before him the vows made in honor of the Madonna who had freed the faithful from some charm.[35]

Episcopal synods and the individual bishops constantly fought against the mixture of Christianity and magic present in the populace, but their efforts to preserve the purity of the faith met with hostile reactions. Only the beginning of mass emigration and the economic development of the South marked a progressive disappearance of magical practices. The sacraments and other rites of the Church had a double symbolism. On the official Church level they represented spiritual salvation; on the popular level, a psychological escape from

an unbearable misery, a refuge against the oppressive environment and
a mixture of theological hope and hope of physical survival in the
midst of exploitation by landlords, a barren land, sickness and high
taxes.[36] The religious behavior of Italian immigrants can be understood only in the perspective of Southern Italian history, popular
culture and the relations between the Kingdom of Naples and Sicily
with the Church. Bishop Nicola Monterisi (1867-1944), a great
southern churchman, summed up the transition from the isolated,
almost primitive southern society and religion, into modern society.
He wrote:

> In the past, the reception of the sacraments and the performance of the
> Easter duty was part of the practices of cult. But little by little the in-
> fluence of modern unbelief has emptied cult of its substance of content.
> What remains is the external aspect and religious formalism only,
> the great disease which corrodes and threaten us with death today. The
> laymen, ignorant in religion, away from the sacraments, often leading
> an irregular life, does not renounce Church and confraternities. Instead,
> prompted by an instinctive spirit of State control over religion, he wants
> to take over. He transforms church, confraternities and religious
> associations into an agency of amusement. He pushes to phanaticism
> the exterior traits and the traditional paraphernalia of cult. He spends
> extravagant sums in firecrackers, bands and illuminations. . . . A conse-
> quence of the cultic mentality is that the Christian people support
> financially only works of cult, and not all of valid cult. The rest (social
> and educational activities) does not count.[37]

In the United States, the religious change which took place among the
immigrants seems to support Monterisi's criticism. But the cultic expressions of the Italian pre-industrial South have been substituted by
parallel urban American manifestations of legalism, nationalism and
authoritarian bureaucracy. The two shell-like forms of Catholicism,
although emptied of much genuine piety in the upheaval of moder-
nization and migration, remained alive enough to stir and shape new
community forms in the complexity of American society.

    All Italians arriving into the ports of the New World declared
themselves Catholics, with few exceptions in the case of Waldensian
Protestants from the valleys of Piedmont and a handful of socialists
and anarchists.

    "Of the total number of Italians arriving during the past year
(1888)," wrote the U.S. Commissioner of Immigration in New York to
Archbishop Corrigan, "all but one twentieth of one percent were
professed Roman Catholics. . . ."[38] These Italian Catholic immigrants, however, were even religiously unprepared for their new environment. The traditional faith of the southern Italian villages could

not be preserved in an industrial society, if it had to depend only on liturgical rituals, customs and familism. To survive, it had to be transformed into a more personalized and articulated religious form or, at least, into a more efficient expression of associational life.[39]

Causes of Emigration.

Peasants and day laborers leaving southern Italy for America were as ignorant of their place of destination as they were totally unprepared for their new environment. They were certain of only one thing: the reason why they were going away.

The American Consul at Catania, Sicily, caught the spirit of these migrants in a report he sent to Washington in 1888. Four fifty-to-sixty-year-old Sicilians presented themselves to the consul, who preserved his dialogue with them:

> "Good morning, Mr. Consul. We are on our way to Palermo to catch the steamer for America. There was a man in our town who assured us that they want laborers in America, paying 15 lire ($3.00) for six hours pay work, or at the rate of 2½ lire (50¢) for every working hour. We are four of us here, but others are ready to join us at Palermo. Do we need any passport from you, sir? The man told us we need nothing; but we want to be sure, not to have trouble. He said, not to see the American consul at Catania, because he discourages old laborers from emigrating, for fear of getting sick."
>
> "In what part of America do you intend to go?"
>
> "We don't know, sir. The man said in America, where they dig gold. Although we are a little old, but we can dig well, as we have been work-ing in sulphur mines."
>
> "Have you there any relatives, friends or acquaintances who would take care of you on your arrival, or to feed you until you find something to do?"
>
> "No, sir," was their sudden reply. "But we have plenty money to live on for two full years, and all we make during that time we save it, and then come back home very rich."
>
> "How much money have you got with you?"
>
> "Well, sir, we have about 160 lire ($32.00) each of us. We sold everything we had to make it."
>
> "That money will just do you to pay for your passage ticket."
>
> "No, sir. The man told us at Palermo they give us the passage ticket for nothing."
>
> "The man is wrong; let him give you the ticket before you leave the country. He wants your money and leave you in misery (sic). You are too old now to emigrate in a very far country, where the people don't speak your language. Take my advice to go home, to live happy and die with your families."

The elderly peasants became bewildered and left, the testimony concludes.[40]

A feverish desire to cross the ocean and to escape social conditions incapable of fulfilling their new aspirations had taken possession of peasants, laborers and artisans. It had penetrated the poverty stricken villages of southern Italy and created a climate of high expectations that pushed the migrants out of the Old Country. The unification of Italy had brought about a serious economic and social upheaval. The artificial equilibrium of the economies of the old states of the Italian peninsula rested on the lack of external competition. The absence of mobility of capital was responsible for a disastrous situation in industry and agriculture affecting particularly southern Italy.[41] The political *Risorgimento* should have been followed by an economic revolution. Such a readjustment, however, the old leadership of southern Italy could not give because it lacked capital and, above all, initiative. The peasants, on the other hand, victims of *la miseria,* malnutrition, malaria and illiteracy, were left with only the capacity to work and a tradition of servitude. Thus, as Faina concluded in a report of the governmental inquiry into the conditions of southern peasants: "In the general restlessness of all classes for the conquest of an economic improvement, the southern peasant was left with only three alternatives: either resign to his *miseria,* or rebel or migrate."[42] The attempt to rebel had failed. The ascetical resignation to a fate of subservience, suffering and poverty had ended as well. A Sicilian *giornaliero* (day laborer) reflected the soul of the people forced out of the island they loved, when he said: "For the inhuman way with which the *signori* treat us, they should all be placed before the mouth of a cannon, with the exception of the Church (not the priests) and the Saints. We must remain subjected to them like slaves."[43] The *Risorgimento* did, in fact, break a secular impasse of bitter fatalism and slowly wrought "the awakening of the conscience of one's own right."[44] Emigration became linked to "a secret and instinctive uprising of the inferior strata of the population toward a greater welfare, forcefully incited by political turmoil and by the bandits' struggles."[45] It became the only feasible choice for the southern peasant.

Journeying toward the United States on the ship *Regina d'Italia,* Father Pietro Pisani had a first-hand experience of immigrants' feelings and conditions. The great majority of the new people embarked in Palermo were farmers, as were three-fifths of those that had boarded at Naples.

> There are, however, he wrote, among the Sicilians, many barbers and dressmakers, that go to refill the barbershops of New York and of the most important centers of North America.

The vast majority of the migrants were illiterate. The Sicilian was impulsive, diffident and ignorant, Pisani continues,

> but generous, extrovert, ready to give you his heart, when he is convinced that you too have one. He is deeply religious, honest, even though that religiosity is manifested, because of lack of education, in exterior acts which are often superstitious to the point of making him even ridiculous in the eyes of those who do not know how to appreciate him. In the familiarity of those conversations, Pisani adds, I had the opportunity to acquire a more exact idea of the causes that push so many peasant families of the South to emigrate. These families represent an immense capital *irreparably* lost to the material and moral prosperity of the country. Hunger, *dira necessitas* (dire necessity), is the first of all causes of emigration. But there is also the greediness of our tax system, made worse in some southern provinces by the particular conditions of labor contracts; by the apathy of many large property owners and *latifondisti* (latifundia owners), for whom the peasant still represents little more than the donkey; by the sollicitations of all those that call themselves ship-agencies representatives or emigration sub-agents, an infinite number, in spite of the law and the wise provisions of the Royal Commissariate. We must not forget, however, that in the last few years the principal agents of emigration are relatives, the *compaesano*, the *compare*, who write themselves or ask others to write for them from America, sending letters, insisting, sending money for the trip, or simply sending to their family the fruits of their sweat.[46]

Escape from oppression and poverty remained the haunting dream of the immigrants. The repeated complaints of Catholic, Protestant and Socialist organizers, in fact, focus on the narrow vision of the quick money of the immigrants. *Il Proletario* editorialized on this feeling in 1905:

> Italians come to America with the only intention of accumulating money. They live like sheep. . . . Their dream, their only care is the bundle of money they are painfully increasing and which will give them, after 20 years of deprivation, the possiblity of a lukewarm life in their native country.[47]

The expectations, however, were soon reshaped by the slums of the big cities of North America. The Italian immigrants found themselves bewildered and lost in an urban environment whose language they did not understand, whose bureaucratic machines scared them, and whose social and religious outlook clashed directly with their traditional world's view. Dreams of quick fortunes turned into nightmares of every day survival. The hard experience of social rejection taught Italian newcomers to overcome family clannishness and to join with other

clans of the same dialect, province and patron saints to find personal
security in the strength of the group. The immigrants, in their total
absence of opportunity for social participation, were forced to re-think
the forms of social experience they had known in their villages, the
institutional type of parish especially. Ignorant of political
maneuvering and of large economic enterprises, burdened by illiteracy,
Italians in the United States seemed to lack the ingenuity and intellectual resources necessary to challenge the future with new institutions.
They had to fall back on and repeat the past. The Puritan Village and
the Urban Village of transplanted Italians offered a striking contrast.
Summer Chilton Powell writing on the formation of a New England
town remarked:

> To emigrate from accustomed social institutions and relationships to a
> set of unfamiliar communities in the way in which Noyes and Ruddock
> shifted from England to Sudbury, and then later from Sudbury to
> Marlborough, meant a startling transformation. The townsmen had to
> change or abandon almost every formal institution which they had
> taken for granted.[48]

The Puritan immigrants had a sophisticated theology to defend, experience of debates and persecutions, a use of courts, common law,
elective offices, which endowed them with a rich background out of
which a new social set up could be structured. Little Italy in the United
States of America, instead, was born as a tentative and temporary substitute for the Old World community. It had the familiar superstition,
smell and slang, and, above all, institutional structure that made the
world understandable again. Necessity, however, which stimulated the
creativity of the Puritans, gave a new twist to the reconstructed world of
the peasants as well.

Four million Italians entered the United States from 1880 to 1924
basically for economic reasons. They criss-crossed the Atlantic and the
United States only with the avowed aims of making money, returning
to their villages, and buying some land. But their expectations changed
as they were realized. Much to the surprise of Americans, who opened

Table 11. *Italians with American Citizenship, 1900*

Place	Born in Italy	Born in America	Total
United States	350,586	257,494	608,080
New York State	138,906	92,324	231,230
New York City	111,696	79,593	191,289
Source: Bollettino dell' Emigrazione, 11, 1905, pp. 3-14.			

the gates to Italian immigration mainly under pressure for a temporary mass of unskilled laborers, the immigrants, who had planned themselves a quick return to their villages, opted for a future in America. (Table 11) They closed ranks and developed new communities. The complexity of their experience is reflected in the various interpretations it provoked.

NOTES

1. Massimo Livi Bacci, *L'Immigrazione e l'assimilazione degli Italiani negli Stati Uniti secondo le statistiche demografiche americane.* Milano: Giuffre', 1961, p. 94. William B. Shedd, *Italian Population In New York.* New York: Columbia University, Casa Italiana, Educational Bureau, Pp. 16.

2. Massimo Livi Bacci, op cit., pp. 10-11.

3. Svimez, *Un secolo di statistiche italiane: Nord e Sud (1861-1961).* Roma, 1961.

4. Immigration Service, *Annual Report of the Commissioner General of Immigration to the Secretary of the Treasury* for the Fiscal Year Ended June 30, 1896 and 1897. Washington, D.C.: Government Printing Office, p. 29, p. 17. Also, *Reports of the Immigration Commission, 1896, 1897.* Washington, D.C.: Government Printing Office, 1911. Vol. III, p. 359.

5. *Letter from the Secretary of the Treasury Transmitting a Report of the Commissioners of Immigration upon the Causes which incite Immigration to the United States.* Vol. I, Reports of Commissioners. Washington D.C.: Government Printing Office, 1892, pp. 224, 226.

6. Egisto Rossi, *Italian Immigration to the United States for the Fiscal Year Ending June 30, 1899. Fifth Annual Report.* New York: Italian Immigration Bureau, 1899.

7. *Reports of the Industrial Commission on Immigration and on Education.* Washington, D.C.: Government Printing Office, 1901. Volume XV, p. 473

8. Felix Morelli to Bishop Giovanni Battista Scalabrini, New York, October 1, 1888, ACSC-USA. Prov.

9. Massimo Livi Bacci, op. cit., p. 18.

10. G. E. Di Palma di Castiglione, "L'immigrazione italiana negli Stati Uniti dell'America del Nord dal 1820 al 30 giugno 1910. Nota statistica con quattro quadri." *Bollettino dell'Emigrazione,* XII, 2, (1913), pp. 98-112.

11. Ibid. p. 109

12. Egisto Rossi, op. cit. p. 6; Ministero degli Affari Esteri. Commissariato dell'Emigrazione. *Emigrazione e Colonie.* Raccolta di Rapporti dei RR. Agenti Diplomatici e Consolari. Volume III, America, pp. 46-53.

13. House of Representatives, 50th Congress, 1st Session, *Testimony Taken by the Select Committee of the House of Representatives to Inquire into the Alleged Violation of the Laws Prohibiting the Importation of Contract Laborers, Paupers, Convicts, and other Classes.* Washington: Government Printing Office, 1888.

14. Ibid., p. 111, Report of Consul Carroll of Palermo.

15. Ibid., p. 121, Report of Consul Jones of Messina.

16. Ibid., p. 123, Report of Consul Camphausen of Naples.

17. Ibid., p. 111, Report of Counsul Johnson of Venice.

18. Ibid., p. 116, Report of Consul-General W. L. Alden of Rome.

19. F. Prat, "Gli Italiani negli Stati Uniti e specialment nello Stato di New York," *Bollettino dell'Emigrazione,* 2, 1902, pp. 14-41.

20. Ibid., p. 39.

21. "La popolazione italiana negli Stati Uniti dell'America del Nord (Con una carta illustrativa)," *Bollettino dell'Emigrazione*, 11, 1905, pp. 3-14.

For an extensive review of Italian emigration statistics a most comprehensive source is: Commissariato dell'Emigrazione, *Annuario statistico dell'emigrazione italiana dal 1876 al 1925 con notizie sull'emigrazione negli anni 1869-1875*. Roma: Edizione del Commissariato dell'Emigrazione, 1926. Pp. 1740.

22. *Annual Report* of the Commissioner-General of Immigration for the Fiscal Year ended June 30, 1901. Washington: Government Printing Office, 1901. (G. E. Palma di Castiglione, op. cit., Table IV.)

23. *Letter of the Secretary of the Treasury Transmitting a Report of the Commissioners of Immigration* . . . op. cit., p. 223, 224, 226.

24. Francesco Coletti, "Dell'emigrazione italiana," in *Cinquanta Anni di storia italiana, MDCCCLX-MDCCCCX*. Milano: Ulrico Heopli, 1911, pp. 93-222.

Humbert Nelli. *The Italians of Chicago, 1880-1930*. New York: Oxford University Press, 1970.

25. Edward McSweeney to Michael A. Corrigan, Letter of November 26, 1900, pp. 2-3. Archives of the R.C. Archdiocese of New York (AANY).

26. *Letter of the Secretary of the Treasury* . . . op. cit., pp. 225.

27. Pier Giovanni Grasso. *Personalita' Giovanile in Transizione. Dal Familismo al Personalismo*. Zurich: Pas-Verlag, AG, 1964.

28. Robert F. Foerster, *The Italian Migration of Our Times*. Cambridge: Harvard University Press, 1919, p. 95. On Southern Italian Familism see:

F. Cancian, "Il contadino meridionale: comportamento politico e visione del mondo," *Bollettino delle Ricerche Sociali* Anno I, No. 3-4, pp. 258-77.

Paul J. Campisi, "Ethnic Family Patterns: The Italian Family in the United States," *American Journal of Sociology*, 53 (May, 1948), pp. 444-446.

Francis X. Femminella, "The Italian-American Family," in M. Barash and A. Scourby, eds., *Marriage and the Family*. New York: Random House, 1970, pp. 127-141.

Edward C. Banfield. *The Moral Basis of a Backward Society*. Glencoe, Ill.: The Free Press, 1958.

Leonard W. Moss & Walter H. Thompson, "The South Italian Family: Literature and Observation," *Human Organization*, vol. 18, 1, (Summer, 1959), pp. 35-41.

Phyllis Williams. *South Italian Folkways in Europe and in America*. New York: Russell and Russell, 1969, pp. 73-79.

Leonard Covello, *The Social Background of the Italo-American School-Child: A Study of the Southern Italian Family Mores and Their Effect on the School Situation in Italy and in America*. Leiden: E. J. Brill, 1967.

Virginia McLaughlin, "Like the Fingers of the Hand: The Family and Community Life of First Generation Italian-Americans in Buffalo, New York, 1880-1930." Unpublished Ph.D. Dissertation, State University of New York at Buffalo, 1970.

29. Leonard Moss and Stephen C. Cappannari, "Patterns of Kinship. Comparaggio and Community in a South Italian Village," *Anthropological Quarterly*, 33, 1, (January, 1960), pp. 24-32.

Joseph Lopreato. *Peasants No More*. San Francisco: Chandler Publishing Co., 1967.

30. See: Nicholas J. Russo, "The Religious Acculturation of the Italians in New York City," Unpublished Ph.D. Dissertation, St. John University, 1968. Pp. 341.

31. Paul R. Baker, *The Fortunate Pilgrims. Americans in Italy 1800-1860*. Cambridge: Harvard University Press, 1964, pp. 154 on.

32. Ibid., pp. 173.

33. M. J. Spalding, *Miscellanea*. Vol. II, Theological and Miscellaneous. Baltimore: John Murphy & Co., 1875, p. 524 and passim.

34. John England, *Works*. Cleveland, 1908, vol. VI, pp. 222.

35. Gabriele de Rosa, *Vescovi, popolo e magia nel Sud*. Napoli: Guida Editori, 1971, p. 58 and passim.

36. Ernesto de Martino, *Sud e Magia*. Milano: Feltrinelli, 1972, p. 137 and f. See also: Gabriele de Rosa, op. cit., p. 162; Leonardo Sciascia, *Feste Religiose in Sicilia*. Bari: Leonardo da Vinci, 1965. Annabella Rossi. *Le feste dei poveri*. Bari: Laterza, 1971. Luigi M. Lombardi Satriani, *Santi, streghe e diavoli. Il patrimonio delle tradizioni popolari nella societa' meridionale e in Sardegna*. Firenze: Sansoni, 1971.

37. Gabriele de Rosa, op. cit., p. 231 and the entire chapter commenting on the writings of bishop Nicola Monterisi.

38. Thomas Fitcher to Michael A. Corrigan, Letter dated December 13, 1899. AANY G-30 H.

39. Per Giovanni Grasso, op. cit.

40. 50th Congress. 1st Session. House of Representatives, *Testimony taken by the Select Committee of the House of Representatives* etc., op. cit., pp. 113.

41. Francesco Coletti, "Dell'emigrazione italiana," in *Cinquanta anni di storia italiana*. Milano, 1911. Vol. III., op. cit.

42. Ibid., p. 121.

43. Ibid., p. 146.

44. Ibid., p. 157. *Atti della Giunta per la Inchiesta Agraria e sulle Condizioni delle Classi Agricole. Relazione per le Calabrie e la Basilicata*, vol. IX, fasc. 1, pp. XV-XVI.

45. Ibid., pp. 157, *Relazione per le Calabrie* etc., op. cit., pp. 66.

46. Sac. Prof. Pietro Pisani, "Vanno in America." *Pro Emigrante*, Anno II, 1908, pp. 5-8. *Pro Emigrante* was the bulletin of the Society of the Missionaries of Emigration of Msgr. Coccolo for assitance to the immigrants aboard ship during their crossing.

47. Ilion, "Americani e Americanizzazione," *Il Proletario*, Anno IX, n. 23 (Giungo 1905), p. 1.

48. Summer Chilton Powell, *Puritan Village: The Foundation of a New England Town* (Middletown, 1963), pp. 142.

CHAPTER **III**

American Views of Italian Newcomers

"America," says the title of a poem by Archibald MacLeish, "was promises." And to the Italians arriving in an uninterrupted flow, America appeared without any doubt as the opportunity waiting to be seized. In the earthy language of the peasants, America was not construed as a theological vision, but, in an equally valid way, as the expectation of a dream fulfilled: sufficient bread for the family and pride in the independence from landowners. "America is vast . . . you can breath there," Carmine Biagio Iannace impressed on his girl friend returning to Campania from his first trip to the United States in 1906.[1]

Allured by their dream, the immigrants came westward to the Promised Land, where other groups had preceeded them and with whom they had to learn to deal. Earlier arrivals saw the newcomers as a possible embarassment, as a threat. After all, as Alfonso Strafile wrote in his *Memorandum Coloniale* in 1910 on the conditions of the Italians in North America, they were poor, illiterate, leaderless. These *braccianti* and unskilled workers were willing to adapt literally to anything, even to the point of undercutting previously established workers.[2] Their coming, marked by the shortcomings and conditions described in the preceding chapter, could not avoid stirring up the imagination of earlier Americans and provoking all kinds of responses. If a judgment can be derived from the expressions of anxiety of people in the host society, the reaction was one of ignorance, misunderstanding and hostility. In the face of this reception, the Italians did not abandon their dreams. They fell back on their own resources to build a community pattern, as far as the new social environment allowed, based on values and institutions they had known and accepted in the old country. The reaction which touched the Italians more directly was that of their co-religionists in the already established and accepted churches. They had settled in the same geographical areas, and the physical proximity was strengthened by the link they shared in the common religion. They took it for granted that a common religious bond would give them a special right of acceptance. The Catholic Church, however, as had the other segments of the receiving society, had its own agenda already sketched out for the newcomers. Reflected in the Church's statements is a deeply rooted conviction that Italians had to become Americans as soon as possible by adopting a Catholicism like that of the Irish.

The Catholic Church wanted to Americanize the immigrants. Other groups of society were intent to show the American dream of democracy and success; to prove and to disprove the benefits of capitalism; to respond to ethnocentric and filiopietistic devotion as a means to satisfy the immigrants' emotional insecurity. In fact, the immigrants discovered that they were not equal in what they had envisioned as an egalitarian society.

Catholic Americanizers.

Edmund Dunne sums up the thinking of the Catholic Church in the United States as expressed by liberal bishops like Gibbons of Baltimore, Ireland of St. Paul, and their followers in the Catholic hierarchy at the time of Italian mass immigration:

> One thing certain, the Catholic Church . . . is the best qualified to weld into one democratic brotherhood, one great American citizenship, the children of various climes, temperaments and conditions.[3]

The Church, officially committed to nationalism, even to the risk of relinquishing its universal prophetic mission,[4] understood well that "Americans have no longing for a Church with a foreign aspect" and that "they will not submit to its influence." Archbishop Ireland stated unequivocally that immigrants, as long as they could be identified as foreign, "shall not encrust themselves upon the Church."[5] The Church was perceived as the essential vehicle for the Americanization of foreigners. This view is reflected in the writings of most historians, like

Ellis,[6] Brown,[7] and Barry,[8] who, like Henry Steele Commager, interpret the Catholic Church during the 1880's and 1890's period as "one of the most effective of all agencies for democracy and Americanization."[9]

Already in 1925 Gerald Shaughnessy had marshalled statistical data to demonstrate that American Catholicism had met the challenge of assimilating the immigrant masses into a firmly knit Church:

> Not one, he concluded, can parallel the phenomenon which occurred only in America. Not another instance in history is recorded where millions of different races and nationalities, of varied national prejudices and leanings, made their way to a strange country, not *en masse* but individually, there to build up what they found practically nonexistent, a flourishing, closely knit, firmly welded Church. . . .[10]

Will Herberg specified the Americanizing role of the Church. As they Americanized themselves, Herberg states, the Irish carried the whole Church along with them and made it an American Church.[11] Latin and Slavic immigrants found a united front on the issue of Americanization. There seemed to exist on all sides a clear line of demarkation determining the boundaries of 'in' and 'out' groups or of morally 'good' and morally 'bad' people. To the eyes of the southern *contadino* the excitement over the Cahensly question and the flag-waving attitude of Irish pastors and bishops were not very different from the ethical judgment of the Protestant ideology pushing them out of the category of the predestined.[12]

Father Bandini, writing on the financing of the Italian St. Raphael's Society of New York for 1893, states his conclusions after years of contacts and dealing with American civic and ecclesiastical officials:

> What is interesting is that people in Italy seem to think the St. Raphael's Society is greatly helped financially by Americans. These persons cannot realize that this project, because of its stated purpose, prompts Americans to think it must be helped instead by those who send us. This project, which facilitates the arrival on American soil of an element that, far from being desired, is one it would be more desirable to expel, represents an activity that must be as welcome to Americans as smoke is to the eyes.[13]

As late as 1917 the Archbishop of New York could be advised by Father Reilly, pastor of Nativity Church, that

> the Italians are not a sensitive people like our own. When they are told that they are about the worst Catholics that ever came to this country, they don't resent it or deny it. If they were a little more sensitive to such remarks they would improve faster. The Italians are callous as regards religion.[14]

From the *Catholic World* we learn that the Italians, at least in 1888, lacked some traits of the American character, "especially," said Bernard Lynch, "what we call *spirit*. . . . They, for the most part, seem totally devoid of what may be termed the sense of respectability. . . . The shame of being thought a pauper is almost unknown among the Italian people of this quarter (Mott and Park Streets, New York City)."[15] The immigrants and their clergy were looked upon with suspicion and hostility because they were poor and foreign. An Irish pastor even remarked: "Italian priests here must be servants."[16] He echoed Cardinal McCloskey's answer to the Poles who had petitioned him for a church of their own and had been told that what they needed was not their own church but a "pig shanty."[17] Linguistic and cultural differences and their social environment of poverty made the Italians too different; they could not "encrust themselves upon the Church" too easily.[18]

In fact, it has been constantly a difficult proposition for the American Church to accept the Italians as Catholics. In 1857, when Sanguinetti attempted to initiate the first organized congregation of poor immigrants, the *Katolische Kirchen Zeitung* commented that there was no need for an Italian Church since most Italians were street organ grinders and '48 revolutionaries, not Catholics.[19] In 1884, the Bishop of Wilmington found it was a delicate matter to tell the Sovereign Pontiff how utterly faithless the specimens of his country coming here really were. "Ignorance of their religion," he added, "and a depth of vice little known to us yet are their prominent characteristics. . . ."[20] The veteran Italian American journalist Agostino de Biasi, responding to Archbishop Canevin's pamphlet stating that the Latin race in general and the Italians in particular had to be blamed if Catholicism had not made greater success in the United States, wrote:

> Italian immigration counts no more than forty years of life. And we dare say that when the Irish and German immigration was forty years old and was as numerous as the Italian immigration today, the Irish and Germans had not built as many churches, schools, hospitals and orphan asylums as the Italians have done.[21]

De Biasi's rebuttal may have been influenced by subconscious ethnocentrism. It was, however, an expression of the feeling and the experience of the Italian American masses.[22]

Recently Vecoli pointed out that the assumption that the Church had positive impact on the acculturation and assimilation of immigrants has been largely untested.[23]

The 'Italian Problem' was many things to many people, Vecoli concludes, but to the Italian immigrants themselves it may have been that
the Church in the United States was more American and Irish than
Catholic.[24]

The Catholic Church could not serve as a primary agency for the integration of the immigrants because of its own definite ethnic
character. The immigrants remained either nominal Roman Catholics
or without church ties of any kind. This will appear even more so,
Vecoli continues, if we keep in mind that even the devotionalism to
saints and madonnas of the Southern Italian peasants was coupled with
a basic indifference to and distrust of the institutional church. Thus,
the approach to the Italian experience in the American Church has
been from the point of view of the Catholic Church as a positive or
negative agency of Americanization rather than a study of the immigrants' institutional response and creativity.

Protestant Christianizers.

The ideological evaluation of the newcomers on the part of the
Anglo-Saxon world was far more radical and destructive than that of
the Hibernian. Southern European immigrants, the necessary unskilled labor needed in the expanding industrialization of the nation,
were feared as a threat to America's free institutions. This fear was
tempered only by the conviction that the alien population could be
evangelized and properly Americanized.[25] Although an Irish Catholic
was preferable to an Italian Catholic, all Irish, Italians, and French-
Canadians were inferior because they were bigoted Catholics who
would not convert. The criteria of inferiority were drawn from the attitude toward conversion and racial origin. The Italian immigrants
scored very low on both accounts because they were Southern Europeans and devotional Catholics. Yet, a true Protestant being identified in the last decade of the Nineteenth Century with a true
American, Italians could not be assimilated without being first
Christianized.[26] It was a duty demanded by the Church and the Republic
"to bring the Gospel in its purity to these masses from Southern Europe, who are, to a large extent, both ignorant and superstitious."[27]
The Italians were obviously destitute of vital religion.[28] Idolatrous and
superstitious as they were, not only did they need the Gospel,[29] they
had also to be made into men:

> The multitude of common people in Poland and Lithuania, Western
> Russia, and Hungary and Bohemia and Italy, are not of the stuff that
> fosters enterprise. Yet they break out of inertia, come to America, and are
> still coming, following one another like sheep, and only waiting to see

that the first comers seem safe. Such migration is one of the marvels of
the age. Are we not justified in seeing in it the hand of God? Long years
He has waited for the learned and powerful of those lands to take in
hand the culture of the mental and spiritual nature in these ignorant
peasants, that they may have liberty to grow and kindly stimulus in
growth. He has waited in vain; and this Twentieth Century of the era of
Jesus Christ sees these poor people still in ignorance of the essentials of
the free manhood that Jesus came to teach. Is it presumption to see in
this great movement a remedy provided by the Almighty? He will move
them for their own good across the ocean to a land where there is opportunity for the downtrodden to rise. He places them at our doors as a
revelation of His will by giving them the kindly help they sorely need in
order to be men.[30]

If Christianized, however, the Italians would qualify for entrance into
American society. This, in turn, would help America to carry out her
messianic task.

These immigrants of the later landing know neither the Bible nor its
morals. It is for us to see that they are kindly and patiently taught.
Otherwise they will tend to retain their ignorance and their wrong
theories and standards, and gradually to lower the mental and moral
and spiritual tone of our own people by the sheer weight of example.
The grave national and social problem which their coming places
before us is thus stated in its simplest form: 'We have succeeded in absorbing Saxon and Scandinavian; can we now digest Latin and Slav
and Hun?'[31]

Once the immigrants were evangelized,

This nation, together with the rest of the Anglo-saxon race, fully
brought under the power of the Gospel and in the spirit of a true consecration going forth to conquer the world for Christ, with God's
presence and blessing would prove irresistible.[32]

The eagerness, however, of Christianizing the immigrants had also a
less idealistic motive:

Public schools, mission schools and churches will do the work (of
evangelizing the immigrants). And it must be done. Business pleads for
it, patriotism demands it, social consideration requires it.[33]

Since bad men cannot be good patriots and since love for and devotion to the country require intelligence, sympathy and character,
observed John Dixon, the problem arises: Whence will these new-
made Americans get these qualities? The answer was clear: surely by
not retaining their language and by being properly evangelized.[34] The
behavior of social workers reflected the ideological convictions of the
first decade of the century. The gap between the foreign colonies in the

large cities and the dominant group was deep. It derived from poverty (close to immorality in the Calvinist tradition) and the different cultural expression of religion of the immigrants:

> with these (Slavs and Italians) we are getting in our State the continental idea of the Sabbath, the socialist's idea of government, and the communist's idea of property, and the pagan's idea of religion. These ideas are antagonistic to those embodied in our civilization and free institutions—our American ideals being largely the outgrowth of our Protestant faith. Hence we believe that the urgent need is that the Gospel be preached to this new immigration.[35]

Missionary work could not be delayed any further. Personnel and money were invested in this direction.[36] At the same time the separateness of the immigrants was deprecated:

> Living their own lives . . . practicing their own superstitions and beliefs, breeding anarchists, communists, socialists, Sabbath-breakers, blasphemers.[37]

The Protestant attitude seemed to be that God had brought these people into America and if America could now save herself, she would save the world: no need to "put up the bars."

> No greater opportunity ever came to the Christian people of America to do mission work than to evangelize, Christianize, Americanize and assimilate these multitudes of immigrants in our midst into one composite people, united, liberty-loving, flag-honoring, God-fearing, Christ-following, Christian.[38]

What will be the end product of Americanization?

> Within the next decade this army of strangers will be assimilated. *They will be American of some sort.* The battle has begun, our only hope is in the immediate action. The unscrupulous politician, the murderous saloon and the Roman Catholic Church, un-American and unscriptural, are after these strangers. Will our Protestantism bear the test?[39]

Norman Thomas, who discovered his call to socialism while pastor in Italian Harlem, shared the ideological commitment of the general Protestant establishment. The social work of the Church and its Extension Committee and Home Mission was "in the interest of both religion and Americanism." Thomas' work in East Harlem, the work at the Jan Hus (Settlement House) and at Labor Temple was "Americanization work of the best type."[40]

Italian-American Protestant ministers and Church workers generally accepted a concept of Americanization that was in line with the official position of the Protestant Establishment. This factor became another cause of isolation of religious dissenters from the main stream of life and institutions of Little Italy. In the view of Italian-American Protestant leaders: "The Italian needs to be Americanized as well as Christianized."[41] For Rev. di Domenica, true Americanism equalled Protestantism:

> The (Protestant) work, he wrote, must be done, not only for the salvation of the Italians, but for the salvation of America as well.[42]

The Protestant ethic of economic and social success as a guarantee of God's choice, in the encounter with the Italian immigrant, could reassure itself of its long-standing evaluation of Latin people as inferior persons and nations.

The Left and the Radicalization of the Immigrant Proletarian.

Socialist and radical left movements reacted to the arrival of Italian immigrant workers in an ambivalent way. The immigrants appeared as a new opportunity to strengthen a revolutionary movement against a capitalist society and, at the same time, as a menace to existing wage and job availability. At the turn of the century, the more vocal Italian American leftists advocated rejection of trade-unionism, organized religion, and American Politics. In a 1909 editorial statement, *Il Proletario* formulated in a clearer form than that in which the usual anarchist-socialist jargon of the few hundred leftist emigrés would normally present it, their view on the role of the immigrant masses in the United States:

> For us, the defense of the immigrants must not be a work of charity; it must not have a religious or political character. It must be a humanizing of the workers' syndicalism. It must be a function of the working class fighting against the capitalist class without preoccupation of the interests of the little bourgeoisie or the *bottegai* (shop-keepers, i.e., priests)—Italian and German—of the various countries.[43]

The Church was seen as opposing the interests of the workers and as an ally of the establishment and the bourgeoisie.[44] The Italian immigrants, as all other immigrants to the United States, were simply victims of an economic system which had international capitalistic support. America was not the land of gold or the civilized land where people of different countries become brothers. It was, instead, "the tomb of the workers, where the best youth come to fall, compelled by famine and need."[45] The workers to whom Italy denied any *lume di cultura* (education) and whom it expelled through starvation, were more exploited and despised here than they had been in the old country.[46] In fact, not only the growing well-being of capitalism but also that of the entire mass of the American people fell on the shoulders of millions of immigrants steadily arriving from Europe in search of a more abundant bread. Americanism was a process of social mobility through the use of technology and through the exploitation of the latest immigrant group by the previous ones in such a way that the immigrants are like colonized people and the Americans like the colonizers. The future socialist society will be the result of the social levelling-off derived from the contact between less civilized people with others more civilized.[47] In rather vague projections, the end of the immigrants' exploitation was to be achieved with their union and their rebellion against existing socio-economic structures. The trade unions had sold out to the system. They were born with a revolutionary purpose, but they had become an instrument of conservativism. They were capable only of stopping all noble aspirations of the working class. Gompers and Mitchell were simply "vampires of humanity and the Italians remain the element marked for the slaughter house."[48]

The ideological plan was hard put to the test for practical success. The Italian immigrants were more interested in easy money-making, in the trade unions and in their political compromises. They were willing to put up with abuses and poverty because their social mobility, already visible in the transition from Italy to America, was for them an evident sign of future success. Besides, the subtle discussions between reformists, socialists, anarchists and syndicalists were foreign to the mind of the immigrants, impossible to be understood.[49] The priest also was an obstacle since he had a "malevolent and preponderant influence on the virgin and illiterate masses" of Italian immigrants.[50] The priest was making proselytes for his cause through social work while the leftist were just talking.[51] Carlo Tresca had to confess that the socialists had done nothing in terms of schools, cooperatives, and social agencies.[52] The average section of the Italian Socialist Federation in the United States had hardly more than 13 to 15 members.[53] Thus, New York had about 200 registered members of the Italian Socialist Federation out of an Italian population of 650,000; Philadelphia had about 100, out of a population of 140,000.[54]

The approximation of the figures notwithstanding, the Italian immigrants certainly failed as a revolutionary proletariat. Through the Progressive Era the Socialist Party could not gain significant support from the Italians or the Irish. A party organizer, Julius Gerber, complained that of all the nationalities in New York, the Italians were the relatively and proportionately weakest in the socialist organizations.

Table 1. *Sections of the Italian Socialist*
Federation in the United States, 1905

State	No. of Sections
Pennsylvania	12
New York	6
Illinois	1
New Jersey	4
Vermont	5
Connecticut	3
Massachusetts	8
New Hampshire	2
Rhode Island	1
Maryland	2
Louisiana	1
Washington	1
Florida	1
TOTAL	52

Source: Il Proletario, April 16, 1905, Anno IX, n. 16, p. 4.

Catholic clergymen were blamed for the failure, as well as for the fact
that the Italians did not bring to America education, community action,
and ideological and political radicalism.[55] The American Socialist Party
was unable to counteract the Church. Besides, some of the socialist
immigrants were at heart political emigrés trying primarily to build a
base for supporting their European movements. The leftist intellectual
leadership was made up of transient people. They were waiting for a call
to go back to Italy and become part of its political scene. In fact, they
could not always hide their antipathy for the glacial practicality of that
nation of businessmen who were the American people, totally uncon-
cerned with their ideologies. The trade unions despised the immigrants.
Industrial socialism (I.W.W.) accepted the immigrants as equals, but
was not able to concern itself with day-to-day union issues, the bread and
butter issues, which affected most Italian and other immigrants.[56]

The activist Mario de Ciampis concludes his memoirs on the Italian
American Socialist movement pointing out how the failure to achieve
any permanent success was due to internal fighting, personal am-
bitions, the polemics that emerged with the start of World War I and

> . . . the fact that the majority of its members, because they were simple
> workers mostly illiterate, did not know how to educate their families to
> the socialist ideology, leaving their children indifferent to the social
> question and in the hands of the priests.[57]

Strafile reported in 1910 that, much to his regret, the poor immigrant mass was exhausting itself in *feste* and processions, which were a show and a business for the personal publicity of the *prominenti*. The cancerous wounds of the Little Italies were: *pretismo* (clericalism), *prominentismo* (the dominance of the *prominenti*), socialism, and Italian-American journalism. Strafile cautioned:

> . . . the Italian priest in America is a power, an impregnable fortress, and constitutes a kind of colonial feudalism.[58]

The leftists advocated the use of immigrants for a revolution. The anticlericals insisted on the Italians' moving out of the deadly circle of Little Italy and plunging into American life. They perceived American life as free from the traditional neighborhood social and sacred values which they considered limiting individual choices.

The priests, however, and the ostracized trade unions as well, were progressively sinking their roots in the ethnic communities by responding to the practical day-to-day needs of the immigrants,[59] and by embodying their values. Group assimilation, then, could not be pursued by adopting the ideological conviction of anti-clerical and leftist groups.

Italian Responses to the Experience of Mass Migration.

Mass migration from Italy provoked a variety of reactions in the people of the Peninsula and in the people who moved out of it. As a major aspect of the Italian national life, the problem of migration touched all sectors of the country: government, landowners, workers, merchants, the Church and the intellectuals. Emigration was interpreted as a

Table 2. *Italian Societies in Selected States, 1910*

State	No. of Societies	State	No. of Societies
New York	453	Ohio	27
New Jersey	113	California	33
Pennsylvania	147	Connecticut	33
Massachusetts	72	Texas	20
Illinois	31	Washington	13
Michigan	35		

Source: "Le Societa' italiane negli Stati Uniti dell 'America del Nord nel 1910," *Bollettino dell' Emigrazione,* 1912, n. 4, op. 19-54.

safety-valve, a business, an expansion of the national territory without the necessity of wars to conquer colonies overseas. It was also seen as a human tragedy to be eliminated or at least alleviated in all possible forms.

The Italian Government.

The attitude of the Italian Government and the Italian ruling class toward emigration to the United States can be best summed up in the words of John B. Scalabrini. In 1887 Scalabrini wrote in *L'Emigrazione Italiana in America:*

> Our countrymen abroad are the least protected. They are often victims of infamous speculations. . . . The Government has very few facts in this regard to record to its honor. So much so that rooted in the hearts of all is the opinion that the least protected of the migrants are the Italians. . . . Government and Parliament have long discussed this vital problem. But the queries of some Deputies and their projects for legislation; the usual yearly recommendation in the analysis of the budget, and the usual answers from the ministers; the circular letters to the provincial prefects; the articles of semi-official newspapers, all these are ineffectual remedies. They leave the situation as it is when they are not translated into wise laws.[60]

If no action was taken by the Government in Italy, where the pressure for protective laws was stronger, the immigrants could not expect much support in the countries of their destination. At first, the Italian Government aimed at preserving a feeling of *italianità* (being Italian) among the masses of immigrants. This effort did not demand any concrete assistance and its exploitation was easy since it found a prompt response in the nostalgic hearts of the immigrants. The Italian ruling class did not realize that for the peasant, who had opposed the political unification of the Peninsula, the concept of *patria* he knew and was attached to was his native village, more than the traditions of art, literature and history the bourgeoisie had in mind.[61] The perspective of the Government was reflected in the diplomatic reports reaching Rome from the United States. The Consuls were considered incompetent and spiteful toward the migrant workers, a class they had not understood in Italy and could not understand abroad.[62] The abstract position of the Italian Commissariate for Emigration and of the Italian Government is manifested in their policy of trying to orient the immigrants to agriculture[63] at a moment when the American rural population was starting its exodus to the city. Besides, there was an absolute absence of capital for investment in rural colonies and no willingness on the part of most migrants to become farmers.[64] Also, the type of leadership in the immigrant elements the Italian ruling class was relying on and concerned with was a leadership in a vacuum. Such leadership was formed by those *spostati* (out-of-place), ex-students, ex-officers and ex-state employees, ex-school teachers, ex-provincial newspapermen and intellectuals, who, despising the peasants, in no way could accept being classified with them or being associated with them on a social level.[65] But the padrone and the priest, the first on the economic level and the second on the social and symbolic levels, communicated with the urban peasants even if they were not recognized by the Italian Government as elites.

The Italian ruling class, in fact, did not value, and often even ignored, the vitality of the socio-cultural institutions of the immigrants, as the parochial church and the benevolent and fraternal societies that flourished around it. It failed to insert iself as a positive guide in the tribal and primordial world of the peasant. Therefore it eliminated any possibility of continuity of contact with the popular element of the Italian culture. Obviously, the official policy of the Italian Government was reflected in its diplomatic representatives. The New York Italian language weekly *La Scintilla Elettrica* caustically commented in 1910:

> To speak clearly, we never place any trust in the representative of the Government of our country, because certain proud barons and counts, relics of impoverished nobility, disdain the contact of the so-called *cafoni*, and, concerned only with their own image, end up by being damaging to the legions of the *lottatori per la vita* (fighters for life).[66]

Prominenti, Padroni and Fraternal Societies.

The attempts at building indigenous institutions on the part of the immigrants was heavily hindered by lack of prepared leadership and *campanilismo*.[67] The Italian *prominenti*, laborers who had made some money in Little Italy, dealt with the average Italian American as with a misfit, whose decisions they had to make and whose needs they had to define. The traditional political line of the Italian American leader has been a legitimization of his position by identifying himself with the *apostolato di Italianita'* through contact with the Italian Government, decorations, and collections for catastrophies in Italy. Thus, the sentimental feeling of the average Italian American was appeased, the leader's position assured, and no action needed to be taken among the immigrants. The Italian Government obviously played along. The myth of *italianita'* created the acceptance of an unreal world within which much of the Italian leadership relegated itself.[68]

The discovery of the real immigrant was a hard psychological itinerary.

In 1911, the New York socio-anarchist magazine *Novatore* reported Massimo Rocca's discovery of the real Italian Americans, those called *cafoni*, in private conversations:

> For three years, Rocca writes, I have been living and travelling in America, and I have begun to realize that I am Italian. I have begun to recognize and reconcile myself with those poor people of the Italian South, that misery has pushed out of their native villages in search of hard-earned bread in distant and deserted lands. I have begun to love those poor illiterates who do not know how to read and write, but who possess a treasury of virgin energy and a gentle spirit, to the point of depriving themselves of even the barest necessities, in order to help their family overseas, which they probably will never see again. Poor people resigned to a triple oppression of class and nationality, offering their necks first to the indigenous capitalistic yoke, then, to the scorn of other nationalities, which condemn them to the lowest and dirtiest jobs; and finally to the insatiable greed of the colonial *prominenti*.[69]

The *padroni* and *prominenti* came under the tight scrutiny of the American Government, both at the federal and state level. Their role lost much of its significance by the time of World War I, even though their shadow remained present in the ethnic community beyond that period.[70]

The benevolent societies, the natural pedestal of *padroni* and *prominenti*, were so fragmented that they never achieved effective political or economic force. They wasted their small funds for monuments and parades, and limited their function to an expressive manifestation of religiosity and patriotism.[71] In New York City, where approximately six hundred thousand Italians lived in 1910, hundreds of Italian societies were all divided:

> I will not say, the editor of *La Scintilla Elettrica* reported, by regions, but even by *campanile*. Instead of societies classified by arts and trades, or true societies for mutual aid, these are only paper societies. They are formed by 50 to 100 members only, all belonging to the same little *comune* of Abruzzi, Basilicata, Calabria or Sicily, whose name they bear. In such a deluge of societies you will not find one with cultural purposes.[72]

The Immigrants Speak for Themselves.

The mass of Italian immigrants was slow to move in any direction. They brought with them to the United States the suspicious caution of their miserable villages, the distrust of almost everybody, and a total lack of confidence in the institutions of the State and the Church. The Americanizers were tempted to consider the immigrants bad, unintelligent, criminal, and superstitious. The immigrants found the requests of outsiders threatening to their ways and to their concerns with survival rather than with ideologies, either leftist or anti-clerical, nationalist or theological.

It appears that neither the Italian Government and its allies nor the Protestant and Catholic established groups were able to read accurately and penetrate the rapidly growing Italian communities in the United States, in order to encourage them toward organizational effectiveness. The fraternal societies were simply small village organizations so local as to be ineffective. The Italian Church, to the extent it became aware and responded to the social conditions of the immigrants, chose to act on a concrete and immediate level where the needs of the immigrants were most urgent: at the ports of departure and arrival, in the crowded neighborhoods of their urban settlements, in sensitizing public opinion on their behalf. It remains to be seen which strategies and allies the immigrants chose in their process of adjustment.

NOTES

1. Carmine Biagio Iannace, *La scoperta dell'America*. Padova: Bino Rebellato, 1971, p. 155

2. Alfonso Strafile, *Memorandum Coloniale, ossia, Sintesi storica di osservazioni e fatti che diano un'idea generale della vita coloniale degli Italiani nel Nord America, con monografia illustrativa della colonia di Philadelphia*. Philadelphia: "Mastro Paolo" printing house, 1910, 1912, p. 26 and passim.

3. Edmund M. Dunne, "The Church and the Immigrant," in C. E. McGuire, ed., *Catholic Builders of the Nation*, Boston, 1923, vol. II, p. 15.

4. Dorothy Dohen, *Nationalism and American Catholicism*. New York: Sheed and Ward, 1967, pp. 209.

5. John Ireland, *The Church and Modern Society.*, p. 73.

6. John T. Ellis, *American Catholicism*. Chicago: University of Chicago Press, 1955.

7. Henry J. Browne, "Catholicism in the United States," in *The Shaping of America: Religion*, eds., J. W. Smith and A. L. Jamison. Princeton: Yale University Press, 1961.

8. Colman Barry, *The Catholic Church and German Americans*. Milwaukee: Bruce Publishing, 1953.

9. Henry Steele Commager, *The American Mind*. New Haven, 1950

10. Gerald Shaughnessy, *Has the Immigrant Kept the Faith? A Study of Immigration and Catholic Growth in the United States, 1700-1920*. New York: The MacMillan Co., 1925, p. 268.

11. Will Herberg, *Protestant-Catholic-Jew*. Garden City, N.Y.: Doubleday, 1960, p. 142 f.

12. Joshua A. Fishman, *Language Loyalty in the United States*. The Hague: Mouton & Co., 1966, p. 318 on.

13. Letter dated February 10, 1893, Fr. Pietro Bandini to Fr. Francesco Zaboglio, ACSC).

14. Rev. B. J. Reilly to Cardinal Farley, New York, March 4, 1917, AANY.

15. Bernard J. Lynch, "The Italians in New York," *The Catholic World*, XLVII, April, 1888, p. 68.

16. Letter dated May 24, 1888, Fr. Marcellino Moroni to Archbishop Michael A. Corrigan, AANY.

17. Joshua A. Fishman, op. cit., p. 335, quoting W. Kruszka, *Historya Polka v Americe*, XII.

18. John Ireland, op. cit., ibid.

19. *Katolische Kirchen Zeitung*. New York; October 1, 1857.

20. Bishop Thomas A. Becker to Archbishop James Gibbons, Wilmington, December 17, 1884, AAB, 78 VI. See also the editorial by John Gilmary Shea, "Catholic Increase by Immigration," *The Catholic News* (New York) March 8, 1891, p. 4.

21. La Martinella (pen name), "Italian Catholics in America. Apropos of Archbishop Canevin's Pamphlet," *Il Carroccio*, Anno IX, n. 10, October 1923, pp. 355-356. *Canevin's Growth in the United States.*

22. cf. also, Grazia Dore. *La democrazia italiana e l'emigrazione in America.* Brescia: Morcelliana, 1964. Pp. 497.

23. Rudolph J. Vecoli, "Prelates and Peasants: Italian Immigrants and the Catholic Church," *Journal of Social History 2, Spring 1969, pp. 217-268.*

24. Ibid., p. 268.

25. John Willis Baer, "The Peaceful Invasion of America: Some Facts; Some Figures; Some Fears," *The Assembly Herald*, X, 5, (May, 1904), p. 233.

26. "Practical Methods of Limiting Immigration," (editorial), *Journal and Messenger*, LXIII (March 15, 1894), 1; Ibid., editorial of LXIV (March 21, 1895), 1 cf. Lawrence Bennion Davis. *The Baptist Response to Immigration in the United States 1880-1925.* Ph.D. Thesis. The University of Rochester, History, 1968. University Microfilms, Inc. 68-15, 831.

27. ——. "Who are Coming?—To What?"; "Character of Immigration," *The Assembly Herald*, IX, n. 2 (August, 1903), pp. 381-384.

28. Dwight Spencer, "Divine Adjustments," *Baptist Home Mission Monthly*, XVII (September, 1895), pp. 334-336.

29. Ellen May, "Why Italians Need the Gospel," *The Missionary Review of the World*, n. 5. 22, November 1909, pp. 817-820.

30. Rev. Henry Otis Dwight, LL.D., "Thy Neighbor the Immigrant," *The Missionary Review of the World*, N.S. XVII, 12, Dec. 1904, pp. 881-894 (with illustrations).

31. Ibid., p. 889.

32. Wilson Phraner, D.D., "The Evangelization of Our Own Land the Key to the Evangelization of the World," *The Assembly Herald*, X, n. 1, (January, 1904), pp. 27-30.

33. Charles L. Thompson, D.D., "Opportunity and Responsibility Today," *The Assembly Herald*, X, 1, (January, 1904), p. 26.

34. John Dixon, D.D., "Problem of the Immigrant," *The Assembly Herald*, XIII, 3, (March, 1907), pp. 5-6.

35. ——, "Synodical Home Mission in Pennsylvania," *The Assembly Herald*, XIII, 3, (March, 1907), p. 117.

36. John Dixon, D.D., "Our Foreigners," *The Assembly Herald*, XII, 8, (August, 1906), p. 388. "Italians! A million and one-half of Italians in our Land! Those coming from Northern Italy are more intelligent than their southern brethren and are very receptive to Protestant teaching. Our over thirty churches have about 900 members. Our work could be very easily increased ten-fold if there were only more equipped Italian ministers." In 1904 the New York Presbytery had begun a new approach toward immigrants. D. J. McMillan, "Work among Foreigners in New York," Ibid., p. 389. "The Home Board and the Women's Board," wrote Dixon, "care for the European races to the extent of thirty-three thousand dollars each year: ten thousand for Italians; sixty-five hundred for Germans; fifty-nine hundred for Hungarians; forty-seven hundred for Bohemians; seventeen hundred for Ruthenians; and the balance in smaller sums for Greeks, Jews, Portuguese, Russians, Syrians and Poles. . . . It may safely be estimated

that the self-supporting synods and presbyteries spend no less than seventy-five thousand dollars every year. Thus fully one hundred thousand is spent annually by our Church for our European immigrants." John Dixon, D.D., "Our Church and the Foreigners," *The Assembly Herald*, XIV, 1, (January, 1908), p. 30. The work, however, was not moving in any significant way. The Presbyterian Italians of Newark were already decreasing. Between 150-240 were showing up at the meetings, when they were 260 in 1901. Davis S. Lusk, "Forming Friendly Centers," *The Assembly Herald*, April, 1913, p. 203. In Detroit, after six years of work, the church services averaged from sixty to seventy men. Rev. Alfred H. Barr, "Work Among South Italians and Sicilians in Detroit," *The Assembly Herald*, XV, 1 (January, 1909), pp. 29-30.

37. Wm. P. Fulton, D.D., "Redeeming the Cities," *The Assembly Herald*, (April, 1913), pp. 191-194.

38. Ibid., pp. 193.

39. Austin H. Folly, D.D., "Who is My Neighbor?" *The Assembly Herald*, (April, 1913), p. 196.

40. Letter dated April 3, 1918, Norman Thomas to Rev. Wm. Adams Brown, New York Public Library, Norman Thomas Papers. (NTP)

41. Rev. Stefano L. Testa, "For the Italian: A Ministry of Christian and Patriotic Appeal." *The Assembly Herald*, XCII, (January, 1911), p. 11. Antonio Mangano, *Training Men for Foreign Work in America*, pamphlet, n.d. n.p., 1917c. For a different view of Americanization in relation to missionary work among Italian immigrants, see the booklet of the Baptist Church, Italian Baptist Missionary Association: *Report of the Committee on Americanization*. New York, 1918, pp. 22.

42. Rev. A. Di Domenica, "The Sons of Italy in America," *The Missionary Review of the World*, Vol. XLI, 3, (March, 1918), pp. 189-195.

43. ——. "I nuovissimi protettori," *Il Proletario*, Anno XIII, 5, (January 29, 1909), p. 1.

44. cf. "Dalle rive del Tevere a quella dell'Hudson. La Chiesa cattolica all'arrembaggio," *Il Proletario*, Anno XVIII, 14, (April 5, 1913).

45. Antonio Fiocca, "Lasciando il martello e prendendo la penna," *Il Proletario*, Anno IX, 15, (April 5, 1905), p. 2.

46. Nicola Barbato, "Le rivoluzione in Russia. La solidarieta degli Italiani. Ai lavoratori italiani degli Stati Uniti," *Il Proletario*, Anno IX, 6, (February 5, 1905), p. 1.

47. Ilion, "Americani e Americanismo," *Il Proletario*, Anno IX, 23, (June 4, 1905), p. 4.

48. Carlo Tresca, "Alla vigilia della conferenze di Chicago," *Il Proletario*, Anno IX, 26, (June 25, 1905), p. 1; Carlo Tresca, "Periodo di crisi: Insidie all'operario italiano," Ibid., Anno IX, 34, (August 20, 1909), p. 1.

49. g.b. "La nostra organizzazione," *Il Proletario*, Anno X, 32, (August 12, 1906), p. 1; Alberto Argentieri, "La nostra azione," *Il Proletario*, Anno XV, 8, (February 24, 1911), p. 1.

50. Carlo Tresca, "Per la F.S.I. L'organizzazione statale. I." *Il Proletario*, Anno IX, 15, (April 9, 1905), p. 1.

51. g.b. "L'organizazzione." *Il Proletario*, op. cit.

52. Carlo Tresca, "Per la F.S.I. L'organizzazione Statale, *Il Proletario*, op. cit.

53. cf. *Il Proletario*, Anno IX, 23, (June 4, 1905), p. 1.

54. "Le nostra organizzazione," *Il Proletario*, Anno X, 32, (August 12, 1906), p. 1.

55. Melvyn Dubofsky "Success and Failure of Socialism in New York City, 1900-1918: A Case Study," *Labor History*, v. 9, 3, (Fall, 1968), pp. 361-75.

56. Charles Lienenweber, "The American Socialist Party and the "New" Immigrants," *Science and Society*, XXXII, 1, (Winter, 1968), pp. 1-25.

57. Mario De Ciampis, "Storia del Movimento Socialista rivoluzionazio italiano, *La Parola del Popolo*, vol. 9, 37, (December 1958-January 1959), pp. 136-163.

58. Alfonso Strafile. *Memorandum Coloniale*, op. cit. p. 26.

59. Grazia Dore, "Socialismo italiano negli Stati Uniti," *Ressegna di Politica e di Storia*, Anno XIV, n. 159, January 1968, pp. 1-6; February 1968, pp. 33-40; March 1968, pp. 114-119.

60. G. B. Scalabrini. *L'Emigrazione italiana in America. Osservazioni di Giovanni Battista Scalabrini, Vescovo di Piacenza.* Piacenza: Tipografia dell'Amico del Popolo, 1887.

61. Fernando Manzotti. *La polemica sull'emigrazione nell'Italia unita*, 2nd ed., Milano: Dante Alighieri, 1969; Grazia Dore. *La Democrazia italiana e l'emigrazione in America.* Brescia: Morcelliana, 1964. Bruno Caizzi. *Nuova Autologia della questione meridionale.* Milano: Comunita', 1962. Pasquale Villari, "Emigrazione e questione sociale nell'Italia meridionale," in Alfio Carre', ed. *Orientamenti e testimonianze sulla questione meridionale.* Trapani: Célèbes, 1965.

62. cf. *Bollettino dell'Emigrazione*, III, 12 (1904) pp. 14-15 .

63. cf. *Bollettino dell'Emigrazione*, III, 9 (1904), p. 57; VI, 6 (1907), pp. 18-19.

64. cf. Ch. II. For the total failure of New Palermo, see G. Moroni, "Lo Stato dell'Alabama," *Bollettino dell'Emigrazione*, XII, 1 (1913), p. 52. Where capable leaders or *padroni* were present, there was success, as for example, in the case of Tontitown, Vineland and the Italian emigration into the rural areas of up-state New York, as reported in Luciano Iorizzo's doctoral dissertation "Italian Immigration and the Impact of the Padrone System," Department of History, Syracuse University, 1966.

65. Cf. *Bollettino dell'Emigrazione*, V, 3 (1906), pp. 45-46; Grazie Dore, op. cit.

66. Editorial, "Le Istituzioni," *La Scintilla Elettrica*, March 27, 1910 p. 1.

67. See chapter II, pp.

68. Cf. *Il Progresso Italo-Americano di Nuova York.* New York: Nicoletti Bros. Press, 1911. Pᴅ. 272.

69. Massimo Rocca, "Il Congresso dell' Ipocrisia," *Novatore*, 11, 5-6 (1-16 Marzo, 1911), p. 24.

70. John Koren, "The Padrone System and the Padrone Banks," United States Department of Labor. *Bulletin*, N. 9, (March, 1897). U.S. House of Representatives. *Letter from the Secretary of the Treasury Transmitting a Report of the Commission of Immigration Upon the causes which incite Immigration to the United States.* 52d Congress, 1st Sess., Ex. Doc. 235, Pt. I.

71. Gerolamo Moroni, "Societa' italiane nel distretto consolare di New Orleans, La.," *Bollettino dell'Emigrazione*, 1910, n. 10, pp. 3-7. "Le societa' italiane all'estero nel 1908," Ibid., 1908, n. 24, pp. 90-123.

72. Editoriale, "le Istituzioni," op. cit.

CHAPTER **IV**

The Emergence and Growth of Italian American Parishes

Italian immigrants reached America when it was already an explored continent. Settlers were no longer free to subjugate nature and organize their lives as they wished. Their religion was no exception. The Irish Church wanted to transform these newcomers immediately into *American* Catholics. The piety of the Italians was too compromising a virtue, either bordering on superstition or making life too earthy and pleasant. Protestant denominations felt challenged to expose Latin Christians to the benefits of the Reformation. They worked hard at converting them to the Protestant faith, and, more importantly, to Protestant social virtues. Italian American intellectuals and radicals, few in number and isolated by their ideological jargon, were out of touch with the immigrant mass. The fraternal societies were impotent congeries of fragments. The *prominenti* had a tendency to use the ethnic community only for their personal success. There seemed to be little hope for an easy assimilation of the Italians. But as one examines the history of their experience, it becomes evident that, in the presence of many trials, the Italian ethnic Church emerged as a central and creative force in the life of the immigrant community.

The historical growth of the Italian parishes follows three major stages of development, after an initial and sporadic religious interest in Italian immigrants, before the heavy immigrations of the 1880's. At first, an attempt was made to include the Italian immigrants in the existing Irish parishes. Then, a policy of clear separation was adopted and a building period followed. Finally, a return seems to take place to a fusion of Italian, Slav, Irish and other groups into a new and still emerging social amalgam defined as 'Middle America.'

Italian Immigrants and the Church, 1850-1880.

On February 17, 1864, the church of Our Lady of Grace was incorporated in Hoboken. In the missionary territory of the State of New Jersey, the few hundred Catholics of the city were proud of their achieved organization. Happier were their priests. The pastor, Father Antonio Cauvin, had arrived in New York from the Kingdom of Piedmont in 1847. After serving the Italian and French population around Canal Street in Lower Manhattan, in 1851 he was sent by Archbishop Hughes to minister to these ethnic groups and to the Irish in Hoboken. For a while, Cauvin had been a tutor in the family of Count Cavour. In fact, Victor Emmanuel, King of Piedmont and Sardinia, presented him with a silver ostensorium, and the Cavour family sent him some liturgical vestments, on the occasion of the opening of the new church, "in recompense for the services rendered by him for so many years to the Italians of New York, especially to the Genoese, whom he attended to in their sickness, instructed, and many of whom continued to come to him for confessions."[1]

Fr. Gennaro de Concilio, a brilliant Neapolitan, disciple of the philosopher Sanseverino, had reached America in the spring of 1860 at the request of Bishop James Roosevelt Bayley of the just erected diocese of Newark. His assignment was to assist Father Cauvin. De Concilio was an alumnus of the Brignole-Sale College for Foreign Missions of Genoa which had sent several outstanding priests to work in the United States.[2]

Northern and southern Italians did not yet form a large colony. De Concilio could act, then, also as chaplain at the nearby Seton Hall University and as professor of logic (1860-1862). This remarkable scholar founded the church of St. Michael and the Italian church of Holy Rosary in Jersey City. He became the treasurer of the St. Raphael's Society for the Protection of Italian Immigrants in 1889. He wrote the famous Baltimore Catechism used for fifty years, without revision, by the children of the immigrants and of their native co-religionists in all Catholic schools and religious classes in the United States.[3]

The organizing of churches for Italian immigrants, however, did not start in New Jersey. Saint Mary Magdalene de'Pazzi in Philadelphia had been organized in 1852.[4] "This church, the first in the United States for the special and exclusive use of an Italian congregation,"[5] had no parochial boundaries. It was originally a Methodist chapel with a small burying ground attached. Father Gaetano Mariani and Bishop Neumann had bought the chapel for the use of Italian immigrants. St. Mary's started as a mission in 1852 and the cornerstone of the church was laid in 1854. On the committee appointed for the occasion were persons of mixed background, with Irish names in the majority.

Already in the 1850's the eastern seaports of New Orleans, Philadelphia, New York and Boston had small Italian communities, mostly of seamen and merchants, and a handful of political refugees. As in Philadelphia, the Italians of Boston were cared for by the priests serving English-speaking congregations. In 1866, twelve Italian clergymen were serving in the diocese of Boston[6] and at least since 1868 an Italian Jesuit was giving special services for Italians at St. Mary's chapel in that city.[7] The tiny Italian colony of Boston had constituted its first fraternal and benevolent society in 1842. It was made up of seamen, musicians, and businessmen whose wealthy financial status and good religious practice were not creating a problem for the church.[8]

In 1855, there were 968 foreign-born Italians in New York City. The largest concentration was in the sixth ward enclosed by Canal Street, Broadway and Chatham Street. The eighth Census of 1860 counted 1,464 natives of Italy in New York. The immigrant community, however, was split in two divergent groups, that would have increasingly moved away from each other: one, educated and wealthy; the other, semi-skilled and poor. The majority of the Italians of New York were fruit and flower hawkers, plaster statuette vendors, organ grinders, rag pickers and boot blacks. They were ignorant of the English language and of little political influence.[9]

In his dispatches to Rome, the Papal Consul General in New York confirmed the impressions of abjection the largest segment of the Italian group was presenting. Sicilians and other Italians, convicted criminals, had been forced to emigrate to the United States. Their presence was alarming the native born. The Consul wrote:

> The number of crimes (always on the increase) perpetrated by Italians begins to attract public attention on the emigration coming from the Italian Peninsula. . . . The state of deprivation of the Italians arriving here without resources is such that consideration of humanity alone should suffice to forever deter directing to this country those forced to

those forced to expatriate. They (Italians) do not know the language and find it a great difficulty to learn it. The abilities they possess are generally insufficient to assure them the necessary means of existence and they fall into a great misery. Brazil, Buenos Aires and the Spanish countries are generally more convenient than any other to Italian migrants, who find there climate, language, customs and traditions similar to those of their fatherland.[10]

A month later, in February 1858, Consul Binse reported to Cardinal Bernabo that a chapel for Italian immigrants was happily commenced by the excellent priest Father Antonio Sanguineti. He added:

But I must confess that the execution of his work is difficult. I don't know how he can manage without creating a mixed church, i.e. taking care both of Irish and Italians. In fact, even admitting that he could procure the means to buy a church, how could he sustain the expenses of cult among poor Italian organ players, figuristes etc. who form the poorest class of our population? Besides, already a miserable *canaille* of a journalist, Secchi de Casali, in his detestable newspaper *l'Eco d'Italia* tries to obstruct Father Sanguineti with all possible means.[11]

G. F. Secchi de Casali belonged to that minority of the Italian community of New York made up of vehemently anticlerical political refugees, intellectuals and professionals, who were mostly interested in their future in an Italy united either under the House of Savoy or the Republicans of Mazzini. This group earned a living by teaching music, the Italian language and literature, and the opera. Secchi de Casali, Eleuterio Felice Foresti, Pietro Maroncelli, Giuseppe Avezzana, Quirico Filopanti and the other less famous Italian patriots might have been afraid of losing their status, if a heavy plebeian immigration from Italy was to take place. The political and literary circles of New York and Boston, in fact, outdid each other in welcoming, entertaining and supporting the Italian *fuorusciti,* the exiles from the various States of the Italian peninsula. As people condemned for their involvement in the revolution for a united Italy, they were received in America as the symbol of freedom from bourbonic and papal tyrannies.[12] In the eyes of the United States, this small Italian community of New York was a worthy and acceptable continuation of the Reformation and of the American Revolution. It overshadowed the larger number of poor and ·unskilled Italian immigrant laborers and projected such an image of Italian religion as to affect the relations between Italian immigrants and American Catholicism for almost a century. The incident which fossilized the stereotype of anticlericalism of the Italian immigrants was the visit of Archbishop Gaetano Bedini to the United States. In 1853 Archbishop Bedini arrived in New York on his way to Brazil where he was sent as papal nuncio by Pius IX. While in the United States, Bedini presented President Franklin Pierce with a letter from the Pope; took care mainly of ecclesiastical affairs; and, to his surprise, had to face the organized demonstrations of the Italian exiles who identified him with political repression in the Papal States. Alessandro Gavazzi, a former priest and chaplain to Garibaldi's army, became the rallying point of the opposition to Bedini's visit. In a series of lectures and street demonstrations, Gavazzi managed to further split the Italian followers of Felice Foresti, a supporter of Mazzini, and those of Secchi de Casali, who endorsed King Victor Emmanuel. He defined Bedini "an ecclesiastical hyena"; aroused a new furious attack on the Papacy; and gave new ammunition to the anti-Catholic and anti-immigration Know-Nothing Movement. Finally, on the emotional appeal of patriotism, Gavazzi stirred the tiny Italian community of New York to the point of plotting Bedini's death. Father Cauvin, who continued his care for the Italians in New York from his parish in Hoboken, had in fact assisted the last moments of a young immigrant, Giuseppe Sassi, who was knifed for revealing to archbishop Hughes the plot against Bedini. As a result of Gavazzi's campaign against Pius IX and Catholicism, Bedini's visit was a failure and an embarrassment to American Catholics. The nuncio was forced to return to Europe in a clandestine and ignominious way at the conclusion of perhaps the saddest period of the Church in American history. American Catholics in New York could blame the turbulance and disorder of nativists groups on the fiery speeches of an Italian ex-priest and on the passionate editorials of the Italian exiles' newspaper, L'Echo d'Italia, which had adopted the strategy of anti-papalism to advocate patriotism.[13]

In the meantime, an elementary school for the Italian children of the Five Points, an area of New York formed by the intersection of what is now Worth, Park and Baxter Streets, was established in 1855-1857 by the Children's Aid Society.[14] When Italian merchants and professionals in New York began to finance it in a significant way by 1863 the fear of Protestant proselytizing once again disturbed New York Catholics.

As the beginning of fraternal and institutional organization, however, was appearing in the immigrant group, the problem of religious assistance was also confronted. From 1847 to 1851, Fr. Antonio Cauvin had labored for the Italians in the sixth and eighth wards out of the French church of St. Vincent de Paul. But the Italian immigrants became caught in the net of larger problems of ecclesiastical politics. The insistence on native clergy and Americanization was forwarded to Rome in 1847. On the same occasion the adamant position of the Irish in defense of the Papal States and the Pope's temporal power was made known to the Holy See. Father Geremias Cummings, a curate of St. Patrick's Old Cathedral of New York, wrote to the Secretary of Propaganda Fide:

> The Holy See has several times expressed its desire that the Church and the clergy of the United States be a national church and clergy. But, to-date, this is progressing slowly. Our best Catholics—who are without doubt the Irish—find it difficult to divest themselves of their affection for all that concerns old Hibernia. Therefore, they would like to establish here an Irish Catholic Church. The Germans set up house on their own and do not want to have anything to do with the Irish. Frenchmen in many cases would like indeed a Catholic, Apostolic, Roman Church. They, however, would like to dress her up à la francaise. Now, the consequence of all this is that Americans, mostly Protestants, profess to consider Catholicism as a foreign merchandise with which, as a consequence, they want to have nothing to do. People capable of thinking, be they Americans, Irish or others, establish what the American church should be: by stating that: 1—We must call and consider ourselves neither Irish, nor Germans, neither Americans nor Frenchmen, but Catholics! Let's take away these odious distinctions. II—If we want religion to take a firm hold in the United States, the same soil must produce its clergy . . . therefore we have to choose Americans as bishops. . . . IV— . . . let's take what is necessary for the expression of ecclesiastical habits (uses) and customs from Rome, thus we will be sure of not erring. . . .[15]

Official Catholicism saw the various national groups as a temptation toward isolation from the surrounding society. The remedy proposed was disciplinary uniformity and nationalism, i.e. Americanization of the Church and acceptance of national ideas and priorities. Cummings, at this time a confidant of Archbishop John Hughes, added:

> Here in New York there is in preparation at the present a public demonstration to honor the Pope and to protest against the occupation of Ferrara. All important men of the City will take part![16]

The poor Italians, crowded in the Five Points area of the city, could not care less for the occupation of Ferrara, a city in the Papal territories. But to Archbishop Hughes and to the Italian political refugees, Papal politics had a direct impact on their views, emotions, and work. To the refugees, in fact, who were waiting impatiently to return to fight in the army or in the Parliament of united Italy, a demonstration for the Pope was one against them. They felt obliged, then, to fight back through their newspapers, their speeches and their counter-demonstrations. In 1849, Cummings, by now pastor of the new church of St. Stephen, reported to Propaganda his impressions of the Italian community:

> One of the preoccupations that I had during my sojourn in New York was to see to it that there was a way to gather the Italians who lived here in a goodly number so to encourage them to practice the duties of our holy religion. I have found some of them good and edifying Catholics as well as respectable citizens. But almost all were at my arrival a dishonor to their beautiful fatherland. I know Felice Forresti. I believe he is basically a crazy radical and probably an infidel regarding belief, but he has kept—as a white-haired and decent man,—a form of behavior worthy of praise. He went to Paris to take part with the rebels, his old friends, but then returned to New York. General Avezzana, another acquaintance of mine, a failed merchant in this city, has also, as we are told, made bankruptcy of his good reputation in Europe. We had here a miserable gang (combricola) called the Societa' di Benevolenza Italiana (Italian Benevolent Society) and another called the Guardia Nazionale (National Guards). The worst of their members returned to Italy. The others are quiet, knowing that sensible Americans hate and despise their revolutionary *cabale*. Some people had joined the Society called Alleanza Cristiana (Christian Alliance), which has also died of anemia. The Protestant Italians, once favored, had to turn elsewhere or return to call themselves Catholics. One of them, during the time of Protestant expansion, was writing letters to the Gazzette as if they were originated in Rome when actually he was living in New York. This man is now a spectacle of compassion and ridicule to all. We had in New York an Italian priest, the excellent Signor Muppiatti, who died lamented by everybody because of his apostolic virtues. The only Italian in our clergy is Don Felice Villanis of Turin sent here by Propaganda. He is loved by everyone, especially by the people of Cold Spring and West Point where he is pastor. He is also one of the most learned and respected priests of our Diocese.[17]

By 1854 a good and zealous Franciscan Missionary, the Sicilian Fr. Francesco Caro, was working out of St. Stephen parish.[18] The following year another priest, a political refugee from the Papal States, Don Nicola Marcocci, excommunicated because of his political republican views, but a reasonable man of impeccable character, joined the same parish.[19]

In the diocese of Newark, New Jersey, in the meantime, as well as in the diocese of Brooklyn, some Italian priests were busy and successful in developing English language parishes: Father Venuta, in Jersey City; Father Biggio, in Bordentown; Father Tarlatini, in West Hoboken, and a score of others in the diocese of Newark. Father Fransioli was instead establishing St. Peter's parish in South Brooklyn in

1859.[20] Already in 1849 Fr. Charles Constantine Pise, perhaps the most brilliant and gifted priest of his time, had established the parish of St. Charles Borromeo, where he remained pastor until his death in 1866. Fr. Pise, born in Philadelphia of an Italian father, had been from 1832 to 1834 Chaplain of the United States Senate, the only priest ever to be elected to that office.[21]

The few hundred Italians of Lower Manhattan, however, were starting a pattern of unorthodox organization, in-group divisions, and external conflicts—a pattern that would remain with them in the future. Factions formed around the various proposals circulating in the small ethnic community. *L'Eco d'Italia* attracted the more educated and anticlerical Italians. The Franciscans wanted to build an Italian hospital. Others were set on the building of a school. Father Sanguineti and his supporters thought the construction of a church was the first priority. The Italian Consul tried to be a power-broker among the various interest groups.[22] The American experience of Father Sanguineti portrays well the incipient efforts and frustrations of Italian immigrant laborers to organize a parish of their own.

On October 13, 1857, Father Antonio Sanguineti had arrived in New York with the intention of immediately returning to Italy,

> but, he writes, having found there so many poor Italians who were leading a most deplorable and miserable life, with no priest to take care of them I had no heart to leave. I stayed, and requested permission to work for the good of those unfortunate. This permission was refused to me. But then, after appeals to other persons, and, better, so God disposing, it was granted to me. . . .[23]

Sanguineti worked out an agreement with the French church of St. Vincent de Paul at first. He took over a mission chapel of the church for the Italians and received room and board in exchange for all offerings from the chapel as the pastor Father Lafont had stipulated.

> While, then, I was staying with Rev. Lafont, Sanguineti continues, since he had sold the church and I could no longer continue with him my congregation because of the great distance existing from the homes of the Italians to the place where the new church was built, he notified me that from that moment on I should think to provide for my people. I found myself with a very great number of Italians that were coming to Mass; a hundred and more children that infallibly were coming to their catechism every Sunday, and not having the heart to abandon them, I promised the construction of a small chapel. The Italians, on the other hand, realizing they were at the point of being forced to scatter and get lost, not consenting to remain abandoned, they united together. After a few meetings they resolved to open a subscription, i.e. to take a collection. A person, in the meantime, since I was not speaking English, had

taken it on himself to inform first of all the Bishop. But then, once we realized this person was not able to reach the bishop, I and a few Italians presented ourselves to the Archbishop who, having made the remarks he thought best, told us to continue and that if we succeeded to have four thousand dollars he would help us to have a church.[24]

The collection started the day after the meeting with Hughes. The joy of the Italians was great. The reaction against the project was also quick.

"Enemies of the church," Sanguineti says, counterattacked swiftly, possibly Italian anticlericals and Protestants. Instead of building a new chapel for the Italians, Sanguineti remained in the old French church of St. Vincent de Paul from May 1, 1858, to the following July. The lay committee in charge of the collection, upset by Sanguineti's independent decision to have some gates made for the altar-rail, assaulted him in church and physically harmed him. The noise of broken pews and the yelling of the priest attracted some nearby people who saved him. From then on, Sanguineti decided to directly take care of collections, but he never saw the money already raised. With the assistance of some Italian, French and Irish Catholics, from July 1858 to February 1859 he continued his work for the Italian community and gave regular account of his income to the Bishop. In March 1860 Sanguineti returned to Italy discouraged after having uselessly attempted by letter, visits and intermediaries to reach the Bishop of New York to show that the accounting of his chapel was improving. Instead of obtaining permission to proceed with his work, Sanguineti had received an order from the Vicar General to sell everything. Reflecting on his American experience, Sanguineti observed that he would gladly spend all his life for the poor Italians. He said:

> . . . because there is in America no place destined for the Italians, there still is now a Roman family with three adult children without baptism. If in America the needs of the Italians had been taken care, probably there wouldn't be so many here who tear the heart of this beautiful land; America wouldn't register so many bad reactions of Italians; and the Church wouldn't lament the loss of so many souls. . . .[25]

Once in Italy, Sanguineti pleaded for help from the Pope for his Italians in New York, especially since the Protestants had already provided a store-front chapel out of which they distributed gifts and proselytized and because the rumor was spreading in New York that it was the Pope who was against the union of the Italians.

> It is sad, Eminence, Sanguineti wrote, that these poor people, with the abundance of churches they had one day in Italy, cannot have a little church in America; it is painful that the Italians who first brought

religion to those lands, defended it and implemented it, cannot now have for themselves the means to practice it, they who were the first who discovered America.[26]

I have nothing against Bishop Hughes. If he has defended me, I am very obliged. I would have wanted that, rather than defend my person, he had protected the work I had started for the benefit of so many poor Italians. The Bishop should not have let me to believe I should stop certain ceremonies (funzionette) considered too Roman and too respected among Italians. We intended to perform those ceremonies in order to better reawaken the faith of the Italians, who for so many years were living very much abandoned, and to attract them more easily to the church.[27]

The case of the Italians and Father Sanguineti provoked an exchange of letters between the Propaganda, to which Hughes had protested, and New York. Sanguineti had left because he had seen an adamant opposition to a church for Italians on the part of the diocese[28] and because of his desire to appeal to the Pope on their behalf. The archbishop accused the priest of financial mismanagement and the Italians in New York of irreligiosity and unwillingness to support their church.[29] Cardinal Bernabo, to shed more light on the whole question, requested information from a trusted alumnus of Propaganda. On October 15, 1860, Father Cummings wrote to Rome on Sanguineti:

I have every reason to believe that during his stay in New York his conduct was without fault. I believe it is my duty to tell you that he is not an individual to whom one should entrust the erection of a church for Italians in this city. He was well received at the beginning and he would have succeeded to do some good had he been prudent. The Archbishop, without directly helping him, let him act; the Italians came in good number, and even I and other friends of the Italians did everything possible to help him. But we had to leave him because he lacks judgment. He had to complain, and with reason, of the conduct of some Italians, but he offended many . . . notwithstanding his great zeal and desire to do good he is a little of a bungler (cianfruglione). His defects have been an heroic obstinacy, imprudence (avventatezza) and indiscretion and bitterness against those who might have offended him and a great lack of tact (del b molle) in the government of his parish. He made another blunder that I often but to no avail told him would be his ruin and the ruin of the Italian parish: making use of any means to attract to his church the Irish, who had already sufficient churches of their own. This procedure offended the Bishop, made the other priests jealous, and angered the Italians who saw the Irish little acceptable to them, being preferred to themselves.[30]

The Italians attending church were very poor. Father Sanguineti overstepped his jurisdiction, even if on the advice of the Papal Consul

General, in order to raise money for his purpose. Thus, poverty, a weak personality, the divisions among the Italians and their priest, the intransigence of the archbishop, doomed the project. There seems to have been a worry about conflict with the government also, apparently the Italian government, since Sanguineti felt obliged to reply to Propaganda:

> I wouldn't know how I could have compromised myself with the government by having done something right, a procedure decided by the Italians, approved by the Sardinian Minister, begun with the consent of the Archbishop, carried out in the company of Italians, and exclusively among them.[31]

Neither the rented former church of St. Vincent de Paul nor the chapel started under the name of St. Anthony of Padua on Canal Street could evolve into a national church. The Italians were divided, some allied with Sanguineti and others with Hughes, but all determined to maintain some lay control over their church.[32] Consul Binse repeatedly stressed the good qualities of Father Sanguineti: "The zeal and devotion of this excellent priest," he wrote to Propaganda, "so disinterested, are truly admirable. It would be a disgrace indeed if the lack of support should cause the failure of the work he has begun with so many difficulties."[33] At the same time, with the selflessness and sweetness of Father Sanguineti there was "a lack of firmness and talent and experience" that made the outcome of the projected Italian church very doubtful.[34] Above all, the lack of leadership in the ethnic community stifled any fast organizational growth. As Consul General Binse observed:

> I must say that the leaders among the bad Italians here are the worst 'canaille' that one can imagine. On the other hand, the Italians who are well intentioned, respectful and attached to their religion, are very poor and very ignorant. It is necessary to do everything for them; they are not disposed to come to the aid of the priest. Father Sanguineti, therefore, has established a small tax of three cents to meet the expenses of cult. But the Italians do not pay it with good will; several of them prefer not to come (to church).[35]

Yet the mass of lower class Italians were the typical immigrants of the future, forgotten by their compatriots with money and learning, and forced to find their way into American life through their peasant common sense.

While the Italian immigrants in New York were busy with internal frictions and the political controversies raging in the Italian peninsula, in the West and in the South of the United States great Italian missionaries like Bishop Rosati, Father Mazzucchelli, Father Cataldo and a score of others, who had implanted the Church in those regions, were slowly aging or vanishing from the scene.[36] Their fading away, however, did not leave the small Italian communities outside of New York without religious care. The early Italian settlements of California did not lack the ministry of Italian priests, especially of the Jesuits. The Italian Consul in San Francisco reported in 1871:

> In California there are no strictly called Italian churches. St. Francis, however, in this city, has two curates, one of them particularly dedicated to our people. He is the Reverend don Giovanni Valentini from Como who arrived here in 1868 from China where he stayed several years as a missionary. He is still young, educated, esteemed by all, and—these are rare as well as important qualities—very charitable and of Italian sentiments.[37]

The Consul, then, points out that in San Pablo, Santa Inez and also Monterrey there were Italian priests. He continues:

> The Jesuit Fathers, the majority of whom are Italians, staff a very beautiful church in San Francisco, the best served in the whole city, surrounded by buildings of their property used as schools and habitations. In Santa Clara, they also own about forty miles south of San Francisco, a large property where they have founded the most beautiful college in the entire California. There are admitted boarding and extern students without religious distinction. The students pay a rather expensive tuition, but in return they receive a solid and extensive education, since the professors are the best.

Forty five Italian Jesuits were listed by the Consul as depending on the Santa Clara house, among them famous pioneers and missionaries like Fathers Accolti, Mengarini, Cangiato and Ravalli. The University of San Francisco, the University of Santa Clara and Gonzaga University are some of the results from the initial labors of these Italian missionaries. The few hundred Italians of Louisville, Kentucky, seemed also without religious problems. At the death of Victor Emmanuel II, the Italian colony of Louisville left aside Church and State antagonisms in the Old Country and they wrote to the Italian Foreign Minister De Pretis in 1878:

> . . . with the sign of mourning already visible on the face of every Italian, we moved in procession to the Cathedral to attend a funeral ceremony, thus showing to these foreign people that the Italians know how to honor, although extinct, the achievements and heroic actions of their now deceased monarch.[38]

The Societa' di Unione e Fratellanza Italiane of St. Louis, Missouri, had the Catholic catechism printed in 1869 for the children of the

Italian community of the city as part of the Italian language textbook adopted by the Society.[39]

But when mass immigration appeared on the Eastern seaboard, a new chapter of Italian presence in America was opening, a chapter social historians would catalogue as the 'Italian problem.'[4] Were the Italians becoming a problem for the Church or the Church a problem for the Italians?

In 1860 the foreign-born Italians in the United States numbered 11,677. A decade later they had increased to 17,157.[41] The concern of diplomats and bishops was aroused by these immigrants, poor, vociferously anticlerical, but Catholic.

Six months after Father Cauvin had seen the incorporation of his church in Hoboken in February, 1864, the Italian Plenipotentiary Minister in Washington, Commendatore Bertinatti, expressed the desire to visit the new Archbishop of New York, John McCloskey. By now Father Sanguineti was in Italy. Father Cauvin was too far away to minister to the Italians of the Five Points and so were the other Italian priests. Father Pamfilo da Magliano, who had led the settlement of the Italian Franciscans in New York State in 1855 and had just established St. Bonaventure University,[42] wrote to Archbishop McCloskey that Bertinatti was

> said to have received an order with promises of funds from his Government, that he must adopt some plan for the amelioration and education of the Italians residing in New York. I may advert, he added, that both he and the Consul General, aside from political difference, are very zealous for the Catholic religion and seem very anxious to save, by some means, their countrymen from the baneful influence of protestantizing societies. The plan that he would submit to Your Grace is to have an Italian church and an Italian school under the care of Italian Ecclesiastics.[43]

In the Spring of 1866, the parish of St. Anthony of Padua was erected for both Italians and Irishmen of the Lower West Side of Manhattan.[44]

Philadelphia, New York, Newark, and Boston had organized Italian congregations by 1875. But from 1870 to 1880 over 43,000 new immigrants had arrived from Italy and from 1880 to 1890 the tide had swollen to almost 268,000.[45] The percentage of returnees was extremely high, however, and the American Census of 1890 registered 182,580 foreign-born Italians for the whole of the United States. Thus, Italian emigration had an almost seasonal character. In any case, Italian colonies were springing up rapidly in California, New England, Louisiana, New York, and Pennsylvania and a critical time had begun for the religious care of these immigrants.

The Ethnic Parishes.

The institutional response to the immigration tide was slow and hesitant. Church conflicts based on different ideologies and interests weighed heavily on the Bishops of the New York Metropolitan area during the 1880's and the 1890's and affected every administrative move they made. The immigrants were unaccustomed to fast change and self-organizing. On the one hand, there was the preoccupation of well-intentioned churchmen entrusted with a pastoral mission of preserving the faith of the immigrants, alleviating their social and moral stress, and building the Church in what was fast becoming the leading modern nation of the Western world. On the other hand, there was the fear of reopening a nasty period of confrontations in the church, as had happened during the quarrels between Irish and German bishops and parishes. There was fear of rekindling nativist accusations against the Church as a threat from a foreign power, as a non-patriotic institution, and as an open menace to the values and traditions on which the Republic was established. In 1896, Father Zucher wrote in defense of Americanization:

> The object of some German Bishops seems to be to Germanize their dioceses, and that of many German priests, to Germanize their parishes. . . .
> The great objection which American Protestants have until now urged against the church—an objection which at certain periods they entertained so strongly as even to raise persecutions—is, that the Catholic Church is composed of foreigners; that it exists in America as a foreign institution, and that it is a menace to the existence of the nation.[46]

Bishops Gilmour and Moore had already written in 1885:

> From the founding of the Republic this imputation of foreignness has been the main imputation made against the Catholic Church in the United States, and periodically with the interval of a few years, very violent attacks are made against the Catholics, this imputation of foreignness forming, as it is well known to everyone, the cry for the assault.[47]

Officially, the Third Council of Baltimore of 1884 had not spoken in favor of nationality parishes, although it recognized the impelling necessity of helping the newcomers from Europe, mostly Catholics, and of providing priests to care for them. In the *Schemata* of the Council it had been suggested that where there were many Italians, churches and schools should be built for them allowing the use of the immigrants' language.[48] But the Council debates insisted on the creation of organizations of socio-religious assistance along the line of the German St. Raphaelsverein. Above all, the Council encouraged the priests to advise the immigrants to move West into farming.[49] Obviously, the Italians leaving the land in their native country out of desperation could not be convinced to move out of the metropolitan areas. Besides, the debate during the council revealed the unwillingness for an all out commitment to Italian immigration problems. The collective pastoral letter circulated by the Archbishop of Baltimore James Gibbons in 1884 in the name of all the Bishops of the Council doesn't even mention immigration.[50] Already in the preparation of the Council the Archbishops and Bishops of the United States present in Rome in 1883 had decided with the Roman Curia that:

> To prescribe a fixed way to provide for the necessities of Italian immigrants is impossible, at least for now. . . .[51]

Archbishop Corrigan had written to his Ordinary Cardinal McCloskey on more detailed plans for the care of immigrants. He reported from Rome:

> With regard to the question of immigration, we advised the formation of Societies in Europe, e.g. in Italy, on the plan of the St. Raphael's Society in Germany. Propaganda promised to send us some good Italian Missionaries from the Collegio Brignole-Sale in Genova, and to interest Religious Orders in the welfare of poor Italians. Then, to write to the Propagation of the Faith to furnish funds to pay said Missionaries. . . .[52]

For its part, Propaganda Fide supported the idea of national parishes. Its rationale was avoidance of useless conflicts between ethnic Catholic groups and a more efficient pastoral care for non-English-speaking people. In 1891, Cardinal Rampolla, Secretary of State of Leo XIII, wrote to Cardinal Gibbons:

> One can provide well for the Catholic migrants from different countries through national parishes as it is already customary.[53]

By the time of the Council of Baltimore, however, the existing Italian parishes were practically mixed, combining a congregation of Italian, Irish and German worshippers. The experiment of Father Sanguineti in New York City, of the parish of St. Anthony of Padua with an Italian and Irish congregation also in New York, of the parish of Our Lady of Mt. Carmel in Harlem, the parish of Our Lady of Victories for Italian and French Americans in Madison, New Jersey,[54] show that the planning was for mixed ethnic congregations. Italians were very poor and could not contribute enough to the support of the

church and the priests. Their traditional anticlericalism and their lack
of familiarity with the voluntaristic system of churches in the United
States made them reluctant to sustain ecclesiastical structures only by
themselves. The Italians of St. Leo parish in Baltimore wrote to Cardinal Gibbons in 1881:

> The undersigned Italians domiciled in this City respectfully lay before
> you a few considerations concerning their spiritual wants:
>   While we feel grateful to Your Grace for the great zeal shown to us in
> the erection of St. Leo's Church, still we feel greatly displeased that our
> priest was forbidden to preach in English.
>   Two are the reasons why we are much displeased with that prohibi-
> tion:
>   The first reason is, because some of us have wives who are either Ger-
> man or Irish or American; and our young men and women, boys and
> girls, all speak the English language, and have a very limited knowledge
> of the Italian language.
>   The second reason is, because we Italians are too few, and mostly
> poor, to be able to support the Church. . . .[55]

Duplex Parishes: A Contradictory Model?

Italians, settling in mostly Irish and German occupied territory, were
taxing the local parishes with requests for new services without bringing new revenues. Almost eighty-five percent of the Italians lived in the
eight states where seventy-five percent of the Irish had settled and they
succeeded them in the same miserable tenements and jobs.[56] The creation of duplicate structures for the newcomers would have caused enor-
mous new expenses for buildings and programs. The administrative
response became oriented toward a new ecclesiastical institution, the
duplex parish. The system of duplex parishes consisted of a combining
of two ethnically different congregations under the same parochial administration. The cultural and class differences seemed to make it advisable to have the English speaking people run their own church and
its societies as the regular, official parish organization. The non-
English-speaking people would have been permitted to use the basement, at some specified days and hours, for their own ceremonies and
gatherings. This system was already in existence in 1880 in the lower
East side of New York, and it became the almost universal transitional
stage toward independent Italian churches in St. Paul, Boston,
Brooklyn, Newark and other cities. Describing the Little Italy extending from the Bowery to South Fifth Avenue and from Bleeker to
Broome Streets in New York, the Jesuit Father Russo wrote in 1896:

> Our Little Italy has a population of from twelve to fifteen
> thousand. . . . Nearly all the southern provinces of Italy are represented

with their different dialects, customs and manners. In former days they belonged to St. Patrick's Church—the old cathedral—the basement of that Church being opened to them. Two Italian secular priests were added to the staff of the parish to look after their spiritual welfare. . . . The results were far from encouraging . . . the parish priest was disgusted, asked the Archbishop to make other provisions for them, and the basement of his church was consequently closed to the Italians. Of course, the willing ones might have gone to the upper church to hear Mass; but, besides being deprived of religious instruction, they were placed in an alternative which was distasteful to them. They had either to pay five cents at the door, like all others, or be refused a seat during Mass. The former attacked their purse, the latter, their pride and sensitiveness.[57]

The Transfiguration Parish in nearby Mott Street was proceeding along the same lines in 1897:

While all that we have spoken of refers to the upper church, let it not be forgotten that we have three Masses in the basement for the Italians of the parish, and that Father Ferretti, under Father McLoughlin's direction, does very efficient work for that portion of his flock. Nearly twelve hundred of the sons of sunny Italy attend these services, besides which they have vespers and evening services without end. Father McLoughlin did his best to make the two races coalesce, by compelling the Italians to attend services in the upper church, but found that far better results could be obtained by having the two people worshipping separately. There are quite a number, however, of the better class who prefer to worship in the upper church. . . .[58]

For ten years, the dark and dirty crypt of the cathedral in St. Paul, Minnesota, became the Italian parish. Rev. Nicholas Odone tried to appeal for funds for a new church by affirming the necessity of terminating their dependence on the upper church:

What a humiliation, he wrote, for us, here, numerous as we are . . . to have to come here in this low and humid hall, placed under the feet of a dissimilar people who sometimes look down on us, in more than one case depending on the humor of others, and more than once of necessity swallowing the bitter and hard-to-swallow pill.Oh, let us reawaken in us the national pride. We are Italians and let us remember we are children of Dante Alighieri. . . .[59]

Monsignor de Concilio, who had been present at the Third Council of Baltimore as a theologian, was seeing in the duplex parish a conspiracy against the Italians. He wrote to Bishop Scalabrini in 1889 that in a meeting they held the Archbishop and the priests of New York had decided not to allow the Italians to be separated from the American parishes where they were living. He added:

The Italian Mission here is surrounded by almost insurmountable difficulties, even when all other circumstances are favorable. Your Excellency should understand how much these difficulties are increased by a silent opposition, antipathy, silent repugnance of the Bishops and priests against the missionaries and the Italians; by their determination to keep them under themselves in mixed parishes, with the pretense of amalgamating them to the Americans; by their deliberate subtle spite that they have for the Italians whom they consider as the disturbing element of their people. . . .[60]

The Rector of Transfiguration Parish, Thomas F. Lynch, was speaking for most pastors when he wrote to Archbishop Corrigan in 1886 demanding the collections taken up in his church basement from the Italian congregation:

The Italians do not constitute a *separate congregation,* but are a *part* of the congregation of this church and should therefore contribute their share toward the expenses. . . .[61]

In Boston, Italians had services of their own in St. Mary's Church by making use of a chapel set aside for them within that church until the new Italo-Portuguese Church in North Bennet Street was organized in 1873.[62] In Brooklyn, the first Italian parish started with a meeting of the congregation in the hall of the kindergarten building of St. Peter's Church, at the corner of Hicks and Warren Streets.[63]

Again, in New York in 1893, there was an Italian priest ministering to his people in the basement of St. Brigid's Church, a practice continued until the Italian parish of Our Lady Help of Christians was built and inaugurated in 1911.

They (the Salesians) have succeeded in gathering quite a congregation of them (Italians), having four Masses on Sunday, and I feel that if they left, it would cause their dispersion. The secular Italian priests don't seem to draw them as well. There is an immense mass, some 10,000, I think, in St. Ann's, Immaculate Conception, and St. Brigid's. The two thousand who come to our basement are from all these places and from the Nativity, and St. Rose's also, and as big a crowd as it is, it is still only about one fifth of the seething multitude. . . .[64]

In the South mixed congregations were also the initial stage of Italian religious organization. The Italians in Memphis were in a miserable condition. When they built their church under the leadership of Father Luisetti, there could be seen many Irish practicing there.[65] In St. Louis the same phenomenon was present in 1889.

In St. Louis there are 18,000 Italians totally abandoned. The Archbishop has Mass celebrated for them in the basement of three

American churches, where some American priest says some words in Italian, and everything stops there.[66]

The problem of fitting Italians into established parishes was further complicated by the impression conveyed by some Italian priests of keeping their flock from assimilation:

> ... he has just asked me if I would object to this man officiating in our basement and giving a sermon there in English every Sunday. The plea is that the Italian children don't understand Italian. There is abundant provision for the children in our school and Sunday school, if they would only send them up to it. But some of the priests attending here seem to be helping to keep them and the people Italian.[67]

The compounded factors of poverty and divergent cultural habits created an impossible situation. Incurring expenses for new land acquisition and new buildings was normally a prohibitive item.[68] The Irish pastors expected an immediate assimilation of the immigrants into the established structures. They expected as well the help of Italian priests in this process, but could not admit the Italians to participate in the same ceremonies, because of the language barrier and inevitable conflict of interests.[69] Italians resented discrimination because of their poverty and their religious traditions, a discrimination symbolized by being relegated into the basement of churches or subsidiary facilities. They resented their lack of equality, as it was expressed in rather strong language by two of the most outstanding Italian churchmen laboring in the United States at this period, Gennaro de Concilio and Francesco Zaboglio. In 1888, Monsignor De Concilio wrote to bishop Scalabrini:

> Since in the United States one worships *Mammona iniquitatis* (money) and one is appreciated more or less for what he is worth financially speaking, even Catholics have absorbed a little of this spirit, and people are appreciated, also by them, for what they are worth financially. Since Italians in the greatest part are very poor and cannot contribute anything for the maintenance of cult, they are literally despised as many paupers and rascals, who cannot ever be down-graded and humiliated enough. This is the reason why the system of the annex or mixed (congregation) will never succeed. No, the Italians must be independent. . . .[70]

In that same year, Father Francesco Zaboglio wrote:

> Your Excellency knows that Fr. Lynch said that here the Italian priests, ours included, must be servants, servants, servants. Fr. Kearney has not said this, but from his behavior of Monday it seems he is trying to put it into practice, and this notwithstanding that Fr. Kearney is said to be a great priest.[71]

Archbishop Corrigan of New York and the Bishops of Brooklyn and
Newark were not in principle against establishing separate parishes for
the various nationality groups. The problem was with the pastors on the
local level. On the one side there were the pastors, almost exclusively
Irish, and on the other there were the immigrants and their priests, both
religious and diocesan. Father Morelli, who started the Columbus
Hospital in New York and several other Italian American institutions,
summed up his experience vis-a-vis the mixed congregation. He wrote
in 1889:

> Day after day our experience proves to our eyes the inconvenience of
> mixed churches. Where there are Irish and Italians, for the Italians
> nothing is done except administering Baptisms and performing
> marriages. A word in the Italian language is never heard; Italians never
> go to confession and this notwithstanding the Bishops remain obstinate
> in preserving these mixed churches in the hope of Americanizing the
> Italians. . . . The Italians because of the abuses (soperchierie) they re-
> ceived in the Irish churches are not going to church. . . . The Italians,
> like the Germans and the French, yearn for churches of their own in-
> stead of the basements of the Irish churches. . . .[72]

In a letter to Cardinal Simeoni, Prefect of Propaganda Fide, Father
Moroni reports the argument of a New York pastor against separate
churches:

> Churches are opened for Italians and then the Irish are served in them
> and the parish is divided. This is fine, Moroni continued, and justifies
> the opposition of the pastors to see Italian churches in the area of their
> parish. But the fault is not with the Italians, but with the choice of loca-
> tion of churches where there are few Italians.[73]

The immigrants were not even in full control of the church basements
they were using and felt compelled collectively to remind
the Bishops to satisfy the desires of the entire Catholic population.[74]
The Italian priests also were convinced that from a pastoral point of
view the mixed church was not effective. Father Domenico Vicentini,
c.s., wrote to Archbishop Corrigan in 1893 that, in principle, it was a
good idea to make use of Italian priests as assistants in English-
language parishes because of the financial difficulties of the Italians
and because of the idea of Americanizing them, "a natural and almost
necessary thing for those who settle in these States." In practice, he
added:

> Many Italians do not take advantage of mixed churches (past experience
> proves it), both because of the idea they have of being despised by the
> Irish, and because in mixed churches American and Italian priests alike

will prefer in their care, the Irish. We are human and it will take a spirit of great dedication to be all to all: to the poor, to the ignorant, to the badly educated.[75]

To the complaint of a pastor, Father Nicholas Russo retorted:

The Italians were not withdrawn from his jurisdiction . . . all the sacrifices we had to make from the beginning, were made only because he refused to look after the Italians.[76]

The English-speaking congregation was also uneasy and anxious to see the Italians vacate its basement.[77] Even when it was reduced to a minority, it could not resign itself to turn over the church to the new-comers.[78]

The attempt to enforce the Americanization model of the established Irish Church was ineffective. In fact, it bitterly antagonized the Italian faithful and their priests. A situation of open conflict began to develop between Irish pastors and Italian priests, Irish and Italian parishioners. To remedy both exploitation and frustration in churches and parochial schools,[79] the concept of the national parish was developed as the next stage of Italian ethnic organization. It appeared useless forcing old structures to serve new social conditions. The mixed church and the annex church were rejected in favor of the independent ethnic church, if not of an independent jurisdiction. Language problems, economic strain for existing parishes, the precedent of German parishes, all of these factors advised the acceptance of Italian national parishes on the part of the American Catholic bishops. Prejudice, however, was not absent as a reason for separating the newcomers from the established churches. In 1898, the pastor of St. Bridgid's parish on Eighth Street and Avenue B in Manhattan wrote to Archbishop Corrigan:

It does seem necessary to have separate churches or chapels for the Italians, as they cannot well be mixed with other nationalities on account of their filthy condition and habits, even if they were willing to come to our churches themselves. . . . I want to suggest to your Grace a plan by which provision might possibly be made for the Italians of the contiguous parishes of the Immaculate Conception & St. Bridgid's without incurring expense for land, which is generally the prohibitive item.

    It is to put up a cheap frame or corrugated iron barn-like chapel over the gravestones in the center of the 12th St. Cemetery—far apart from other buildings. . . .[80]

Separate Parishes: A Sectarian Model?

The failure of the Third Council of Baltimore to resolve the issue of the nationality parishes for non English-speaking immigrants did not silence the demands and protests of newly arriving Catholics. The Italians could only exchange comments among themselves on their subordinate position and remonstrate occasionally with a written protest to their bishop. But the Germans could speak through some of their own bishops within the American hierarchy.[81] The debate on the nationality parishes took on a new national and even international proportion. Carefully prepared arguments and counter-arguments began to fill the pages of diocesan and secular newspapers and the private correspondence of bishops until the turn of the century. In 1886 Cardinal McCloskey of New York wrote:

> If these German Prelates are allowed special legislation as Germans, great injury is likely to follow to the interests of religion. We will be looked upon as a *German Church* in an *English-speaking country.* Let the Italians fancy a German element in the Church of Italy, riding rough shod over the Italians. How would your Cardinals and the Pope fancy it?[82]

That same year, Father Abbelen, Vicar General of the diocese of Milwaukee, could present very logical reasons for an opposite view. He wrote to Cardinal Gibbons, archbishop of Baltimore:

> Your Eminence is aware that the relation between Non-English and English speaking Parishes and Priests is in an unsettled state, and a cause of friction and animosity, especially between German and Irish priests, as also a source of many evils for the faithful. The fact is that there is a tendency on the part of a great many Irish priests to hold that the German Churches are subordinate to theirs, that the German priests have, strictly speaking, no parochial rights, that their services for their people are certainly very necessary and, also, welcome, as long as the Germans retain their language and their customs: but the sooner these disappear, the better. This tendency finds its clearest expression in the postulatum that there should be only one Parish, properly so-called, in one district; that the English-speaking church should be the Parish Church, and the others its dependencies.
>
> Now, the whole German sentiment is directly opposed to this, especially for the following reasons:
> 1) Canon Law is on our side . . .
> 2) The subordination, as claimed, is an injustice and an insult to the Germans. They are perfectly equal with the others, under our Constitution, before the Civil Government: on what ground have they deserved to be treated as unequal before the laws of the Church? Neither their numbers nor their social standing, nor their share of work and sacrifice in the building up of our young Church, nor their domestic and Christian virtues would warrant such treatment.
> 3) All direct and violent efforts to deprive the Germans of their language and customs, to "americanize" them in a quick way, are nothing but fatal means of leading them away from the Church. Let us leave this "americanization" to its natural course, to a gradual amalgamation.

> It will come of itself, especially when and where immigration ceases. Self-interest is its most potent, irresistible factor. But let no one force it, and least of all, a Catholic Bishop and Priest. The German is tenacious: The German Catholic is proud of his country, especially since the glorious "Kultur-Kampf:" the German Catholic,—unlike the Irish—is surrounded by countrymen, who, as Protestants, infidels, secret-society-men, do everything in their power to lure him away from his church. If they could taunt him with being considered, here in America, only as a second-rate Catholic etc.—the consequences, Your Eminence, would be too sad to think of.[83]

On September 28, 1896 a printed Latin summary of the German argument for independence was circulated. Abbelen and his supporters were seen not so much as protesters, but as a threat to the whole Church. Bishop Keane quickly urged Gibbons to counterattack:

> A clear and strong word from your Eminence in regard to the alleged injustice to the Germans would be of very great utility. It is a question involving the most vital interests of the Church in our Country. J.J.K.[84]

The Church was thus identified with its Irish wing. The battle had started from very spiritual premises: the salvation of souls, which the Germans saw in the preservation of their language and culture and the Irish in the conversion of America. Foreign identification, however, was hindering conversion, as already in 1878 Father Willard, a Wisconsin priest, had written to Archbishop Gibbons:

> These (German) priests seem to forget the Unity and Catholicity of the Church to perpetuate the curse of Babel in *Language*. Their great endeavors to make everything foreign and German, make them very obnoxious to Americans. So long as the priests care more for sauerkraut and its concomitants than they do for the souls of the Americans, they are not very likely to convert them. . . .[85]

Father Willard had remarked to Gibbons that both of his parents' families were in the United States before the Declaration of Independence and had taken part in the War of the Revolution:

> The fact of my being an *American, not an Irishman,* as also speaking the German language, has led them (Germans) to repose more than the usual confidence in me, hence I have been made cognizant of many of their plans.[86]

It was also at this time that the Germans became the symbol of all ethnic groups within the Church. A collective letter from a group of Wisconsin pastors to Archbishop Gibbons stated in 1878:

> Hereafter we shall class the Irish and their descendants and any other English speaking nationality as English-speaking; and the Germans, French, etc., as German-speaking . . . although the vast number of these

Germans, French, etc. can speak the English language, and many of the native born among them understand it better than the language of their fathers. . . .[87]

These pastors were complaining of discrimination in reverse on the part of the Germans and were asking for a non-German Bishop. When the controversy became a national issue, the problem lost its German identity and became the problem of nationality parishes. The presence of large masses of Italians and Eastern European Catholics probably decided the tipping of the balance in favor of a clearer canonical legislation. The Third Council of Baltimore was still in preparation when significant numbers of Italian immigrants began to arrive. In the Irish controlled dioceses of the Eastern Seaboard the Italians, as we have seen, were directed into a mixed congregation system. The American Bishops seemed satisfied with that and with encouraging the presence of Italian speaking priests in some of the areas of settlement of the Italians. In 1884, Cardinal Gibbons had summarized the thinking of his colleagues when he wrote to Archbishop Elder of Cincinnati:

I do not think it practicable to establish colonies for Italians as nearly all that come to our shores congregate in the cities and do not take to farming. The Ordinary can provide a priest for them whenever their number demands a priest of their nationality. In our conferences in Rome, the American Prelates unanimously proposed that it would be most expedient to establish in the sea-board the care of emigrants after the model of the St. Raphael Society which is doing so much good for the Germans. It was also proposed that corresponding societies—for the Italians— should be established in Genoa, Naples etc. and that the European societies would correspond with the sister societies in America, and thus the emigrants on departing from home and arriving here would receive friendly attention and advice.

The Cardinal Prefect promised to bring the matter, when asked, to the attention of the ordinaries of Genoa, Naples, etc.

With regard to some missionaries for Italians in our large cities, it was stated at our meeting that the College of Genoa would furnish priests and that Don Bosco could be appealed to. I think a priest is already charged in New York with the special care of the emigrants. . . .[88]

After the Council of Baltimore, from 1884 to 1890, the Abbelen Memorial in defense of the Germans and the answers to it on the part of Bishop Ireland and Keane brought the Holy See more directly into the picture. This national issue became international.[89] Cardinal Simeoni of Propaganda Fide was requested to authoritatively answer the letter of an American Bishop on the issue of national parishes. The bishop, as his predecessors had done before, had erected parishes on the basis of the language and nationality of the faithful:

... convinced this was best for the spiritual welfare of the faithful, for the preservation of the faith, and to avoid any occasion of insults and conflict among them, which might easily arise in the contact of people of different origin and cultural background.[90]

The practice was now challenged as illegal, since in the same territory it was not possible to establish several independent quasi-parishes. The quasi-parish should have been made dependent on the existing territorial parish. The petitioning Bishop's doubts were formulated in two questions:

1. Would it be possible to establish several real and totally independent parishes in the same geographical area according to the various languages of the population?

2. Would a bishop act against ecclesiastical legislation if he decides that children living in the family of their parents who belong to a specific parish should be obliged to remain attached to that parish while they are minors or until the bishop decides differently in view of special circumstances?[91]

After receiving favorable comments from the Archbishops of Boston and Baltimore, Propaganda Fide sent its own favorable decision for both queries to Gibbons on June 8, 1887.[92] Although by 1887, acknowledgement of inevitable assimilation to American ideas, habits and politics were forthcoming from both sides, the "horrible curse of national feeling," as Archbishop Gross of Oregon City called it, was still enkindling endless disputes among clergy and liaty. The melting-pot concept of assimilation was warmly espoused by the liberal English-speaking Bishops, who, in the fire of battle, failed to realize that the nature of group life in the structure of American society was deeper than the language use and the "external culture" of the immigrant groups. Archbishop Gross more clearly stated that:

anyone acquainted with the American people knows that they believe and trust that the various nations pouring into our country's bosom will become amalgamated into the one great American Nation; that these peoples coming here will leave behind, gradually at least, their German, French, Dutch, Irish, and other national European customs and adopt the American ideas, habits, and politics. But Archbishop Heiss here makes no secret of his determination to perpetuate German habits on American soil and tries to make the Catholic Church an advocate of the same un-American views. He does not (from this statement) acknowledge an American nationality as even existing. According to him Bishop Spalding is an Englishman; Archbishop Elder is a Briton; His Grace of New York an Irishman—and as for poor me—well, I have no nationality at all! . . . All know that the enemies of the Church from the days of the Roman emperors down to the leaders of Know-

Nothingism have endeavored to bring the reproach that the Catholic
Church is a foreign establishment. And Archbishop Heiss makes every
Bishop and Archbishop in the United States an Englishman, Frenchman,
Irishman, German, or Belgian—there is not an American among us.
Your Eminence knows so well our country—knows that just now there
are great exertions being made to have another political crusade against
Holy Church, and this document of Archbishop Heiss will do more than
anything else to strengthen the attack.[93]

Archbishop Heiss had formulated most of the points that were made
by the German Catholics and would have been used by all other
successive non-English-speaking immigrants:

1) Total independence of German parishes from the Irish, also exluding
   the jurisdiction of Irish priests on any German of a German parish.

2) Resentment that German parishes (in St. Louis, especially) be called
   Ecclesiae succursales or of secondary role.

3) Rejection of the assumption that the Irish are so much better as
   Catholics than the Germans that they should be preferred to them
   even in rights and privileges.

4) Interpretation of Americanization as a slow and natural process,
   since a fast pace would damage the faith of the Germans.[94]

In this line of thinking, at the end of 1887 the idea of Apostolic
Vicariates for Italians, to make them independent from the Bishops,
was circulating in the New York Metropolitan Area. Influential people
had espoused the idea and were putting pressure on Rome for its implementation.[95] The American bishops, however, who had gone on
record as opposing even the nomination of language Vicar Generals,
could certainly not respond favorably to the new proposal.[96]

For Monsignor de Concilio action was imperative to achieve independence:

The true remedy is to subtract the Italians from the ordinary jurisdiction
of the Bishops here and to proclaim (establish) either an Apostolic
Vicariate or a Superior of the Italian Missions with exclusive jurisdiction over all the Italians.[97]

In a famous pamphlet written in 1888, de Concilio further elaborated
his proposal for the remedying of the religious conditions of abandonment the immigrants were beginning to find themselves in, and he
presented the system of a "Mother Church." Opposition to the existing
system of mixed congregations and annex churches was restated. The
system was seen as useless, impractical and humiliating. The immigrants' habits could not be changed overnight and the majority of the

Italians could not be reached through that system. There would be no rapport unless the priest belonged to the same nationality as the people. The Italian priest would not enjoy freedom of initiative in his work for the newcomers. To meet the spiritual need of the Italians in the United States, in every major city of the union there should be one or more "Mother Churches" exclusively Italian. The "Mother Churches" would be independent parishes located where the majority of the Italians live. Attached to these churches there would be a house for the priests, schools, and other social services. Chapels distributed in smaller Italian colonies far from the church would be served from the "Mother Church." Propaganda Fide would authorize the American Bishops to give faculties to Italian priests only for the Italians. The financial help collected in Italy by Propaganda Fide should be distributed for the Italian work in the United States.[98] To carry out his project, de Concilio turned to Bishop Scalabrini in Italy. He wrote in 1889:

> May Your Excellency complete his work and bring to the attention of His Holiness the enormous necessity of such a measure. An Apostolic Vicariate would solve entirely the Gordian Knot. However, for the time being at least, there should be a superior who could give unity, encouragement and direction to all the missions, who could deal with the Bishops, with authority. The American Bishops, who would probably make some noise against an Apostolic Vicariate, could not say anything against a superior with almost the power of an Apostolic Vicar.[99]

The double jurisdiction entailed by de Concilio's proposal came under stronger attack in 1891. The Archbishop of New York wrote to bishop Scalabrini, who explicitly favored national parishes. He complained of the maneuvering of French-Canadians, Italians, Greek-Catholics and Poles for their own bishops and apostolic vicars and, in particular, of de Concilio's pamphlet, which was sent to all Italian bishops and to the cardinals in Rome.[100] Archbishop Corrigan was confronted at the same time with the demands of the immigrant communities of his immense diocese and with the controversy raised by the Lucerne Memorial, which strengthened the claims of the ethnic communities. On December 9-10, 1890, an international conference of the St. Raphaelsverein, an organization founded by Peter Paul Cahensly in 1871 for the care of German Catholic emigrants, was held in Lucerne, Switzerland. The conference modified and adopted a document prepared in Piacenza by Bishop Scalabrini's collaborators and which suggested practical pastoral approaches for the care of immigrants in the United States. The document, signed by officials of the Society from seven different countries, petitioned the Pope for parishes, priests and bishops suitable to the nationality of the immigrants. It emphasized the great desirability for the Catholics of each nationality, wherever possible, to have several bishops of their own background in the eipscopate of the country of their immigration.[101]

Scalabrini and his delegates to the Lucerne Conference, Fr. Francesco Zaboglio and Marchese Giovanni Battista Volpelandi, were well acquainted with the Italian situation in the United States. Scalabrini's own priests, introduced to the American Bishops by a special letter of Leo XIII in 1888, had repeatedly written on the needs of the immigrants and the difficult relationship encountered with American priests. Other laymen and priests as well, de Concilio among them, were in correspondence with Scalabrini. Father Alphonse Villeneuve, a French-Canadian priest from New York State, through personal visits and detailed correspondence, had especially brought home to Scalabrini and to Cahensly the dangers affecting the faith of Catholic immigrants in the United States. At the 1890 International Social Congress in Liege, Belgium, he impressed on the participants his claim that twenty millions Catholic immigrants had either turned Protestants or indifferent in America. Villeneuve saw the root of the problem in the lack of acceptance of immigrants' representation in the structures of the Church. In April of 1890 he wrote to Scalabrini:

> I know that the various nationalities which suffer in the United States are anxious to know if, at long last, the Holy See will deign to witness to them that it does not want to treat them like pariahs, but like affectionate sons; that it wants (the immigrant groups) to have in the hierarchy the part due to them; that it never had in mind to make the American Episcopate an exclusive episcopate, accessible only to Irish and to some occasional German and Belgian. . . .[102]

Villeneuve interpreted a pluri-ethnic hierarchy as a sign of justice and universal pastoral care on the part of the Holy See and as an enrichment for the American Church. He continued:

> The addition of the Canadian element to the hierarchy of the American Republic will graft the tree with a vigorous, strong sap full of the best promises for evangelical fruits.[103]

At the end of 1890 the Bishop of Ogdenburgh, New York, died. Villeneuve once again wrote to Scalabrini pleading for his intercession with the Pope for a French Canadian appointment. If an Irish bishop were named to the diocese of Ogdenburgh, the immigrants will understand that

> it is the Irish element which will soon dominate the Church in the United States. And they know that such a domination certainly wipes out

all nationalities with the consequent loss of an immeasurable multitude of souls.[104]

According to Father Villeneuve's information, the Irish clergy planned to fully control the episcopal sees and all the parishes, with limited toleration for national parishes and elimination of Catholic parochial schools. Thus, they "would Americanize everything in the anti-American meaning of the word given by the Irish bishops." Clearly, Villeneuve referred to naturalized Canadian American bishops and insisted for Scalabrini's support in Rome for this cause. After all, he wrote,

> it is question of the common salvation. The cause of the immigrants is binding on all. The immigrants have a common enemy: the Irish. I cannot reproach myself for saying this time and again. Your Excellency should write to the Holy Father directly; speak to him frankly and plainly; tell him the Irish are not the only Americans, that the other immigrants are also Americans and that it would be a sin against justice to deliver the Church of the United States to only one race. . . .[105]

Scalabrini, Villeneuve reassured, would not be alone in pleading the cause of the immigrants. Monsieur Ribot, Minister of Foreign Affairs, had given assurance of a diplomatic intervention at the Vatican on the part of the French Government. In the middle of January 1891, Villeneuve was in Florence on the way to Rome. He wrote to Scalabrini on the developments of the Lucerne Conference.

> Special news that I have from my friends in Rome makes me believe that Your Excellency will obtain from the Holy Father all the reforms and measures desirable for the salvation of our dear immigrants. . . . A letter received this morning from Cahensly tells me he will be in Rome with the marquis Volpe Landi at the end of the month and that the princes Isenbourg-Birstein and Scwarzenberg will sign the petition to the Holy Father. . . .[106]

On April 16, 1891, the Lucerne Memorial was presented to Pope Leo XIII by Cahensly. The following May, the Memorial exploded in the press with inaccuracies and distortions which provoked a fierce denunciation in the United States of Cahensly and the nationality bishops. The Memorial was presented in the United States as advocating a double jurisdiction in the Church: American bishops for the Americans and nationality bishops for the immigrants. This false assumption has affected the development of the church and pastoral care of migrants in the United States until today.[107] The Lucerne Memorial simply requested what was already accepted in principle: equality for the ethnic

parishes and priests and participation in the hierarchy of the entire
Catholic population, not separate jurisdiction, as the seventh point of
the Memorial states:

> It seems very desirable that the Catholics of each nationality, wherever it
> is deemed possible, have in the episcopacy of the country where they im-
> migrate, several bishops who are of the same origin. It seems that in this
> way the organization of the Church would be perfect, for in the
> assemblies of the bishops, every immigrant race would be represented,
> and its interest and needs would be protected.[108]

The primary target of the Bishops' response to the Lucerne
Memorial were the German Americans. The Holy See worked to quiet
down the American Bishops: too much weight had been given in
America to Cahensly's Memorial, and his project of an international
episcopate was of impossible implementation.[109] Cardinal Rampolla,
the Pope's Secretary of State, in turn, wrote to Cardinal Gibbons to
reassure him that the Holy See did not consider opportune the idea of
giving to each immigrant group a representative in the Episcopate.
National parishes were sufficient.[110] The Holy See rejected the political
contention of the Bishops that the immigrants should cease to feel
bound to the country of their origin. Rather, it saw its role in looking
equally after all without taking any account of nationality, American
or European.[111] The Archbishop of New York, most interested in the
whole debate because of the huge number of immigrants in his diocese
was also becoming an ally of conservative forces in the Church. He was
honorary president of the St. Raphaelsverein for the Germans and active president of the St. Raphael's Society for the Italians, as well as the
supporter of the two main efforts undertaken on behalf of Italian immigrants: the new religious congregation of the Bishop of Piacenza,
Scalabrini, and that of St. Francis X. Cabrini. He wrote to Cahensly dis-
approving both the Lucerne Memorial and the Memorial of Cahensly
and Volpe-Landi to Cardinal Rampolla, which had been submitted
shortly after the first. With profound grief Corrigan stated that the
Memorial was "based on a total misconception of the genius of the institutions of this country;" that it kept alive "the scorn continually
hurled at us that we are aliens;" that to have Bishops from minority
groups would be unfair to the majority of American-born Catholics.
After all, the Holy See was on his side. The loss of Catholics was three
and a half million only, and this because of lack of priests and
churches.[112] To Bishop Scalabrini the whole international incident
seemed blown out of proportion. At the request of Cahensly and
Volpe-Landi, he sent a letter to the Archbishop of New York trying to
tone down his preoccupation:

My dear Bishop, let me tell you, in this whole issue one has raised a tempest in a teapot. It was in no way the intention of these gentlemen (Marquis Volpe-Landi and Peter Paul Cahensly) to infringe on the rights of the American Bishops. They never dreamed, I can attest to it, to ask the Holy See for a *double jurisdiction*. Their plan was very simple: to obtain that the various European nationalities could have among the American Bishops a representative, and this one not a foreigner but an *American citizen*. Isn't this after all what had already been suggested to the same American Bishops by the great wisdom and practical knowledge of things that so much distinguishs them? Isn't this really the existing policy? Aren't there in the United States German Bishops? Wasn't there as a Bishop also Msgr. Persico, who was even born in Italy? And, if I am not mistaken, isn't there even now a Bishop who is Italian?

With the issue reduced to these dimensions, as it was in fact, Your Excellency can well see that no inconvenience of any kind could have come about. I rather believe that such an arrangement would have greatly benefited the body of Bishops. Bishops, in fact, must provide for all Catholics subject to their jurisdiction without distinction. They would have received from the national representatives accurate and reliable knowledge of the customs, the aspirations, the needs of the respective nationalities; it would have been much easier to take care of them; the masses would have been much more satisfied; and religion would have derived a much greater advantage.[113]

With great frankness Corrigan answered his friend in Piacenza. The Memorial was a moral insult to the entire American Episcopate, much more so because the people writing were not acquainted with the American situation. Indeed, the request for *double* jurisdiction was implied. Even the German-American Bishop of Newark, W. Wigger, protested the Cahensly Memorial. Archbishop Corrigan continued:

. . . the American people, educated to freedom, to national independence, advance in Catholicism as they progress in liberty. But entering the church does not leave outside the door the idea of national independence, and the American Episcopate must try its best so that this independence may not (be) invaded in the religious field: it would bring about most serious damages. People used to such an education would not resign themselves to be subjected to a foreign Bishop. . . .[114]

Cardinal Gibbons tried to settle the dispute in his address at Archbishop Katzer's Reception of the Pallium in Milwaukee on August 20, 1891.[115] He pointed out that in "God and Country" were summed up the American Catholics' religious and political faith. The press, however, and the private correspondence of the interested parties kept Cahenslyism alive. Thus, the *New York Catholic,* rejecting the Lucerne Memorial, commented:

... if we are to judge by the acts of the people of Italy, and by what we see of the Italians who came to the United States, the losses there have been the greatest of all."[116]

But Scalabrini, Cahensly, Villeneuve and all the persons working with immigrants from Europe were pursuing their mission of securing independent parishes.[117] Nationalism, American or European, was not the issue for them as it was for some spokesmen of the American Catholic hierarchy. Their priority and preoccupation was the pastoral care of the immigrants and the integrity of the faith.

In October 1891 Villeneuve could write to Scalabrini:

It would be desirable that your Excellency maintain the greatest reserve with this bishop (of Providence) and that you will not inform him at all about the Prevost affair, the Conference of Lucerne, the memorial to the Holy Father, my poor person, etc. . . . The cause of our reforms has great sympathy here. The first excitement is gone. The spirits are calmer. The public realizes it has been deceived by our adversaries. Several newspapers which the Irish led to fight the Memorial refuse to continue the battle. Thus, we can hope the good Lord will enable justice to triumph. . . .[118]

For his part, Bishop Scalabrini was a strenuous defender of episcopal authority. He rejected the more extreme advice of de Concilio and Villeneuve and negotiated for the pastoral care of Italians in close dependence on the local American bishops. The triumphant reception he received from the immigrants and the bishops during his pastoral visit to the United States in 1905 confirmed his wise policy.

As the air cleared, the assessment of the Cahensly question showed to the Holy See the need to send a papal representative to the United States even against the wishes of the liberal Bishops and to encourage the creation of national parishes, even though safeguarding the universal territorial jurisdiction of the Bishops. De Concilio's suggestion for Apostolic Vicariates, the claim for nationality Bishops and a system of double jurisdiction, and the pastors' choice of mixed or annex immigrant churches, all these organizational forms receded into the background in the ideological debate over Cahenslyism. The more practical choice of the immigrants became a viable alternative.

In fact, the Bishops, including those of the New York Metropolitan Area, were committed to fast assimilation on an ideological level. In practice, their administration moved forward allowing the formation of national parishes and the Italian priests proceeded to the task.

Italian National Parishes

Already in 1883 the Passionist priest Gaudentius Rossi had forwarded an urgent letter to Archbishop Corrigan of New York pointing out that a stable form of religious assistance to Italian immigrants had to be established:

> Having learned from various organs of the public press that Your Grace is one of the members of the American hierarchy honored by our Holy Father, Leo XIII, with a special invitation to Rome, I have several times felt interiorly moved to write to you on behalf of many thousand spiritually destitute Italian Catholics in this vast Republic, many of whom are in the state and diocese of New York. On various occasions I witnessed the spiritual wants of these poor, though industrious and well disposed people, in Pittsburgh, Pa., Louisville, Ky., Chicago, Ill., and more recently, in Baltimore, Philadelphia and New York, preaching for them and administering the sacraments to them. But during the short period of a mission or retreat, the spiritual good effected cannot be of a lasting duration without a sufficient number of zealous pastors, able and willing to take care of the flock. In New York City, in his great zeal His Eminence the Cardinal Archbishop has entrusted the care of Italian Catholics to several Franciscan Fathers, who have for some years labored much for them. But these Italians of late have so rapidly increased in number by immigration, that more spiritual help becomes a pressing necessity. This want is almost daily augmented by new arrivals from Italy in different parts of these United States, and more especially in New York. . . .[119]

Rossi suggested to Corrigan to obtain a missionary band from Don Bosco in Turin; he informed him that he would also urge Bishop O'Hara of Scranton, who was about to leave for Rome with Corrigan, to do the same.

On October 10, 1883, Archbishop Corrigan left for Rome. He had attempted in 1880 to induce some Italian priests to join his diocese, but without complete success. As soon as he arrived in Italy, he approached Don Giovanni Bosco for help, which, at the moment, could not be given. Corrigan raised the issue of Italian immigration at the Vatican and possibly with other churchmen in Italy. He certainly discussed the problem with the American Archbishops who were in Rome with him for a series of meetings in preparation for the Third Plenary Council of Baltimore. The assembled members of the American hierarchy concluded that there was no reason why the Italians should not be urged to attend existing churches if Italian-speaking priests were provided for them. However, a new situation was emerging. Missionary bands and mixed congregations were no longer an adequate response. A new system had to be adopted along the lines of the ethnic parishes already tried for German Americans. Inter-ethnic conflicts were intensifying. The Italians were pressuring for independent churches they could call their own. The mixed congregations began to turn into exclusive Italian congregations. The congregations meeting in the basement of Irish churches started to organize their own parishes. Father Gambera's insight, derived from forty years of work in the Italian colonies of New Orleans, Pittsburgh, New York, Philadelphia, Boston and Chicago and reported in his *Autobiografia,* further illuminates the situation:

> The hundreds of thousands of immigrants, from the beginning, were in need of churches, schools, old age homes. Since at that time they were poor and unaccustomed to supporting the church, many abandoned her rather than submit to that sacrifice. Many were saying: the little Padre makes us lose our faith; he wants money; one has to pay as in a theater. The American Bishops and the clergy of all nationalities, with rare exceptions, did not care for Italians. They excluded them from the churches, because they were slow to give and sometimes also misbehaved; and not rarely their Irish churches resounded with humiliating accusations against Italy and its citizens. This very grave condition demanded an assistance that was *ours*. . . .[120]

Italian churchmen were looked upon with suspicion by a good part of the American clergy because they were introduced and recommended by Papal letters, and

> we were suspected, Gambera continues, as secret agents and therefore, instead of receiving us with courteous, fraternal trust, they avoided us with unjust diffidence.[121]

The issue of Americanization, intertwined with the allegation that millions of immigrants had lost or were losing the faith because they lacked their own clergy and parishes, softened the attitudes of many bishops and favored the creation of national churches for the Italians. With the internationalizing of the problem, not only the Holy See was forced to take a stand on the issue of national parishes, but also the Italian Bishops, who began to organize some pastoral assistance for their countrymen overseas. In 1884, Cardinal Sanfelice of Naples circulated a letter to several Italian and American Archbishops announcing the formation of committees for the protection of Italian immigrants in America.[122] At the request of Archbishop Corrigan of New York, the Congregation for the Propagation of the Faith in Rome began to scout around for pious, zealous, and educated priests to be sent to assist the immigrants in America. In 1887 Bishop Scalabrini of Piacenza began an intense, intelligent campaign on behalf of the immigrants. He founded the Congregation of the Missionaries of St. Charles for this purpose.[123] The Salesians began to send their priests from Turin.[124] The priests of the Catholic Apostolate, who arrived in 1882, intensified their activity.[125] The Italian priests overcame their first impulse to ally themselves with the Italian Government and the American Catholic Hierarchy who were inclined to direct Italian immigrants into agriculture. They would have isolated themselves ideologically from the urbanizing mass. Instead, they responded to the expectations of the migrants and settled with them in the squalor of the city slums. (Table 7) In New York, Newark, Philadelphia, Boston, Chicago, Cleveland, wherever the Italians tried to rebuild their villages during the 1880's and until the enactment of the quota system of the immigration legislation of 1924, a network of Italian parishes emerged that would have linked the Italian colonies all over the States.

The Italians of East Harlem in New York wanted a decent place of worship away from the courtyard where the Society of Our Lady of Mt. Carmel was forced to have its celebration. They obtained their parish in 1884. The parish of the Holy Rosary was erected for another segment of the same colony within the same year. In 1882 the Italian colony of Hamilton Ferry in Brooklyn organized its parish exclusively on ethnic lines. In 1886 the Italian parish of St. Raphael's was erected on 41st Street in Manhattan. The following year, the second parish of Our Lady of Mt. Carmel was established in Brooklyn. In July 1888, two large stores were rented on Centre and Mulberry Streets in New York's Lower East Side where most Italians were conglomerating and were dedicated to St. Michael and the Resurrection of the Lord. These two chapels became the base for the parish of St. Joachim that opened on December 25, 1888. They were also the point of departure for missionary activities among Italians from Boston to New Orleans carried out by priests sent by Bishop Scalabrini of Piacenza. In 1898, the parish of St. Philip Neri was opened in the Bronx. The first Italian parish in the City of Newark was organized in 1886 by Conrad Shotthaefer, who also founded two other Italian churches in that city, Our Lady of Mt. Carmel and St. Lucy's in 1891. The first Italian national parish in the Newark diocese, Holy Rosary, Jersey City, was erected in 1886. St. Francis' in Hoboken was founded in 1888.

Interfering with the immigrants' desire for independent parishes was their cultural background.

> The contagious fever of building private chapels, the pastor of St. Francis wrote to Bishop Wigger in 1898, by the Italians in Hoboken is on the increase. Another son (T. Damelio), a *good man* taken by this kind of spirit, is building another chapel on his own property, and at his own private expense.[126]

Table 1. *Immigrant Clergy Admitted to the U.S.*
From Italy, Poland, and Ireland 1899-1930 (Fiscal year ended June 30)

Country	1899	1900	1901	1902	1903	1904	1905	1906	1907	1908	1909	1910	1911	1912	1913	1914	1915	1916
Italy—North	1	2	2	8	18	43	52	36	35	30	20	13	31	21	28	31	22	8
South	16	23	40	26	42	61	69	77	89	94	39	38	75	65	61	73	38	19
Poland	2	4	3	2	3	30	30	27	30	31	11	18	25	31	20	30	11	6
Ireland	19	13	20	10	45	142	177	155	81	157	99	114	123	155	127	139	140	144

Country	1917	1918	1919	1920	1921	1922	1923	1924	1925	1926	1927	1928	1929	1930
Italy—North	5	2	12	35	14	17	46	15	11	19	17	18	27	12
South	8	3	7	93	85	75	57	58	22	36	30	29	25	28
Poland	2	1	3	13	38	22	44	75	13	10	14	16	10	22
Ireland	114	73	107	160	155	148	157	176	90	121	120	119	102	132

Source: Reports of the Immigration Committee, III Table 22 (1899-1910)
Annual Reports of the Commissioner General of Immigration (1911-1930)

Table 2. *Italian Immigrants and Priests Who Arrived in the U.S., 1899-1930*

	Italian Immigrants to U.S.	Italian Clergy to the U.S.	Number of Immigrants per Clergyman
1899-1910	2,223,431	874	2,543
1911-1920	1,109,484	637	1,899
1921-1930	455,315	641	707

Source: Reports of the Immigration Committee, III Table 22 (1899-1910). Annual Reports of the Commissioner General of Immigration (1911-1930).

The chapels dedicated to the patron saint or the Madonna of the immigrants' villages were attempts by each tiny group of persons from the same locality to recapture the rural parochial world, thus dispersing the resources needed for a national parish in the urban environment of their settlement. By 1899, mostly as a result of Scalabrini's action in Italy and of his correspondence with various members of the American Hierarchy, there were several parishes and chapels functioning for Italians exclusively.[127]

Either fraternal societies under the name of a patron saint[128] started the procedure for their own church, or little ad hoc groups of immigrants applied directly to the Bishops. A letter typical of the latter approach was sent in 1908 to Archbishop Farley of New York.

As Catholic faithful, we feel the duty to call to the attention of Your Excellency ·that in this area of Van Nest—West Farm—there exists an Italian colony numbering almost 2,000, that lives completely forgetful of its Christian obligations.

The cause is the lack of Italian churches or chapels in this part of the city where a priest of the same nationality, preaching the word of God, may keep alive in the hearts of all the sentiment of true Catholics. The people, eager to satisfy their religious duty, but ignorant of the English language, are forced to walk five or six miles to go to an Italian Church. This condition, as Your Excellency will understand, can not be met by all, nor is it always possible.

It is for this reason that the Italians of this area would be happy to have their own Chapel with a good Italian priest. With this letter, through us, they made an appeal for their own church to Your Excellency, certain that you will meet their ardent desire.[129]

Other groups, tired of using the basement of Irish churches, wanted their own church and succeeded in their appeal in obtaining one.[130]

Table 3. *Italian Churches in the New York Metropolitan Area, 1899*

Archdiocese of New York				
	Churches	Chapels	No. of Italian Priests	No. of Non Italian Priests
Diocesan Clergy	1	2	5	1
Franciscans	3		8	3
Cong. of St. Charles	2		6	
Jesuits	1		4	
Salesians	1		3	
Pallotines	1		2	4
Sub Total	9	2	28	8
Diocese of Brooklyn				
	Churches	Chapels	No. of Italian Priests	No. of Non Italian Priests
Diocesan Clergy	3		6	
Vincentians		1	3	
Pallotines	1		1	1
Sub total	4	1	10	1
Diocese of Newark and Paterson				
Diocesan Clergy	11		12	3
Passionists	1			1
Franciscans	1		1	
TOTAL	26	3	51	13

Source: G. Gambera, C. S. "Missioni Italiane negli Stati Uniti d' America, 1899." A Manuscript, ACSC—USA—Prov. 1892-1910.
In 1900 there were in New York City 220,000 Italians. In Newark there were 13,000 Italians.

The ethnic parish system, to be sure, was not closed to the significant segment of the Americanizing population who wanted to identify with English speaking parishes. It did not succeed either in drawing back into the fold all the people of the first generation who had become in-different, nor the tiny minority (approximately between 0.5 and 1 per-cent) which had converted to Protestantism.[131] It became, however, the most relevant institutional organization supporting the immigrants in their encounter with the surrounding groups and the dominant society.

After the turn of the century, the continued flow of immigrants was constantly keeping alive the problems of the first generation. But churches, as well as other social service activities, increased steadily. From an already existing Italian parish, priests would go forth to hold services in a store front in the center of the newly formed Italian colony for a few months. Then, the new parish would be regularly erected.[132]

When the process of building ethnic parishes was concluded, New York City, for example, had seventy-four Italian churches, distributed as follows:

Table 4. *Italian Ethnic Parishes and Chapels Established in New York City, 1866-1961*

Years	Manhattan	Brooklyn	Bronx	Queens	Staten Island	
1866-1900	8	5	1	—	—	14
1900-1924	21	9	7	1	6	44
1924-1961	1	9	4	2	—	16
Total	30	23	12	3	6	74

Source: Thomas B. Kenedy, ed. *Official Catholic Directory.* New York: Kenedy & Sons, 1967.

Fifteen other Italian churches were established in the Archdiocese of New York, but outside the city limits.

Official statistics on national churches report smaller figures than actually existed.[133] Yet, the Catholic Directory for 1918 reports the ex-istence of 580 Italian churches and chapels for an Italian population of 3,028,000.[134] Churches were built not only in the cities where Italians lived in congested, overcrowded neighborhoods, but also in rural areas and small towns. Luigi Villari, in a 1908 consular report for the district of Philadelphia, whose jurisdiction extended over Pennsylvania, Delaware, Maryland, Virginia, Georgia, North Carolina and South Carolina, noted that there was an Italian population of less than 300,-000 served by forty Italian churches. He adds a description of the social environment of these ethnic churches:

> Among the manifestations of colonial life, the religious processions, the so-called "parades" of the Societies, are to be noted, and above all, the banquets. Banquets are tendered on all occasions, opportune and inop-

portune: for marriages, and baptisms; to celebrate the feast of the patron saints; for the departure of a barber who goes to spend a couple of months in Italy, and then to celebrate his return; to console a countryman on the eve of his departure for prison for some crime or other, and then to congratulate him when he has finished serving his time. For funerals one spends fabulous sums; one has even seen processions of forty carriages for the funeral of a new-born baby. Sometimes lectures, theatrical representations, or concerts are given, but almost always without success, because there is an absolute intellectual apathy even in the affluent class.[135]

In the South, the most exceptional case was the parish of Tontitown, Arkansas. Here Father Bandini was pastor and mayor of a town composed exclusively of Italian settlers. Aside from this unique case, Italian churches were also erected in Alabama and Louisiana. Reporting on his trip in 1903 through the southern states, the Italian Ambassador Mayor Des Planches mentioned several Italian churches. Despite the fact that the official policy of the Italian Government at that time was anticlerical, the Ambassador repeatedly commented upon the ways in which the church was serving the immigrants. A curious example is offered by the experience of the Italian Sylvestrine Benedictines of Kansas. In 1910 the two priests who came to work among the miners were met by rocks and rotten vegetables thrown at them by those they came to serve. Then slowly, in the following seventeen years, seven Italian churches were built, and the Italian priests moved away only after the mines had closed and the miners had reemigrated.[136]

In North Michigan and North Minnesota, as we learn from the *Bollettino dell'Emigrazione,* there were Italian churches in Calumet, Iron Mountain, Vulcan, Hibbing, Duluth, Eveleth.[137]

In the Northeast of the United States there was no colony of any importance without its church, especially in Massachusetts, Connecticut, New Jersey and Pennsylvania. In New York, Italian churches were erected all across the state up to Lake Ontario.[138]

Where the small number of immigrants or the active interest of local parishes could not warrant the building of independent Italian churches, Italians were cared for through regular missions, as those given by Fr. Morelli, Parolin, Biasotti and a score of others around New York.[139] For example, the missionary band of *L'Apostolato Italiano* had worked over a period of nine months in 42 parishes in 15 Eastern dioceses where there were an estimated 150,000 Italians. Of these as many as 19,970 attended the mission sermons and 14,980 took advantage of the occasion to receive the sacraments, in great part after many years of indifference.[140]

Table 5. *Italian Churches in the New York Metropolitan Area, 1918*

	Religious Priests	Churches	Chapels	Diocesan Priests	Churches	Chapels	Italians
New York	57	15	3	74	23	10	500,000
Brooklyn	9	3	1	35	13	2	250,000
Newark	7	3	1	49	31	3	250,000
Trenton	4	4	2	15	9	4	80,000
	77	25	7	173	76	19	1,050,000

Source: Thomas B. Kenedy, ed., *Official Catholic Directory.* New York: Kenedy & Sons, 1918.

The slow process of growth of ethnic ecclesiastical organization was having some results. Thomas Meehan, in the turmoil of the 1903 immigration movement, summed up the achievements of the Italians in the boroughs of Manhattan, Bronx, Staten Island, and the suburban counties under the jurisdiction of the New York diocese: 18 parishes; 2 chapels; 7 churches used in part by Italians; 52 priests; 133,100 parish members; 8,670 baptisms; 1,902 marriages; 6 schools; 3,316 pupils; and 5,770 in Sunday School.[141] Along with the parishes, there were societies, orphanages, newspapers, hospitals, and missions bands.

By 1918, the situation in the New York Metropolitan Area was reported as described in Table 5.

After the parish church, and at the urging of their priests, the Italians moved toward building some Catholic schools. In no way, however, could the Italian immigrants succeed in establishing a network of parochial schools comparable to that of German and Polish immigrants. Poverty was a major difficulty. Even greater obstacles were the absence of an ethnic identity more extensive than the village of birth; the total lack of interest in preserving any link with the Italian State; and a religious culture which rested on folk traditions and personal piety rather than on nationalism.[142]

Conclusion: the National Parish as a Quasi-sect.

Keeping in mind the constant strain placed on the Italian communities by uninterrupted arrivals of poor relatives from Italy, their miserable income, their inexperience at organizing, and the infallible co-opting out of the community of its members who met with success both in terms of education and money, the immigrants seem to have done rather well for themselves. Their church had a much deeper significance than that acknowledged by bishops and local pastors,

Table 6. *Italian Parochial Schools in the New York Metropolitan Area, 1917*

	No. of Schools	Pupils	Teachers
New York	11	8,101	163
Brooklyn	4	1,945	34
Newark	7	1,468	31
Trenton	2	726	12
TOTAL	24	12,240	240

Source: Manlio Ciuffoletti, *Le scuole parrocchiali negli Stati Uniti d' America e in particolare le italiane.* Rome: Istituto Pio IX, 1918, pp. 20-21.

Table 7. *Number of Children of Italian-born Fathers in Schools of Twenty-four Cities in 1908**

Cities	Number of Children	
	Public	Parochial
Baltimore	879	255
Boston	7,347	922
Cleveland	2,089	65
Detroit	635	268
Duluth	199	17
Fall River	282	8
Haverhill, Mass.	143	24
Kansas City, Mo.	695	8
Los Angeles	840	144
Lowell, Mass.	75	4
Lynn, Mass.	197	41
Manchester, N.H.	10	2
Meriden, Conn.	279	21
Milwaukee	532	18
Minneapolis	85	6
Newark	5,645	815
New Britain, Conn.	114	24
New Orleans	1,865	390
New York	59,645	8,301
Philadelphia	6,705	3,742
Providence	3,544	30
San Francisco	3,431	101
Scranton	561	193
Shenandoah, Pa.	57	—

*Calculated from: U.S. Immigration Commission, *Reports of the Immigration Commission* (Washington, D.C., 1911), Vol. XXIX, pp. 8-13, 144-145.

Protestant organizers and leftists. Many parishes, as it will be pointed out, had responsibility for large groups of Italians. What is amazing is not so much the number of difficulties that emerged, but that in store fronts, beer-houses, basements of private homes and churches, the immigrants and their priests asserted their self-respect. Their peasant intuition was correct. Their process of integration into American society came about through group solidarity which their own church could guarantee by transcending their families and their villages and putting all their different Saints to work together.

The expectations of immediate acceptance of the existing church structures and life would have demanded of the immigrants a capacity to transcend their village-like world's view. In a rag shop (cf. Appendix I), in a saloon or in a store front, the immigrants preferred to control their religious life without either abandoning the officially established Catholic Church or their particularistic orientation. Besides, it was in the context of their peasant religion that they felt as being human.[143] The institution that emerged was the first they could call their own, a new sociological type of religious institution, a quasi-sect.

Duplex parishes of Irish and Italians were attempts doomed to failure, if we consider that even separate mission churches for German Americans, dependent on Irish parishes, had been violently rejected. On the one hand, the Italian immigrants resented the disdain and disrespect evident in the treatment the Irish were giving them. On the other hand, they were incapable of responding to an Irish style of a more socially aggressive and disciplined religion. The effort toward immediate Americanization provoked a negative reaction of diffidence toward the hierarchical church on the part of the immigrants unwilling to surrender their culture. Bishop Joseph Dwenger of Fort Wayne expressed the feelings of all immigrants when he wrote to Propaganda Fide in 1886:

> . . . if one takes into account the present condition of the Church in the United States of America, there will be no difficulty to convince oneself of the necessity to establish missions distinct among themselves not by territory, but by language, and mutually autonomous. Anyone acquainted with America knows that the present populations of almost all the American dioceses and vicariates are' not formed by people of the same origin, belonging to the same nation; but instead that they are diverse among themselves in character, customs, habits, language, nationality. The sum of these different qualities form the character proper of each people. Thus, one distinguishes itself from the other; one does not harmonize with the other. To guide the newcomers with success, it is necessary that they group in special and distinct communities. Mixing them together, would prove to be extremely dangerous. It would be like joining totally heterogeneous elements. To avoid, then, dangerous competition, clashes and fights, that from small beginning could get out of hand at the contact of persons so different among themselves; and to provide efficacious spiritual care, it is convenient to institute quasi-parishes, according to nationality and language. There is no doubt, anyway, that each ethnic parish must enjoy fullness of parochial rights; must be antonomous and independent. Recourse to the expedient of erecting missions according to nationality, but in such a way that one is principal and the others succoursal—therefore in some way dependent and subordinated to it—doesn't seem advisable. The general rule, it seems, could be summed up in this formula: mutual independence of the missions of one nationality from those of another. The pride of the national sentiment of one people would feel hurt if the pastor of one nationality was to be placed in con-

ditions of dependence on the pastor of another. It is well known that hurting of the national sentiment causes very serious consequences. Always, and among all peoples, the national sentiment has been strongly felt. For various reasons this sentiment has now become sensitive to the extreme and exaggeratedly excitable . . . to disregard these circumstances in the government of a diocese, it would most seriously jeopardize its religious interest. . . .[144]

The pastoral awareness of Bishop Dwenger, however, found a formidable difficulty in the very multiplicity of the immigrant groups. Together with the Italians, Poles, Slovenes, Slovaks, Lebanese and Syrians and several other Catholic groups were entering the country. The American bishops feared their church might be labeled a foreign institution. This fear bordered on paranoia when the Cahensly question was picked up by the national media which reported a foreign control of the church. The subtleties of the confrontation between religion and nationalism, however, escaped the Italian immigrants, who spontaneously proceeded to establish chapels and churches of their own. The American bishops, however reluctantly they accepted it, after 1887 had a legal directive from Rome to approve national parishes. But their approval usually came as a concession to long and painful insistence on the part of the immigrants for formal recognition of a creative work they and their priests had devised for their own spiritual care and social identity.

In fact, the Italian immigrants created a form of spiritual and religious life marked by a substantial continuity with the life prevalent in their villages in the Old World. The old dialects and language, religion, traditions and customs were preserved to protect the immigrant group from social disorganization and the shock of adjustment to the new culture. Failing to have their needs met even in churches of their own faith, the Italian immigrants established new ones, where they could find meaning to their isolation, poverty, cultural differences, desire of solidarity and *rispetto*, i.e. equality.

David O. Moberg, discussing the rise and growth of churches, remarks that the social purpose of new sects may be viewed as a defense of the needs and interests of marginal population segments.[145]

The ethnic parish quite appropriately, therefore, can be seen as a quasi-sect. Its shortcomings notwithstanding, it became the place where immigrant Italians who were on the religious and social periphery of society, could fulfill their religious needs, find opportunity for self-expression, preserve their self-perception of being human in face of an unknown social environment.

Appendix

RAG SHOP CHURCH

St. Joachim's, in the Heart of the Bowery,
the Italian Religious Centre

Of the hundreds of thousands of persons in the great multitude that surge to and fro in the vicinity of Park Row daily few there are who know that within's a stone's throw stands a church with as quaint a history as may be found anywhere in the entire city. At 26 Roosevelt Street, in the heart of the Bowery district, is the Roman Catholic Church of St. Joachim, of which Father Peaer (sic) Sinopoli is pastor, assisted by Fathers Quadrenti and Dinonno. The members are Italian exclusively.

Many of the communicants are rag-pickers, and until recently the lower part of the church had been rented for the storage of their goods. Not long ago a fire occurred in the basement, due, probably, to spontaneous combustion. Since then the building has been abandoned as a place of business by the members.

Years ago, when Roosevelt Street was not so squalid and so overflowing with human beings as it is today, this church belonged to a Methodist Episcopal congregation. There were merchants, solid men of downtown New York, living there, and the neighborhood was eminently respectable. Now the church stands with a cheap lodging house on one side and a typical slum grocery store on the other. A nest of tough saloons is near by, up and down the street.

CROSS ALMOST HIDDEN

The church of St. Joachim came into existence in 1888, and the Italian population thereabout grew so rapidly that within a short time the institution had one of the largest congregations in the city. The building is of brick, dingy and dirty. It is only by standing across the street that one can see a small cross on the roof, the only thing about the edifice that suggests its religious character.

Before commercial transactions were discontinued, a person looking in on the first floor would have witnessed a curious spectacle. The whole depth and breadth of the floor was filled with rags. Rags loose, rags in piles, and rags in bales ready for shipment, were all about. Big cranes and chains for hoisting purposes ran here and there. Half buried in these piles of rags were men, women and children—the men and women busy assorting rags, and the *apt,* brown youngsters tumbling about in play or sleeping, as the case might be.

It was the biggest rag shop in the city. It was wholesale and retail in the sense that here the individual rag pickers of the town disposed of their wares, which were assorted and baled and sold for manufacturing purposes. The pastor of St. Joachim's, who was at that time Father Vincent, now in charge of a congregation in Jersey City, rented at a good figure the lower floor to the company that conducted this rag business, and indeed, were it not for this the mission would have suffered.

A part of the church building and adjacent property belonging to the institution are now rented out to about 130 families, netting approximately $1,000 a year, all of which goes toward the support of the church. Up to the time of the discontinuance of the rag-picking industry, the rental of the lower part of the building amounted to several thousand dollars annually, and the loss of this source of income was keenly felt. The congregation is now struggling under a debt of $176,-000 a part of which it hopes soon to cancel.

The church proper was on the floor over the rag shop, and this in itself gave an odd character to the services at times. On week days the men would be at work in the basement when the services were going on upstairs, and one could plainly hear them joining in the responses and chants during the celebration of the mass. On one occasion, while the writer was present, one of the rag-pickers in the basement sang a hymn to the Virgin during the service, and his voice was of rare sweetness and purity.

Now at certain hours of the day laborers come in, set their picks and shovels in a corner, and join in the devotions. The peanut venders and fruit stand keepers in the neighborhood always attend the services for at least a few minutes each day. Bootblacks wander in with boxes on their backs and say a few brief prayers. Thus the Italian population comes and goes. Five masses are said every Sunday. From five hundred to one thousand persons attend each mass, so that many thousands worship in the little church each week.

The position of the parish priest of St. Joachim's is that of a patriarch. Not only does he marry his parishioners, baptize their children, and bury their dead, but he is their constant adviser in other matters. He settles disputes of all kinds among them, from business differences to lovers' quarrels.

SOLOMON FOR LOVERS

One trouble the priest has to contend with is the manner in which his charges get married. Coming from Italy, where civil marriages are the proper thing, the Italians believe that the same laws obtain here. As a result the Italian quarter is filled with professional marriage brokers and matchmakers.

They bring couples together for a fee, then steer them to the City Hall, where two men have for years done a steady business securing aldermen to marry couples, in getting certificates for them, and arranging all other details. The pastors try to impress upon their people that they will marry them for nothing, but they still flock to the City Hall. Many of them buy pictures of the building and send them to Italy, that their friends may see the palace in which they were married.

From:
The Globe and Commercial Advertiser, New York, Monday, November 27, 1905, p. 4.

NOTES

1. Joseph M. Flynn, *The Catholic Church in New Jersey.* Morristown, N.J., 1904, pp. 65-166. Also, Edwin Vose Sullivan, ed., "An Annotated copy of the Diary of Bishop James Roosevelt Bayley, First Bishop of Newark, New Jersey, 1853-1872." Ph.D. Thesis, Department of History, University of Ottawa, 1956. Vol. II, pp. 42-43. Fr. Cauvin returned to Nice and died there in 1902. Peter Condon, "Rev. Anthony Cauvin, Founder of the Church of "Our Lady of Grace" of Hoboken, N.J.," *United States Catholic Historical Records and Studies,* 111 (January, 1903), pp. 155-167.

2. Edwin Vose Sullivan, ed., op. cit., Vol. II, pp. 156-157; Vol. I, entry for April 10, 1860. Cf. Academy of American Franciscan History, *United States Documents in the Propaganda Fide Archives; A Calendar,* by Finbar Kenneally, Washington, D.C., 1966—3 volumes.

3. Letter dated April 18, 1885, Fr. de Concilio to Bishop W. Wigger, AAN. St. Raphael Society Papers, Center for Migration Studies, Staten Island, New York.

4. Giovanni Schiavo, *Italian American History,* vol. II, *The Italian Contribution to the Catholic Church in America.* New York: Vigo Press, 1949, pp. 354.

5. *Historical Sketches of the Catholic/Churches and Institutions of Philadelphia.* Philadelphia: Daniel H. Mahoney, 1895, pp. 99-100.

6. Robert H. Lord, John E. Lexton, Edward T. Harrington, *History of the Archdiocese of Boston in the Various Stages of its Development, 1604 to 1943.* New York: Sheed and Ward, 1944. Vol. III, p. 223 f.

7. *Sadlier's Catholic Directory, Almanac and Ordo, 1870.* New York: D. & J. Sadlier & Co., 1870, p. 127.

8. Robert H. Lord et al., op. cit.

9. Robert Ernst, *Immigrant Life in New York City, 1825-1863.* New York: King's Crown Press, 1849, p. 85.

10. Letter dated January 8, 1858, Papal Consul Binse to Cardinal Bernabo, PFC, American Cent. vol. 18, f. 23.

11. Letter dated February 6, 1858, Papal Consul Binse to Cardinal Bernabo, PFC, American Cent. vol. 18, f. 120.

12. Robert Sylvain, *Alessandro Gavazzi, 1809-1889: Clerc, Garibaldien, Prédicant des Deux Mondes*. Québec: Le Centre Pedagogique, 1962. 2 Voll. Pp. 587.

Francesco Moncada, "The Little Italy of 1850," *Atlantica* (January, 1933), pp. 160-61, p. 176.

13. Peter Condon, "Monsignor Bedini's Visit to the United States. The Official Correspondence," *United States Catholic Historical Records and Studies*, 111 (1903), pp. 149-154.

14. Robert Ernst, op. cit., p. 274.

15. Propaganda Fide Calendar, vol. II, Congressi (Vol. XIV) America Centrale, Section I, Fol. 639—Letter dated November 24, 1847, Jeremias Cummings to Mons. Bernabo' Silarato.

16. Ibid. fol. 638.

17. PFC, vol. II, Congressi (vol. XV) America Cent. Fol. 208. Letter dated May 29, 1849, Jerimias Cummings to Card. Franzoni.

18. PFC, Congressi (vol. XVI), America Cent., fol. 955. Letter dated March 22, 1854, Jeremias Cummings to the Prefect of Propaganda Fide.

19. PFC, Congressi (Vol. XVII) America Cent. Fol. 360, Letter dated June 25, 1855, Jeremias Cummings to Mons. Bernabo', Secretary of Propaganda Fide.

20. Giovanni Schiavo, op. cit. Also, for other Italian priests Rev. Walter T. Leahy, *The Catholic Church of the Diocese of Trenton*. Princeton, N.J., 1907c. pp. 441.

Citizen (Brooklyn), Sunday, August 7, 1887. *Eagle* (Brooklyn), October 18, 1890: "The Rev. Father Fransioli Passes Quietly Away." For Rev. M. Marco's work in Long Island City, see *The New York Times*, November 26, 1870 and March 25, 1871. For the work of Father Cassella, see *Freeman's Journal*, December 11, 1869.

21. "Death of Charles Constantine Pise, D.D." *New York Freeman's Journal*, June 2, 1866, p. 5.

Sr. M. Eulalia Teresa Moffatt, *Charles Constantine Pise, 1801-1866*. M. A. Thesis, Catholic University of America, 1930. Pp. 65.

22. Rev. A. Sanguineti to Archbishop J. Hughes, Letter dated August 21, 1858. AANY, A-14.

23. PFC. Congressi (vol. XVIII), America Cent., fol. 1532. Letter dated October 27, 1860, Rev. Antonio Sanguineti to Card. Alessandro Bernabo'

24. Ibid., fol. 1533.

25. Ibid., fol. 1534.

26. Ibid., fol. 1535.

27. Ibid., fol. 1536.

28. Ibid., fol. 1537.

29. Letter dated September 1861, Archbishop John Hughes to Father Smith, AANY, A-9: same, March 1861, A-7.

30. PFC, Congressi (Vol. XVIII), America Centrale, fals. 1607. Letter dated October 15, 1860, Jeremias Cummings to Cardinal Bernabo'.

31. PFC, Congressi (Vol. XVIII), America Centrale, fol. 1537. Letter dated November 5, 1860, Rev. Antonio Sanguineti to the Prefect of Propaganda Fide.

32. PFC, Congressi (Vol. XVIII), America Centrale, fol. 1521, "Rapporto dell'Arcivescovo di N. York intorno al Sacerdote Italiano di nome Sanguineti; e *supplica* degli Italiani intorno al medesimo Sanguineti," 1860.

33. PFC, American Centrale, vol. 18, fol. 1269. Letter dated March 23, 1859, Papal Consul Binse to the Prefect of Propaganda Fide.

34. PFC, America Centrale, vol. 18, fol. 325. Letter dated August 14, 1858, Papal Consul Binse to Cardinal Bernabo'.

35. Ibid., fol. 325r.

36. Andrew F. Rolle, *The Immigrant Upraised. Italian Adventures and Colonists in an Expanding America.* Norman: University of Oklahoma Press, 1968. Amalia Capello, *Notizie storiche e descrittive delle Missioni della Provincia Torinese della Compagnia di Gesu' nell'America del Nord.* Torino, 1898. Frederick J. Easterly, *The Life of the Rt. Rev. Joseph Rosati, First Bishop of St. Louis, 1789-1843.* Washington, D.C.: Catholic University of America Press, 1942. Samuel Mazzucchelli, *The Memoirs of Father Mazzucchelli, O.P.* Translated by Merie M. Armato and Mary J. Finnegan, Chicago; Priory Press, 1967. XXI, 329 p. Giuseppe M. Sorrentino, *Dalle Montagne Rocciose al Rio Bravo. Brevi appunti storici circa la missione gesuitica del Nuovo Messico e Colorado negli Stati Uniti d'America.* Napoli: Federico e Ardia, 1948. Pp. 307.

37. S. B. Cerrati, "Sulle colonie italiane in California," *Bollettino Consolare* pubblicato per parte del Ministero degli Affari Esteri di S.M.il Re d'Italia. Vol. VII, Parte I, Firenze, 1872. Pp. 54-5. John Bernard McGloin, *Jesuits by the Golden Gate: The Society of Jesus in San Francisco, 1849-1969.* San Francisco: University of San Francisco, 1972, 111 & 309 pp.

38. Nicolo Nicholis to On. De Pretis, letter dated February 23, 1878, from Louisville, Ky. Archives Italian Ministry of Foreign Affairs, Serie Politica (Copy at Centro Studi Emigrazione, Rome).

39. Societa' di Unione e Fratellanza Italiane, *Libro di letture graduate con le prime nozioni elementari, per uso delle scuole di lingua italiana con un secerto di elementi di aritmetice,* in Saint Louis, Missouri. St. Louis: M. Seiffarth, printer, 1869, pp. 146-153 and 213-218.

40. Henry J. Browne, "The 'Italian Problem' in the Catholic Church of the United States, 1880-1900." *Historical Records and Studies,* vol. 35, 1946, pp. 46-72.

41. U.S. Department of Commerce, Bureau of the Census, *Fourteenth Census of the United States, 1920.* II, p. 695. Washington, D.C., 1922.

42. Province of the Most Holy Name, Order of Friars Minor, Archives, reels 4 to 22 containing the material concerned with the Custody of the Immaculate Conception before 1901, and the houses and activities which started them. Friedsam Memorial Library, St. Bonaventure University, St. Bonaventure, New York.

43. Letter dated August 27, 1864, Fr. Pamfilo da Magliano to Archbishop John McCloskey, AANY.

44. *Note di Cronaca sull'origine e progresso della chiesa di S. Antonio (151 Sullivan Street, N.Y.)* Napoli: Tipografia Pontificia M. D'Auria, 1925.

45. U.S. Department of Labor, Bureau of Immigration. *Annual Report of the Commissioner General of Immigration, 1920.* Washington, D.C., 1920. Pp. 181-182.

46. Rev. Fr. George Zurcher, "Foreign Ideas in the Catholic Church in America," *The Roycroft Quarterly,* Nov. 1896, No. 3, p. 8.

47. Riccardo Gilmour, Vescovo di Cleveland, and Giovanni Moore, Vescovo di S. Agostino. *Memoriale sulla Questione dei Tedeschi nella Chiesa di America.* Roma, 1885, p. 6.

48. *Schemata Decretorum Concilii Plenarii Baltimorensis Tertii.* Baltimore, 1884, p. 69.

49. *Acta et Decreta Concilii Plenarii Baltimorensis Tertii. A.D. MDCCCLXXXIV.* Baltimore: Typis Joannis Murphy Sociorum, 1886, pp. 130-132.

50. Rev. Peter Guilday, *The National Pastorals of the Merican Hierarchy: 1792-1919.* Westminster, Md.: The Newman Press, 1954. Pp. 226-264.

51. *Relatio Collationum quas Romae coram S.C. de P.F. Praefecto habuerunt Archiepiscopi pluresque Episcopi Statuum Foederatorum Americae.* 1883. p. 28.

52. Corrigan to McCloskey, Rome, December 2, 1883. AANY, "Material for Arch. Corrigan Life."

53. Card. M. Rampolla to Card. J. Gibbons, Letter of June 28, 1891, Prot. N. 2450, p. 2. Copy, AANY.

54. The parish was started in 1884 by Bishop Wigger of Newark for the French and the Italians. Shortly after, English-speaking parishioners were added. Bishop Wigger, however, disagreed. AAN, Register, II, p. 252.

55. Giacomo Pessagno et al. to Most Rev. James Gibbons, Baltimore, October 6, 1881, AAB.

56. cf. John B. Duff, "The Italians," in Joseph P. O'Grady, ed., *The Immigrants Influence on Wilson's Peace Policies.* Lexington, Ky.: University of Kentucky Press, 1967, p. 112. U.S. Bureau of the Census, *Fourteenth Census of the United States: 1920, Population, II, p. 904.*
cf. *Reports of the Industrial Commission on Immigration.* Washington, D.C.; Government Printing Office, 1901, Vol. XV, pp. 465-492.

57. Fr. N. Russo, "The Origin and Progress of Our Italian Mission in New York," A Letter, Jan. 29, 1896. *Woodstock Letters,* XXV (1896), p. 135-36.

58. *Souvenir History of Transfiguration Parish—Mott Street, New York, 1827-1897.* pp. 44.

59. Libro degli Annunzi, Odone Papers, Immigration Archives, University of Minnesota quoted in Rudolph J. Vecoli, "Prelates and Peasants: Italian Immigrants and the Catholic Church," *Journal of Social History,* vol. 2, n. 3, Spring 1969, pp. 217-268.

60. Gennaro de Concilio to G. B. Scalabrini, Jersey City, April 30, 1889, ACSC, USA, Sup. Prov., 1889.

61. Rev. Thos. F. Lynch to Rt. Rev. Msgr. Preston, V.G., letter dated Sept. 20, 1886. AANY, D-8b.

62. Robert H. Lord, John E. Sexton, Edward T. Harrington, *History of the Archdiocese of Boston,* New York: Sheed & Ward, 1944. Vol. III, p. 224.

63. *Citizen,* Sunday, August 7, 1887: "St. Peter's. The Largest Parish in the Brooklyn Diocese," n.p.

64. E. McSweeny, *A New York Pastor of the Latter Half of the Nineteenth Century.* Reprint from Historical Records and Studies, April 1908, Philadelphia, p. 19.

65. Letter dated September 16, 1887, Valley Spring, Miss., Fr. Defendente Monti to Fr. F. Zagoglio, ACSC. USA., Inizi, 1888.

66. Fr. F. Beccherini to Fr. G. Gambera, Detroit, February 25, 1899. ACSC. USA, Missioni Cessate, St. Louis, 1899-1907.

67. Letter of Fr. McSweeny to Archbishop Corrigan, October 26, 1893, AANY, Box I-9.

68. Letter of Fr. McSweeny to Archbishop Corrigan, October 24, 1898, AANY Box D-1.

69. see Ch. V, Conflict and Cooperation, pp. 00.

70. G. de Concilio to Bishop G. B. Scalabrini, letter dated from Jersey City, May 27, 1888.

71. Francesco Zaboglio to Bishop Scalabrini, June 28, 1888, ACSC. USA. 204 Inizi, 1888. Fr. Lynch was pastor of the Church of the Transfiguration and Fr. Kearney of Old St. Patrick's in Manhattan.

72. ACSC—USA—Inizi, 1888-89. Fr. Felice Morelli to Bishop John B. Scalabrini, New York, October 6, 1889. On the experience of the Italians in Church basements in New York City, see also Fr. Marcellino Moroni to Archbishop Michael A. Corrigan, New York May 12, 1888, AANY, I-39. Fr. Marcellino Moroni to Bishop John B. Scalabrini, New York, February 17, 1888, ACSC—USA. Inizi, 1888. Moroni refers also to open prejudice ("Italian, laymen and priests, are considered inferior to the American clergy and people") and even of discrimination in the administration of the sacraments. Fr. Marcellino Moroni to Bishop G. Bonomelli, New York, January 27, 1888. ACSC—USA. Inizi, 1888.

73. ACSC—USA—Inizi, 1888. Fr. M. Moroni to Cardinal Simeoni, New York, May 16, 1888.

74. Giovanni Canbino et al. to Archibshop M. A. Corrigan, New York, January 8, 1894, AANY, D-8b.

75. Domenico Vicentini, C. S. Provincial, to Archbishop M. A. Corrigan, New York, November 4, 1893, AANY, I-40.

76. Nicholas Russo, S. J. to Archbishop Corrigan, New York, February 22, 1898, AANY, G-35.

77. James B. Curry to Bishop John M. Farley, New York, March 19, 1908, AANY, D-4. The work of the Italian priests in the church basements was usually successful. In St. James Church basement (Oliver St., New York City), for example, Father de Ponte started the first service in 1905 with 7 persons present and after 32 months of work he had an attendance of 2000 people. Rev. Antonio de Ponte to the Archbishop of New York, New York, March 6, 1908, AANY, D-4.

78. Archbishop M. A. Corrigan to Bishop John B. Scalabrini, New York, January 11, 1902; September 17, 1901, ACSC—USA—Prov.

79. Rev. A. Monselle to Archbishop M. A. Corrigan, New York, April 3, 1894, AANY, D-6.

80. Deborah Beatrice Honig, "The Church of Mary, Help of Christians, New York City: The National Parish as a Solution to the "Italian Problem"." M.A. Thesis, Columbia University, Faculty of Political Science, 1966. Pp. 101. McSweeney to Corrigan, October 24, 1898, AANY, D-1.

81. Colman J. Barry, *The Catholic Church and German Americans*. Milwaukee: The Bruce Publishing Co., 1953. pp. 1-85.

82. McCloskey to Smith, Louisville, December 16, 1886 in Colman J. Barry, op. cit., p. 67.

83. AAB, Abbelen to Gibbons, Milwaukee, Oct. 4, 1886, 82-B-1

84. AAB, 54 Il. encl. 2.

85. George L. Willard to James Gibbons, Fond du Lac, Wisconsin, May 7, 1878. AAB 73 S1.

86. Ibid., AAB 73 Sl.

87. P. F. Petit et al. to James Gibbons, Milwaukee, May 8, 1878. AAB 73 S2.

88. AAB, Letterbook of Gibbons, pp. 77-78, Letter of Gibbons to Archbishop Elder, May 8, 1884.

89. Colman J. Barry, op. cit., p. 289 f.

90. J. Card. Simeoni to J. Gibbons, letter of December 15, 1885, Prot. n. 5698 AAB 79 W10.

91. Ibid.

92. AAB, 82 S 5. For a detailed and accurate description of this period of Catholic history and the whole German nationality question, see Colman J. Barry, op. cit., 62 f.

93. AAB, 83-J-6, Gross to Gibbons, Portland, Aug. 30, 1887.

94. *Petition to Rome from Archbishop Heiss of Milwaukee in the name of German Bishops in regard to Germans in the U.S.*, Oct. 3, 1886.

95. Fr. Marcellino Maroni to Archbishop M. A. Corrigan, New York, March 16, 1888, AANY, I-39. Moroni was asked to enlist the support of Bishop Scalabrini for this project but was of the opinion that the Apostolic Vicarietes could not work because of the regional divisions among Italians and the lack of cooperation of the pastors.

96. John Ireland—John J. Keane, *La Question Allemande dans l'Eglise des Estets Units.* Rome, 1887. pp. 28.

97. G. de Concilio to Bishop G. B. Scalabrini, Jersey City, December 28, 1888, ACSC—USA. Prov. 1888.

98. Monsignore Gennaro de Concilio, *Su lo stato religioso degli Italiani negli Stati Unite d'America. Alcunee riflessioni.* New York: Tipografia J. H. Carbone, 1888. Pp. 32. Also. Fr. Marcellino Moroni to Bishop John B. Scalabrini, New York, May 25, 1888, ACSC—USA. Inizi, 1888. Moroni, with reservations on the idea of the Vicarietes, accepted the pamphlet as "a treasure . . . pure truth." Also, Fr. Marcellino Moroni to

Archbishop M. A. Corrigan, New York, May 21, 1888. AANY, I-39. Fr. Marcellino Moroni to Archbishop M. A. Corrigan, New York, March 24, 1888, AANY I-39.

99. Gennaro de Concilio to Giovanni Battista Scalabrini, Jersey City, April 30, 1889, ACSC—USA. Prov. 1889.

100. Michael Augustine Corrigan to Giovanni Battista Scalabrini, New York, April 3, 1891, ACSC—USA. Prov.

101. John Tracy Ellis, *Documents of American Catholic History*. "The St. Raphaelsverein Protests the Neglect of Immigrant Catholics in the United States, February, 1891." Pp. 496-499.

102. Villeneuve to Scalabrini, Letter dated Florence, April 8, 1890. ACSC, B-IV, 1890, p. 24.

103. Ibid.

104. Villeneuve to Scalabrini, Letter dated Paris, December 20, 1890, ACSC, B-IV, 1890, p. 29.

105. Ibid.

106. Villeneuve to Scalabrini, Letter dated Florence, January 15, 1891.

107. cf. "Regulating Migration," *New York Herald*, May 28, 1891. "Cahensley Mission to the United States," *New York Herald*, June 1, 1891, p. 5; "Regard it Menace: Foreign Interference in Affairs of the Catholic Church," *Milwaukee Sentinel*, June 20, 1891.

108. Colman Barry, op. cit. p. 314.

109. Giovanni Card. Simeoni to Michael A. Corrigan, Rome, June 27, 1891, Propaganda Fide, Protocol N. 2699, AANY, I-41.

110. Mariano Card. Rampolla to James Card. Gibbons, Rome, June 28, 1891, Prot. N. 2450, AAB, 88 R-9, for the repercussions of this polemic, see also D. J. O'Connell to Cardinal Gibbons, Rome, July 1, 1891; August 3, 1891, AAB, 88S1, 88U2).

111. Ibid.

112. Michael A. Corrigan to Peter Paul Cahensly, New York, July 22, 1891, Copy, AANY, C-18.

113. Giovanni Battista Scalabrini to Michael Augustine Corrigan, Letter of March 18, 1891, AANY, I-39.

114. Michael Augustine Corrigan to Giovanni Battista Scalabrini, New York, August 31, 1891, ACSC-USA-Prov. The same objections in Fr. N. Russo, S.J. to M.A. Corrigan, n.d., AANY, C-36.

115. AAB, 88U7/1.

116. "Our Catholic Losses," *The New York Catholic*, November 22, 1891.

117. Peter Paul Cahensly to Michael A. Corrigan, September 6, 1892, AANY, C-41. Also letter of October 31, 1892, AANY, and the attached Memorandum stating that the European Raphael Societies do not want for their countrymen territorial bishops, neither do they object to the original nationality of numerous immigrants being after some generations identified with the American nation. For the nationality bishops and the Poles, for example, see Wenceslaus Kruszka to bishop McDonnel of Brooklyn, Rome, October 27, 1903, ADB.

118. Villeneuve to Scalabrini, Letter dated New York, October, 1891 ACSC, B-IV, 1890, 39

119. Letter dated July 31, 1883, Fr. Gaudentius Rossi to archbishop M. A. Corrigan, AANY.

120. Giacomo Gambera, *Autobiografia*, p. 34. ACSC.

121. Ibid., op. cit., p. 35

122. Letter dated July 15, 1884, Giovanni Cardinal Simeoni to Archbishop M. A. Corrigan, AANY.

123. Letters dated August 18, 1887; January 7, 1888; February 27, 1888, Giovanni Battista Scalabrini to Archbishop M. A. Corrigan, AANY.

124. Ernest Coppo, "Salesians of Don Bosco," in *The Catholic Church in the United States of America*. Vol. I, Religious Communities of Men. New York: 1912, pp. 388-390. Also, Sac. Stefano Trione, *L'emigrazione e l'opera di Don Bosco nelle Americhe*. San Benigno Canav.: Scuola Tipografica Don Bosco, 1914. Pp. 24.

125. Domenico Pistella, *La Madonna del Carmine e gli Italiani d'America*, New York, 1954, pp. 167. Nicholas J. Regan, "The Italian Custody of the Immaculate Conception," in *The Catholic Church in the United States*, vol. I, op. cit., pp. 236-239. Mario Francesconi, c.s., *Inizi della Congregazione Scalabriniana, 1886-1888*. Roma: Centro Studi Emigrazione, 1969, pp. 179 (mimeo). Sac. Giuseppe Capra, "L'opera dei Padri Francescani nell'America del Nord," *Italica Gens*, VII, 1-6 (Jan.-June), 1966. pp. 39-56. Sac. Giuseppe Capra, "I Padri Scalabriniani nell'America del Nord," Ibid. pp. 1-14. "Le Missionarie del Sacro Cuore in America," *Italica Gens*, I, 3, 1910, pp. 119-124.

126. AAN, Letterfile, 1898, Marzetti to Wigger, Hoboken, August 9, 1898.

127. For the founding of churches were consulted the diocesan archives of New York, Brooklyn and Newark and the Catholic Directory. Also, Giovanni Schiavo, *Italian-American History*, vol. II, op. cit.; John K. Sharp, *History of the Diocese of Brooklyn, 1853-1953*. New York: Fordham University Press, 1954; Aemilianus Zepf, DD, "Rev. Aemilian Kirner, P.S.M., the First Pallottine Missionary in the United States," *The Pallottine News*, vol. I, 1928, n. 6, pp. 1-6; *Analecta Piae Societatis Missionum*, vol. I, n. 11, July 1911, pp. 270-283; Rev. Dr. Conrad M. Schotthoefer to bishop W. Wigger, Newark, December 17, 1891; Letterbook, II, 142, December 2, 1886; Register, III, 8, all in AAN. Carl Derivaux Hinrichsen, "The History of the Diocese of Newark, 1873-1901," A Doctoral Dissertation for the Catholic University of America, History, 1962 (microfilm); *Nel XXV anniversario dell'Istituto dei Missionari di San Carlo per gli Italiani emigrati*. Rome, 1912. Pp. 80 Provincia Minoritica dell'Immacolata Concezione del Nord America, *L'opera dei Francescani Italiani a favore degli emigrati negli Stati Uniti d'America, 1888-1925*. Rome, 1926, pp. 96.

128. Domenico Pistella, op. cit., p. 45. G. Gambera, *Autobiografia*, op. cit., passim. Lawrence Pisani and Paul Falcigno, "The History of St. Michael's of New Haven," in *75th Anniversary St. Michael's Church*. New Haven, 1965.

129. Letter dated May 17, 1908, Angelo Rezzano et al. to Cardinal Farley, AANY. Also, cf. letter signed by 46 heads of family to the bishop of Brooklyn: "I Pasquale Manfre of 380 Montauk Avenue, Brooklyn, New York, inform You that the undersigned fathers of families desire an Italian church in City Line, Brooklyn, to hear holy and divine Mass on Sunday and to have our children instructed in the holy doctrine so to live in the holy fear of God . . ." Pasquale Manfre et al. to bishop Charles McDonnell, Brooklyn, June 2, 1910 ADB.

130. Letter dated December 9, 1914, G. Valentino et Alii to Cardinal Farley, AANY.

131. Henry D. Jones, *The Evangelical Movement Among the Italians in New York City. A Study*. New York, 1934, pp. 39. This research was done for the Comity Committee of the Federation of Churches of Greater New York and the Brooklyn Church and Mission Federation. Rev. Frederick H. Wright, D.D., "How to Reach the Italians in America. Shall They be Segregated, Missioned, Neglected or Welcome?" *The Missionary Review of the World*, N.S. XXX, August 1917, pp. 589-594: "There are over three million Italians in this country and the work of evangelization, although thirty or more years old, has only touched the outer fringe of the problem." Minnie J. Reynolds, "The Religious Renaissance in Italy," *The Missionary Review of the World*, N.S. XXIV, August 1911, pp. 597-603: "There are today 220 Italian Protestant Churches in the United States. In over 100 of them the first nucleus was a group of Italians who had been Waldensians in Italy." Rev. Chas. E. Edwards, "Our Latin and Slavonic Populations," *The Assembly Herald*, August, 1901, pp. 300-302. Rev. G. P. Williams, "Italian Work in Chicago," ibid., p. 303. "Italian Work in and near Newark, N.J.," ibid., pp. 306-307. The Montclair Italian Evangelical Missionary Society, *First Annual Report*, combined with an address by Mr. Alberto Pecorini on the Italian Immigrant Problem, delivered at the Annual Meeting, November 30, 1903, pp. 16. Rev. William Wynkoop McNair, "The

Evangelization of our Italian," *The Assembly Herald*, IX, (August, 1905), pp. 404-409. Rev. Robert Bonner Jack, "Italians in Lehigh Presbytery," Ibid. p. 414. Rev. Samuel McLanahan, "New Jersey and Her Foreigners," Ibid. pp. 414-415. Antonio Mangano, *Sons of Italy: A Social and Religious Study of the Italians in America*, New York, 1917, pp. 163-166. John Visceglia, Th.D. *Italian Evangelical Pioneers*. Kansas City, Mo., 1948, pp. 14-17.

132. cf. Rev. Ottavio Silvestri to C. C. McDonnell, Brooklyn. October 29, 1914; P. Manlio Ciufoletti, *History of St. Joachim Church in New York City*, New York, 1938 c. Pp. 31 ACSC-USA-Missioni Cessate, St. Joachim. *Il Crociato*, October 25, 1958, pp. 32, a special issue reporting the history of all Italian churches in the Diocese of Brooklyn. John Casagranda et al. to Bishop Thomas J. Walsh, Union City, Aug. 27, 1934, AAN.

133. Francois Houtart, *Aspects Sociologiques du Catholicisme Américain. Vie Urbaine et Institutions Religieuses*. Paris, 1957, p. 51.

134. A. Palmieri, *Il grave problema religioso italiano negli Stati Uniti*. Firenze, 1921, p. 46. In this valuable pamphlet and in his other writings Palmieri strongly advocated an efficient ethnic church to remedy evident ethnic conflicts. Without ambiguity, however, he points out that "the Catholic faith was solidly rooted in the hearts of the immigrants," and was transmitted to the second generation; that some Irish bishops took the initiative in erecting Italian parishes and schools; that ethnic religious organizations were functional and temporary; that the future trend would be toward an American Catholic group made up of people of different ethnic backgrounds. The debate between mostly Irish and Italian priests on the pastoral needs of Italian immigrants had begun at the time of mass immigration. Gennaro de Concilio began writing on this problem in 1886 and was slowly followed by several articles and pamphlets describing the religious conditions of the Italian immigrants, the lack of clergy and the lack of religious instruction. Bernard J. Lynch, "The Italians in New York," op. cit. John T. McNicholas, "The Need of American Priests for the Italian Missions," *The Ecclesiastical Review*, XXXIV, December 1908, 681-682; D. Lynch, "The Religious Conditions of the Italians in New York," *America*, X, March 21, 1914, pp. 558-559. "Catholic Italian Losses," *The Literary Digest*, XLVII, October 11, 1913, p. 636. H. J. Desmond, *The Neglected Italians. A Memorial to the Italian Hierarchy*, Milwaukee, 1900 c. p. 11; "Our Italians, *The Catholic Messenger*, December 3, 1914, p. 6; Rev. J. Gambera, "Our Italian Immigrants," *The New World*, February 25, 1911, p. 2. Gambera's article is a rejoinder to an article on Italian immigrants by Rev. J. J. Loughram, *Catholic Citizen* of Milwaukee, February 4, 1911; Rev. Dr. Salvatore Cianci, *Il Lavoro sociale in mezzo agli Italiani*. Milwaukee, 1913, pp. 20; P. Francesco Beccherini, *Il fenomeno dell'Emigrazione negli Stati Uniti d'America*. San Sepolcro, 1906 pp. 35; Rev. J. Zarrilli, D.D. Ph.D., *A Prayerful Appeal to the American Hierarchy in Behalf of the Italian Catholic Cause in the United States*. Two Harbors, Minn., 1924, pp. 26; Rev. Gioacchino Maffei, *L'Italia nell'America del Nord*. Valle di Pompei, 1924. Pp. 164.

135. Luigi Villari, "L'emigrazione Italiana nel distretto consolare di Filadelfia," *Bollettino dell'Emirazione*, Anno 1908, n. 16, pp. 26-50. F. Prat, "Gli Italiani negli Stati Uniti e specialmente nello stato di New York," *Bollettino dell'Emigrazione*, Anno 1902, n. 2., pp. 14-41. Although the *Bollettino* was an official publication of the Italian Government, at this time openly anticlerical, Prat does not hesitate to write: "In the United States there exists a good number of Italian Catholic priests. In New York and Brooklyn there are seventeen Italian parishes or churches with about fifty Italian priests. We can testify that, generally speaking, there work is efficacious, not only for the religious' assistance of the immigrants, but also for the preservation of our language. . . ." He adds that the visit of Bishop Scalabrini will certainly renew the spirit of *italianita'* in the Italian colonies; that there are very few Italians of Protestant faith; and that Italian migrants are not prone to change religion.

136. P. Pietro Bandini, "Origine della colonia italiana di Tontitown nell'Arkansasn," *Bollettino dell'Emigrazione*, anno 1903, n. 1. pp. 61-62. Giovanni Schiavo, op. cit. p. 495. *The Springdale News* (Springdale, Washington County, Arkansas), May 15, 1908.

Souvenir number, Section Two. E. Mayor des Planches, *Attraverso gli Stati Uniti. Per l'emigrazione italiana.* Torino, 1913, pp. 321. Roger Baudier, *The Catholic Church in Louisiana,* New Orleans, 1939.

137. Attilio Castigliano, "Origine, sviluppo, importanza ed avvenire delle colonie italiane del Nord Michigan e del Nord Minnesota," *Bollettino dell'Emgirazione,* anno 1913, n. 7, pp. 3-22.

138. Mons. Gherardo Ferrante, "Chiese e scuole parrocchiali italiane," in *Gli Italiani negli Stati Uniti d'America,* New York, 1906, pp. 89-94. William Pizzoglio, D.D., *St. Mary of Mt. Carmel Church Utica, N.Y. Its History and Progress from the Beginning to the Present, 1896-1936,* pp. 64 Pio Parolin, *Diario,* Center for Migration Studies of New York. Giovanni Sofia, *Missioni Scalabriniane in America,* Rome, 1939, pp. 223. Pio Parolin, *Ricordo del venticinquesimo anno della fondazione della chiesa de San Pietro in Syracuse, N.Y.,* Syracuse, 1920, pp. 58. P. Costantino Sasso, *Parrocchia della Madonna di Pompei in New York (1892-1942),* pp. 102.

139. cf. Fr. Roberto Biasotti to bishop Charles McDonnell, New York, May 8, 1914; November 5, 1914; May 2, 1916, etc. ADB; Fr. Giacomo Gambera, *Autobiografia, 1889-1934,* ACSC.

140. *L'Apostolato Italiano,* report of July 7, 1913, published in *L'Italiano in America,* clippings, ACMS.

141. Thomas E. Meehan, "Evangelizing the Italians," *The Messenger,* III, Fifth Series, 1903, pp. 16-32. "Our Duty to Our Fellow Catholic Italians," Ibid., pp. 89-92: "Experience shows that there is little difficulty in getting the Italian parents to send their children to Catholic schools." (p. 91)

142. Dino Cinel, "Scuole italiane all'estero," *Selezione CSER* (March-May, 1972) pp. 1-218.

143. Charlotte Gower Chapman, *Milocca: A Sicilian Village,* Cambridge: Schenkman Pub. 6., 1971, p. 193 and f.

144. Sacra Congregatio de Propaganda Fide, *Relazione con sommario e voto intorno all'elezione di quasi-parrocchie distinte per nazionalita' negli Stati Uniti d'America.* Ponente l'Emo. e Rmo. Signor Cardinale Camillo Mazzella. April 1887. Vol. 251, p. 215 and f.

145. David O. Moberg, *The Church as a Social Institution. The Sociology of American Religion.* Englewood Cliffs, N.J.: Prentice-Hall, 1962. P. 107f.

CHAPTER V

The Italian American Parish in Action

As a quasi-sect, the Italian ethnic parish carried out the primary function of preserving the faith of the newcomers. The immediate occasion and the most evident reason for ethnic parishes was indeed the preservation of the 'sacred cosmos,' of the immigrants. God and the Saints, however, were not the only elements in the immigrants' 'sacred cosmos,' which were lending significance to their individual life in its totality. Thomas Luckmann's definition of sacred cosmos is helpful in this context to understand the general order of existence as religiously symbolized by southern Italian immigrants. "As part of the world view," Luckmann writes, "the sacred cosmos stands in a relationship with the social structure as a whole. The sacred cosmos permeates the various, more or less clearly differentiated, institutional areas such as kinship, the division of labor and the regulation of the exercise of power . . . determines directly the entire socialization of the individual and is relevant for the individual biography."[1]

For the majority of Italian immigrants, many sectors of society and culture were not yet removed from the domination of religious institutions and symbols. The process of secularization would have followed the process of urbanization and assimilation into American society. Individual acts of piety, of sacramental participation, or of legal adherence to ecclesiastical precepts, were of secondary relevance to the immigrants. The defense of their "sacred cosmos" was the dominant concern; for its protection the immigrants built the ethnic church, which, in turn, transcended a strictly religious role. The ethnic church appears as a factor strengthening the internal structure of the community, to the extent that it was a symbol and a carrier of immigrant culture; as a strategic structure for integration; as a source of leadership. Conflict was not foreign to the ethnic church. In its context, however, it played a positive role in the process of integration of the immigrant group.

The Symbolic and Cultural Role of the Ethnic Church:

"Independence: here is the first victory!" Father Morelli wrote to Bishop Scalabrini a few weeks after his arrival among the Italians of the Five Points in Lower Manhattan.[2] As the Italian immigrants began to clamor for their own parishes, they could not formulate sophisticated rationalizations for their claims. They intuitively demanded autonomous parishes to safeguard the values around which their lives were built: the family and the feeling of security that the God and the Saints of their tradition were conveying to them in the preservation of an acceptable interpretation of the universe in a strange environment. In 1888 a group of immigrants wrote to Father Moroni, recently arrived from Italy:

> For a long time the Italians have desired to have a church of their own in this locality (Mott Street, New York City), directed by Italian priests, where the education of our children and the sermons are in the mother tongue, without extending the work of their ministry to the Irish who have their own churches and pastors . . .

And for such a project they were willing to pay.[3] At the same time, another group of Italians wrote to Italy to Bishop Scalabrini:

> . . . , until we have a church all ours . . . our Italians will not be fully satisfied.[4]

In Hoboken, the Italians protested to Bishop Wigger in the name of religion and for the peace of the colony. The complaint referred to a church, built by the immigrants with the understanding that it was going to be Italian in name and fact and where the teaching of Catechism and the sermons were to be in the Italian language exclusively, but which was now changing its policy. The priest was using English. He had chosen non-Italian advisers; he was not convoking the Italian societies of the parish. The Bishop should as soon as possible provide the Italian colony of Hoboken with an Italian priest who could take care of the Italians, but *italianamente,* in an Italian style, as many other Italian priests in America were doing.

> With this, it is not that we want to proscribe American intervention in our church, the Italians observed, but we want the Italians, who built their own church, to listen to the Word of God in their native language, rather than to listen to insults directed to them. . . .[5]

The Italians of the Bronx also wanted their own Church to preserve their *sentimento* of true Catholics.[6] After all, the American Church was totally non-understandable. In 1915, Mario Terenzio felt obliged to inform Cardinal Farley of New York on the feelings of Italian immigrants:

> A short time ago in the church of St. Matthew, West 69th Street, an Italian mission was given by the Rev. Fathers Biasotti and Greco. This was a splendid success, a real awakening of the Italian colony in this part of the city. . . . Given an Italian Church with services in the Italian language, our people would not be so negligent in the observance of their religious duties. They are for the most part very poor and feel ashamed to attend the American Church, which they cannot even understand and which does not appeal to them in any way, and seems altogether a different thing from the Church so highly revered and respected in their own country. Here, in my humble opinion, lies the reason that the parents are so indifferent to the church, and their children even more so. . . .[7]

The Italian community of Corona was even more explicit in their petition to Bishop McDonnell of Brooklyn in 1914:

> For several times the Italian people of Corona, L.I., have presented formal request to Your Excellency to have an Italian church. In the past summer the same request was renewed with 60 more signatures added, but in vain we waited for your answer. Now, the same Italian people, gathered in religious congregation under the title of Maria SS. Assunta in Cielo in Corona, L.I., in its extraordinary meeting of yesterday, February 13, nominated a Committee charging it to beg Your Excellency to consider the following:
> The Italian people of Corona, L.I., do not have a Church in which they may be instructed in the faith according to the traditional, glorious, millenary *decoro* of which Italy is the noble example to the world.
> The Italian people, as any other people, share in the benefits derived from the passion of Jesus and the sorrows of Mary.

Since they have only one soul to save and since they must receive the sacraments, they need to have a church in their language and not in a foreign one.

Two lots are ready where we can build; and therefore we ask your authorization and the ritual blessing at the proper time.

We have two Italian priests, who, having given us proof of their correct behavior, prudence, and priestly zeal through the school of Italian and music, deserve our satisfaction and our gratitude.

We of the Committee hope to have a consoling and decisive answer that we demand in the name of Jesus and Sorrowful Mary.[8]

As throughout the Metropolitan area, so even in Brooklyn the pastor of St. Michael's church reported that the Italians did not "care to go to a church which is not their own."[9] There was no satisfaction unless the Italian church could be the center of the immigrant community. The Italians of Fort Lee, N.J., in a mixture of dialect and Italian, submitted their petition to the Bishop of Newark:

The entire Italian colony in Fort Lee, N.J., beg Your Excellency for what we desire. We hope you will concern yourself with this (request) as you did for the other villages. A list of names is enclosed, names of families. It is not necessary for us to send all the names, between three and four hundred families. We all desire to have an Italian Catholic Church. If it cannot be large, even small as in all other villages, because we want to save the Italian religion and we have no other possible means and thus we beg you first. All we Italians will contribute what we can but with your cooperation. Here in Fort Lee we have a Society of St. John the Baptist, founded in 1916. Its feast is celebrated every June 24 and we have no pleasure (soddisfazione) without our Italian church. We beg, therefore, Your Excellency, to take care of this as in all other villages. We await your answer. . . .[10]

Once the Italian churches began to be established, the Italians did not refuse to contribute what they could, even by depriving themselves of the necessities of life. In 1875, some Italians wrote to archbishop Corrigan on the beginning of the parish of St. Anthony of Padua:

About eight years ago, we Italians dwelling in New York, knowing how difficult it was for our compatriots recently arrived to satisfy their religious duties even in a foreign land because of the diversity of the language, erected a church with the consent of the Archbishop Msgr. McCloskey. It was hoped that this church, cared for by Italian Fathers, might serve as a temple consecrated to the obligations of our religion. God only knows the many sacrifices that it cost us, and how many were the fathers of families that deprived their children of supper in order to contribute a few more pennies to the work of charity that was in the process of construction. . . .[11]

The Italian priests were just as eager as the immigrants to see independent churches. De Concilio alerted Scalabrini to send his priests for the immigrants only on the condition they could be independent from the Irish pastors and able to control their own parishes. To do otherwise, the priests would be despised, vexed, treated as abject servants without being able to do any good. In 1888, de Concilio wrote:

> I have proofs at hand . . . it would make your blood boil to see how Italian priests have been treated by American pastors.[12]

The Jesuit Father Piccirillo was also in favor of Missionary Centers and churches for Italians only.[13] De Concilio himself had been in the United States for some thirty years and personally knew half of the Catholic Bishops. In his view, the Archbishop of New York would not have opposed separate parishes, but the pastors, he added, "do not want to let the Italians free." Even if the Holy See were to intervene, De Concilio stated, the Bishops would not be able to do much. "They will say, 'Rome, Rome!' in public to blind the eyes of Rome and those of inexperienced people, but everything will proceed as before."[14] The Pallottine and Jesuit priests working with immigrants were advising the same stand on independence for effective action, avoidance of conflict, and satisfaction of the immigrant community.[15] Scalabrini's representative in the United States, Father Zaboglio, was saddened to observe how even in the smallest town national Catholic Churches existed. Not only German Churches (of which there were a great number), but also French, Canadian, Polish, Bohemian and Hungarian Churches were erected. On the other hand, Italian national Churches had to be established with difficulty. Italians had rights equal to those of other Catholics, and that made more inexplicable the antagonistic behavior of the New York Catholic Pastors, even though the clergy in New England and in other areas of the country was much more understanding.[16]

Bishop Scalabrini subscribed to some of the ideas coming to him from the Italian priests in the States. He wrote to archbishop Corrigan:

> If it were possible to subtract the Italians from the parochial jurisdiction and entrust their spiritual care to my missionaries, everything would be successful in a wonderful way. . . .[17]

The Archbishop of New York, reversing the position he had taken at Baltimore in 1884, assured Scalabrini:

> Everyday I am concerned with our dear Italians. I wish very much to give them a national church of their own where they will be totally independent. This is my firm will. Only and for a while I must be prudent to insure the necessary means. . . .[18]

The immigrants and their priests wanted independence for similar, but not identical reasons. The priests were more concerned with ecclesiastical politics, their equality in the diocesan structure, and freedom of action. The newcomers wanted a feeling of assurance, a canonization of their world evidenced by their children's respect and the celebration of feasts. Most of all they wanted a social institution they could call their own in a strange world of work and politics they could in no way control. Even Freemasons, in fact, were willing to help in obtaining funds, promising to circulate a subscription list among the people in the Italian colony on behalf of an Italian church.[19]

Indeed the religion of the immigrant demanded a physical, ritualistic point of reference. Its content was made up of manifestations of piety oriented toward rites of passage to insert the individual in the group and of communal celebration to strengthen the solidarity of the group. The existing English-speaking churches rejected a return to, or acceptance of, rural and tribal Mediterranean ritualism. In this way they created a vacuum in the immigrant community and in its expectations posited the conditions for conflict by the consequent emergence of a parallel set of religious institutions.

The objective of independence, then, was to serve in an expressive way to signify the moral world of the Italian peasant.

In 1910, the entire Italian colony, located in Brooklyn on Hamilton Avenue between Hicks and President Streets and in the adjacent areas on Columbia and Van Brunt Streets as well as in Commerce Street, complained to Bishop McDonnell of Brooklyn that they needed a resident priest in their old Church of the Sacred Hearts. From the time the parish had been moved to another church, the moral conditions of the neighborhood had deteriorated, and young people were not growing up to be good. Many more Italian families were moving in. They could never have thought that their little church, assuring them peace, would have been left without a priest. Until the church was going to open again, no contributions would be given.[20]

Novenas were attended to church capacity, as were the feasts of the Patron Saints of the villages of origin. There was both a continuity with the old world and religious immediacy. Father Morelli, reporting from the Five Points area in New York City on the success of novenas and on the need for a simple, familiar style of preaching, pointed out from this experience the necessity to start assimilating the Italians into the more sacramental American form of Catholicsm:

> The people come in crowds to the instructions. . . . Through the novenas that are very well attended we will try to inculcate and make known the necessity to frequent often the sacraments, a defect of these Italians. . . .[21]

During the novenas the people "were electrified to hear those popular *cantilene* (slow, rhythmic songs), even if off-tune, in which they used to take part in the church of their village." [22]

The Italian priests were regularly requesting relics, holy pictures, medals, statues and devotional booklets from Italy to distribute them among the immigrants. [23]

The public processions in particular were the most eventful manifestations of the social life of the colony and the most resented by the surrounding society. In 1892 Father Lynch replied to the archbishop of New York:

> ... in reference to public processions of Italians carrying statues of Saints through the streets, I would say that no such procession has ever gone forth from this church. The procession of St. Donatus (which we forbade) was held on last Monday with all the noise of brass band and fireworks in the streets of the 6th and 14th wards of the city. This procession passed the Church of the Transfiguration about ten o'clock. A priest (in cassock and surplice) and four altar boys came after the brass band. Then came the statue of St. Donatus carried on the shoulders of four men. Women and small girls followed with large and small candles and the men of the society brought up the rear. . . . The whole church was decorated with tinsel. The Italian girl selling pictures at the door of the church gave me all the necessary information to prove that these priests had disobeyed your orders. [24]

Some Americanized Italians and other Catholics of Newark remonstrated against processions in an even more vivid way in 1915:

> The undersigned American citizens, respectfully petition Your Excellency as follows:
>
> That in the matter of so-called Italian religious celebrations in this city, we have viewed with some concern their increase, and do now protest against their future continuance.
>
> These performances are in no wise religious; as such they would be celebrated in their churches, their homes, their hearts. On the contrary they desecrate the Sabbath and all other days with their brass bands, public begging (on a Sunday there will be soon a brass band or two with six men carrying trays making the rounds of the streets begging from house to house; the same thing being done on the day of the celebration) and raising obstructions all along the line.
>
> These celebrations are nothing short of nuisances, with the strident noises of the bands, the shooting of fireworks the whole live long day in front of everybody's houses, whether the owners want it or not; bandstands and vendors' booths erected on sidewalks and streets, stretching decorations across roadways and leaving the highways full of powder smoke and dust and dirt. And what shall be said of tender children who are compelled to march bare headed in a broiling hot sun

for hours! Holy statuaries and sacred vestments are paraded repeatedly, not before the faithful and believers, but before scoffers and unbelievers.

The majority of the members of societies do not go to church, not even on these days do they go in, the most of them remaining out during the religious ceremony.

There is no religious fervor in the whole business. It is a simple case of transplanting a custom from some little town in Italy, and verily there is more rivalry in it between the different towns-folk than religion.

. . . Yearly we see the spectacle of a street not large enough to accommodate daily traffic, on certain days blocked by thousands of people gathered to see fireworks shot off right in their midst, blocking or congesting traffic for hours. That more damage is not done or accidents happen is a marvel. . . .

In view of these facts, we call on the proper authorities to aid us in putting a stop to it. . . .[25]

But it was especially on occasions such as these that the parish was becoming the point of reference of the entire ethnic community. Immigrants from different villages, even though honoring the same Saint on the same day, demanded separate liturgical celebrations right in the same parish. Some churches in Italian areas could be seen with five or six statues of the Blessed Virgin donated by different groups and all statues were jealously guarded. The Italian parish, by accepting this reduplication of statues and ceremonies, slowly incorporated and fused into one community the fragmented Italian immigrants of the same American neighborhood.[26] When the great feast days and processions were celebrated, men also attended church in much larger numbers than on the regular holydays. But it took several years before the conviction died down that sacramental participation was primarily for women.[27] Processions started from the hall of the society organizing the feast; went to the church for mass and *panegirico;* then, through the streets, well decorated and crowded, returned to the point of departure.

Under pressure from the local pastors the bishops opposed the processions, especially public illuminations and fireworks. The police normally endorsed the bishops on giving and refusing permits.[28] Describing the poverty and sickness tormenting the Italians crowded in the slums of New York City in 1910, Father Pietro Pisani noted how their folkloristic religion was tolerated by the Italian pastors to the limits of any possiblity, even though the Apostolic Delegate, the bishops, Archbishop Farley of New York as leader, had forbidden all processions.[29]

The alliance between the Saints and the immigrants extended beyond the celebration of processions and *feste.* When a new statue was brought into the church, on the occasion of its blessing one could become the *compare* or *comare* (sponsor) of the Saint by making a certain offering. Another sign of friendship with the Saints was pinning dollars on ribbons hanging from their statues or on their vestments.[30] Loyalty was shown by defending one's patron Saint's right to become the titular of the Italian parish. In the latter case, there were naturally competitions and compromises. An example happened in Newark. The Societa' di San Gerardo wrote as late as 1926:

> The church to be built should possibly be given the title of our glorious St. Gerardo Maiella. Out of sentiment of our dutiful respect for the pious and miraculous St. Lucy and not wanting to unjustly exclude this present titular of the Church, we thought of combining the two names by having the parish under the name of St. Lucy and also make the Church a shrine under the second name of St. Gerardo Maiella.[31]

Father Gambera agreed that "the most sacred institution, the venerable monument for an emigrant abroad is the church. It is the first and authoritative school of religious and social obligations." He added, however, that "unfortunately in our colonies, especially the more fortunate and educated class, of the so-called *prominenti*, the representatives of our Government included, with rare exceptions, were giving a general example of irreligiosity."[32] Gambera confirmed the custom of the Italian colonies in the manifestation of their religiosity and did not hesitate to express his surprise and his interpretation of a form of piety as strange to him, a northern Italian, as it was for the Irish and the other Americans. He wrote:

> Many societies have the name of the Patron Saint of their *paese*. They celebrate the annual solemnity with colorful and noisy parades, with Mass and the *panegirico*. Rarely, however, are the societies present in church. Everything begins and everything concludes exteriorly. And in these exterior comedies is all the practice of their religion . . .
>   . . . in those parades there were no prayers and no religious songs, but only some yelling of disorderly exclamations. Some women (donnicciole) in their ignorant simplicity, were holding candles and walking barefooted. The zealous collectors were passing from door to door. Many were making generous offerings, while to the church they were refusing even the most modest one. The statues were carried only for publicity, and they pretended, in order to do better business, to have a priest present.[33]

But the religious southern Italian customs were all the immigrants had by which to express their social life, even though outsiders could not grasp their implications.

The immigrants were Italians and Catholics in the sense that to be Sicilian, Calabrese, Neapolitan or Pugliese implied to be a participant, even though unconsciously, in the events and history of the Italian nation. But they were not Italians in the sense that they possessed a culture made up of remembrances of a past world or of a national reality which was in formation and ferment. The immigrants were not the Italian political class. They had only some myths, and these, too, very fragmentary, of the Roman civilization and of the Renaissance. As for the political unification of Italy, they had opposed it. The very fact that they did not have a common language, but only various dialects, often incomprehensible among themselves, demonstrated with evidence their cultural heterogeneity of sentiments and traditions, which were becoming unified only to the extent that they were expressions of a culture of a tribal and rural background.

Violently transplanted into an urban-industrial society that valued and exploited them as a reservoir of manpower, cheap and unskilled, the immigrants were still able to provide themselves and their children with a minimum of economic security. But their new occupations in the mines and the factories could not be easily re-inserted and re-interpeted in that clearly defined and static view they, as farmers and day laborers, possessed in the rural, feudal and unchangeable society to which they were accustomed. The norms of production activity to which they had to submit no longer fell under the jurisdiction of the family and the natural community that was the *paese*. The dissociation between work and traditional norms of behavior made it impossible to rebuild in the host country the same type of community the immigrants had left behind. The ship which had forever separated the immigrants from the land of their ancestors, signified more than physical detachment and séparation. It was the beginning of an irreversible process, except for those, mostly failures, who were returning.[34] The only meaningful link with the past the immigrants could find on the American soil was their religious faith, and this too subjected them to an increasing process of Americanization. Ethnic communities grouped around the church and found the security, identity and the appropriate environment they needed to move from one civilization to another. The Germans had a common language and a significant middle-class; the Irish had a faith that was an expression of their historical national experience. The Italians had their ethnic church as a key element in their transition into the urban life and culture of America.

In this context, Father Pietro Bandini, whose experience and competence were recognized by the most divergent ideologies, wrote:

> Persons of some erudition, who know the history of our achievements, the glories of our heroes and geniuses, may have within themselves that spark necessary to keep alive in the heart the fire of love for the

fatherland and clear in mind the admiration for its greatness. But we should not expect to find these things in the little education of the vast majority of our immigrants. So, how would you warm up their heart and maintain alive that flame, that once was burning, of love for their land of birth? Will you try to call to their memory the greatness of the fatherland's institutions, the *decoro* of the fatherland's government?

Let's speak clearly. Let's not deceive ourselves. We must go slowly with such people in rekindling the memory of the fatherland with these arguments. They have maintained fresh the memory of the hardships in which they lived; the poverty they suffered; and the taxes they had to pay to the government. . . . There are, however, other arguments, more in tune with their minds. There is a way not entirely closed and through which you can reach their hearts. . . . Speak to them of their little church on the mountain-top, witness of their past happiness. Recall to their minds the joyous feste in which they participated around the church. Talk of that cemetery with its broken down walls, where in the shadow of the cross rest the remains of their dear ones. Do not even forget the old pastor. He took so much care of them in their young years; caressed them; gave them wise counsel mixed with tears, when good and simple, they left their native village to go to foreign lands looking for the bread that had become too scanty in their own land. Then you will see how the face of many will begin to blush. Their little church, the joys enjoyed once, are the only elements they can recall and which re-awaken the affections of their heart toward a land that had occupied their soul so greatly.[35]

The behavior of Italian immigrants seems to confirm Oscar Handlin's observations on the 'new immigration':

The more thorough the separation from the other aspects of the old life the greater was the hold of the religion that alone could survive the transfer. Struggling against heavy odds to save something of the old ways, the immigrants directed into their faith the whole weight of their longing to be connected with the past.[36]

The ethnic parish accepted the folkloristic religious manifestations of the immigrants; justified their moralism; never rejected their *italianita'*. It re-created, therefore, a cultural community in which the immigrants were aware of "being-of-a-kind," of participating in a common patrimony of symbolic meanings, myths, memories, traditions and values. In fact, this mutual sharing is directly conditioned by an adequate communicability between the members of the group. Karl W. Deutsch wrote:

The community which permits a common history to be experienced as common is a community of complementary habits and facilities of communication. It requires, so to speak, equipment for a job. This job consists in the storage, recall, transmission, recombination, and reapplica-

tion of relatively wide ranges of information; and the 'equipment' consists in such learned memories, symbols, habits, operating performances
of these functions. A larger group of persons linked by such complementary habits and facilities of communication we may call a people.[37]

The Italian parish was the sociological place of communicability
around which the immigrants met physically and culturally. It made
them a 'people' in the social context of the American society, where
belonging to a people or to an ethnic group was a condition for adjustment and mobility.

*The Ethnic Church as an Institution of Pluralization
and Integration.*

The social importance of the Italian parishes in the United States
does not appear as universal as their cultural significance. Yet, to the
extent that the ethnic identity of the immigrants persisted, it was in
large part a direct or indirect consequence of the structural change the
emergence of Italian national churches brought about. Italian labor
unions, the Italian language press, and the fraternal associations have
also preserved ethnic awareness, sometimes in alliance and sometimes
in latent and open conflict with the church. The national parish,
however, was pivotal on the whole question of ethnic pluralism
because it generated for the Italian immigrants the subcommunity they
made up.[38]

With the building of the Italian churches, campanile-like
(*campanilismo*) attitudes and the feeling of superiority which Northern
Italians felt over their compatriots from the South began to die down.
Under pressure from Archbishop Corrigan, Father Morelli had called
Southern Italians to his church, which initially had been opened by
Northerners. He wrote:

> They came immediately, but the Northerners opposed them; they did
> not want them in church. They (Genoese) do not want their statues,
> their feasts, nothing. . . . I opposed this always. . . . I always insisted I
> could not make distinction between Italians and Italians. . . .[39]

Once the Italian church was opened, the ethnic succession in the immigrant neighborhood became more evident. The old non-Italian
residents of adjacent and nearby streets moved out. The Italians moved
in and bought their own houses as a symbol of security, independence
and achievement. Then social life developed: mutual aid societies were
formed, banks were opened, ethnic shops multiplied, professional people established their offices. In this movement of men and in these
situations, the more intelligent and dynamic persons had a chance to

know each other and to make themselves known. Thus, from the migrant mass emerged the future leaders. Immigrants were encouraged to become American citizens. The poor were assisted and the children educated.[40]

For Ciufoletti, the Italian parish and school counterbalanced American nationalism:

> In the confessional, school, and catechism classes we speak with respect, in fact with admiration, of the religious traditions—that almost always are also civic—of the fatherland of the parents. . . . In the public school one doesn't speak of anything else but civics, Americanization, the unique greatness and power of America: the American fatherland is almost idolatrized, and patriotism worshipped as religion.
>
> One should recall Stephen Decatur's thesis that is also the motto of the great *Chicago Daily Tribune:* "Our Country! . . . may she always be in the right; but our country, right or wrong." This, we must keep in mind, is the thinking of the great majority of the people.
>
> It is not surprising, therefore, if often our youth grown up far away from the sweet and healthy influences of the church, are ashamed of their name and americanize it; are ashamed of their parents and despise them.[41]

After a tour of Italian parishes in the United States in 1915, Fr. Capra was amazed that little more than twenty parishes, with less than one hundred priests, could work successfully with an Italian population of over three hundred thousand people in their territory.

> The parish, he reported, is not only a more or less elegant and comfortable church, where religious life is carried out. The parish besides the church, often has the school, where one learns Italian and love for the distant fatherland along with religion. It takes care in the kindergarten of the children of working mothers. . . . It has a hall for the meetings of the numerous societies which somehow relate to the church. Sunday school is taught there. Evening *feste,* and entertainment for the families and their children, are also held in the parish hall, where a variety of activities for assistance to the Italians have their office.
>
> The parish house is the house of everybody. . . .[42]

The church was serving a dual role, religious and social, in the coal mine-fields of Pennsylvania, in Buffalo, New York City, in the smaller centers of New Jersey and elsewhere.[43] Three Italian orphanages and three kindergartens were functioning well by 1910, supported by Italian parishes and Italian religious communities:[44] in East Harlem, on the Lower East Side of New York, West Park, N.Y., and Kearney, N.J. In response to the needs of the laborers of the community who, during working hours, were compelled to leave their small children home, or on the streets, without anybody to look after them, the Italian

church in Woodhaven also opened a kindergarten for them in 1907
following the example of the Italian churches in Manhattan.[45] By 1915
two more kindergartens were opened by the Italian churches of the
Lower West Side of Manhattan.[46] Other Italian parishes followed the
trend in the care of children. The Italians of Williamsburgh, Brooklyn,
expected the church to provide the hospital as well. All the Italian
societies of the area had met to decide the building of a new church
capable of serving all the twelve thousand Italians of the
neighborhood. In the days of the great parades, not even half of the
members of the societies could fit inside the old church. The colony
needed, the Italians agreed, a new church, a building for the school and
a hospital.[47]

A hospital had been started in Manhattan by the Italian church of St.
Joachim already in 1888. It was developed by Frances X. Cabrini, and it
became Columbus Hospital.[48] Sewing classes, recreational activities,
meeting rooms for the societies, night classes in English were often
regular activities of Italian churches for the purpose, as Father Vogel
wrote, of elevating the immigrant standards of moral and social life.[49]

The intense social activity of the Italian priest was even used in the
Italian Parliament as an argument on the part of a socialist deputy
against the government:

> Foreigners realize the inferiority of the action of our consuls compared to
> that of the Missionary, who does not close himself in his office waiting for
> the needy, but goes out looking for sorrows and miseries, before sorrows
> and miseries come to knock at his door.[50]

Other forms of socio-religious assistance for the community were
organized from the Italian parochial network. Already in 1891 Italian
pastors in New York were notified by a pastoral letter of Archbishop
Corrigan[51] that the St. Raphael's Society for Italian immigrants had
started its work to assist newcomers at the moment of their arrival by
taking them away from the exploitation of agents and *padroni*. The
Society, legally incorporated on July 6, 1891, immediately carried out
its statutes' mandate of finding jobs and homes for the newcomers,
providing religious assitance and, in particular, taking care of women
and children.[52]

Until 1924, the St. Raphael's Society continued to operate with alter-
nating success through the support of the Italian parishes of Our Lady
of Pompei and St. Joachim in particular, not only assisting the immigrants, but also advising on appropriate immigration legislation
both in the United States and in Italy. For some representatives of the
Italian Government, however, the St. Raphael's Society was limited by

Table 1. *Italian Immigrants Who Landed
in New York from July 1st, 1891, to June 30th, 1892,
and the Number Assisted by the St. Raphael's Society*

Arrivals	58,617
Sent back by the Bureau of Immigration	496
Assisted by the St. Raphael's Society	20,000
Provided with temporary home, Men...............................	73
free of charge by the Women...........................	34
Society Children.........................	218
Deaths during the voyage	5
Deaths in the Immigrant Hospital	9
Marriages...	7
Baptisms .:..	2

N.B. Many Italians landed at New Orleans and Philadelphia; others at Boston and in Canada.

Source: Rev. Fr. P. Bandini, *First Annual Report of the St. Raphael's Italian Benevolent Society* (July 1st, 1891, to June 30th, 1892.) New York: 1892, p. 28

"its character of a religious organization." At the same time the effectiveness of the Society in protecting the immigrants and in helping them was fully acknowledged. Consul Prat wrote from New York to the Foreign Ministry in Rome in 1903:

> No other institutions take care of the Italian immigrants in the United States, except the recognized Italian Bureau located at n. 17 State Street, and the St. Raphael's Society that has its quarters on Bleeker Street. . . .[53]

It seems ironic that the Society, whose purpose was to "cooperate to keep alive in the hearts of Italian migrants the Catholic faith and with it the sentiment of their nationality and their affection toward the fatherland," could appear as 'limited' in the eyes of the Italian political ruling class. This class again misjudged the immigrants who could not identify with it in any way.[54]

From the just established church of Our Lady of Pompei, Fr. Bandini was instrumental in obtaining from the authorities of the Barge Office permission to start a Labor Bureau in Castle Garden. The Labor Bureau became a key office on which depended the acceptance and refusal of Italian immigrants arriving in New York and their settling in the United States.[55] The significant role of the St. Raphael's Society can be gathered in part from the following letter from the Office of the U.S. Commissioner of Immigration in New York:

> Some two years ago we had correspondence which resulted in according to the St. Raphael Society certain privileges for the Immigration Station at this port, which it has since held. On the first proximo, by the direction

of the Honorable Secretary of the Treasury, the official bureau of the Italian Government, which has been maintained here for over five years, will be discontinued, thus leaving the St. Raphael Society alone in the field to look after the spiritual welfare of Italian immigrants and to perform the usual missionary services for them.

Of the total number of Italians arriving during the past year, all but one twentieth of one percent were professed Roman Catholics; and in view of this fact I desire to call the matter to your attention in order that you may, if deemed advisable, give the subject your consideration.

It is my earnest desire that every class of incoming immigrants shall be properly represented; and my experience has convinced me that the missionary societies which are established here and run on a proper basis, have been of the greatest advantage both to the immigrants and to the Immigration Service as well; and I will gladly welcome any organized effort on the part of the Italians which would secure for them representation free from any pecuniary or sordid considerations, and similar to that now enjoyed by other nationalities.[56]

The Italian Franciscan Fathers, who staffed the parishes of St. Anthony and Precious Blood in Lower Manhattan, organized the American Italian Protectory of the Sons of Columbus Legion—Charity Society for the Free Legal Help and Assistance of the Poor. Father Bonaventure Piscopo, writing to Archbishop Corrigan from the office of the Protectory in Grand Street, explained the motivation of his action.

When sixteen months ago, among many oppositions of the spirit of evil, I started the Charity Society of the above title, my first object was not only to help the needy Italians, but principally to oppose the great power of freemasonry, whose entire control upon the Italians, through a sectarian charity work was greatly detrimental to religion carrying them away from Catholic Church to Protestantism and atheism, and precluding to us the way of coming in contact with them.

I may be mistaken in my opinion, but the facts have shown, during these sixteen months, that my path was not entirely the wrong one; because during this time, on the pretext of charity, I came in contact with thousands of people who would never otherwise have approached a priest, and I had an easy way of impressing upon their hearts and attracting them back to religion.[57]

From November 1897 to December 1898 the American Italian Protectory had committed 360 orphans to different Catholic institutions and 125 sick people to hsopital; it had given employment to 425 immigrants and discharged 260 from the Immigration Bureau; freed 6 persons from jail; obtained citizenship papers to 68 persons; helped 455 poor families with clothing, groceries, coal and cash. In the first quarter of 1899 another 882 similar cases had been taken care by the Protectory.[58]

The *Italica Gens,* a federation of all Italian Missions overseas for the material and social assistance to Italian migrants, was also operating out of the Italian parochial network through special secretariats for migrants. The task of the secretariats was to serve the migrants in finding jobs, writing home, obtaining official documents, hospital assistance, education. By 1910 *Italica Gens* had fifty-four secretariats active in the United States, mostly in conjunction with Italian parishes. There were secretariats in Atlantic City, Bayonne, Elizabeth and Hoboken; five in Manhattan; one in Brooklyn; one in Hawthorne, N.Y. and one in White Plaines.[60] A typical six-month work of a secretariat of the *Italica Gens* in New York is given in a 1910 report of the secretariat directed by the Salesian Fathers (29 Mott Street). There were visits to tenement houses, information distributed at the door of the church on how to fight tuberculosis, help in obtaining indemnity for accidents during work. Then, 96 families (315 members) were helped through the St. Vincent de Paul Society; 86 cases of finding jobs had been completed; 20 children from the Catholic Protectory were returned to their families; 30 Italians repatriated gratuitously; 20 interventions in court; 18 cases of immigration directed to the St. Raphael's Society; 12 people recovered in the hospital; two children adopted by well-to-do families.[61]

The Italian Auxiliary, established in 1922 as an affiliate of the Catholic Charities of the archdiocese of New York and as a replacement for the St. Raphael's Society and the secretariates of the *Italica Gens,* continued the social work among the immigrants in a more systematic and organized fashion. The local initiative of the Italian parishes became integrated into the diocesan plan of social action. But the parish and the Italian priests remained the natural base of activities. Monsignor Germano Formica, Director of the Italian Auxiliary since 1924, wrote in 1926 to the Italian American priests that they were a decisive force in the successful operation of the Italian Auxiliary, its home and services. The Italian immigrants abroad instinctively sought the help of their priests. Formica felt that "around the priests spontaneously grows a movement which responds to the inner aspirations of the Italian people." He continued:

> The parish is the natural center of the religious and social life of our colonies, as the priest is the trusted and sure guide, because in his goodness and wisdom the immigrant re-lives the joys, sorrows, hopes, all the vicissitudes happy and sad of his life of exile. Nothing worthwhile is done in our communities without consulting the priest. Difference of class and political opinion cannot interfere with this collective devotion to him, who is the friend and the confidant of all.[62]

The Italian parishes could direct to the Italian Auxiliary their needy cases, provide for immigrants at their arrival in the port of New York, where the Auxiliary was present to receive them, and supply legal advice and even employment, as the annual reports of the Auxiliary document. (Table 2) The Italian Auxiliary, as an official arm of Catholic Charities, marks the transition of local neighborhood ethnic services into the bureaucracy of diocesan structures, another aspect of the progressive integration of the ethnic parish into the established church.

Notwithstanding the high degree of illiteracy of the immigrants, the Italian-Catholic press started, even if in a rudimentary form, at a very early stage. In 1889, Father Morelli, founder and pastor of St. Joachim church in New York, was convinced that an Italian Catholic newspaper was indispensable for the United States.[63] A few months later, *L'Armonia* was published weekly for the Italian American people and was distributed in various churches in New York City, New Haven, and elsewhere. Eight bishops were subscribers, and few hundred copies were on the various stands of the City.[64] But apparently *L'Armonia* did not last long. Around 1890, while acting pastor at the Precious Blood Church in New York, Dr. S. De Santi started the publication of *La Fenice Italo-Americana*, a weekly Catholic newspaper of religion, politics and culture. The paper lasted at least three years.[65] By 1900 L'Unione Italo-Americana Pub. Co. was publishing *L'Italiano in America*, backed mostly by the parish of Our Lady Help of Christians and other Italian parishes of New York.[66] The newspaper had been organized by the Italian American clergy of New York City[67] and had seen its first publication on December 8, 1900.[68] *L'Italiano in America* was still publishing in 1915. At that time the inter-parish monthly *Bollettino Mensile* for Italian and mixed parishes was distributed in Brooklyn with a circulation of 18,000 copies.[69] In 1918 both *L'Italiano in America* and the *Bollettino Mensile* were in crisis, but they survived at least until 1920.[70] Other parishes or groups of parishes had their own press vehicles. In New Jersey, *La Verita'* and the *Mt. Carmel Bulletin* was in its tenth year of publication in 1915. *Il Carroccio*, embodying the ideal of religion and *italianita'* of most Italian pastors of the Metropolitan area, had started in 1914 and lasted into the 1930's. A bimonthly publication, *Il Carroccio*, was perhaps the best of all Italian-English and Italian language publications for its editorial quality and its ability to portray the feelings and aspirations of the average Italian American, including their sympathy for Fascism. But all the Italian language Catholic press died out with the passing away of the first generation.

Table 2. *Case Work of the Italian Auxiliary of New York City, 1926-1931*

	1926	1927	1928	1929	1930	1931
1. Immigration cases handled, visas and re-entry permits secured	673	1,326	1,839	1,972	2,699	5,582
2. Naturalization cases	137	145	311	479	771	795
3. Telegrams sent, affidavits and other correspondence	1,452	2,617	3,762	4,624	6,036	7,299
4. Military pensions secured and Consular tickets obtained for repatriation	107	215	289	421	1,225	2,593
5. Certificates and other legal papers	54	49	55	53	67	87
6. Immigrants located in America for relatives in Italy	608	875	870	909	961	1,099
7. Insane persons re-patriated	3	5	12	7	—	—
8. Special baggage matters handled	6	8	39	64	214	254
9. Telegrams sent to relatives for arriving immigrants	971	—	2,938	3,829	2,619	—
10. Employment secured to immigrants	152	445	603	632	577	243
11. Transient Lodging at Italian Auxiliary home	935	2,002	3,437	4,233	3,203	1,869
12. Immigrants assisted to and from piers, railroad stations and the Italian Auxiliary home	1,223	3,843	8,524	12,880	10,406	6,133
TOTAL CASES HANDLED	6,321	11,530	22,679	30,103	28,776	25,953

Source: The annual reports of the Italian Auxiliary, Inc., published in *La Voce dell' Emigrato*, voll. IV-IX, 1927 to 1932. Other services listed in the reports are: Mass at Ellis Island every Sunday and Holyday; visiting the Italian patients at Ellis Island Hospital during the week, when necessary; performing marriages for the immigrants.

Table 3. *Spiritual Report of Selected Italian Parishes, Brooklyn, December 1923*

	St. Roch	Our Lady of the Rosary of Pompeii	St. Rita (Brooklyn)	Our Lady of Solace	Our Lady of Loreto	St. Rita (L.I. City)	Sacred Heart	Our Lady of Mt. Carmel
Sunday Masses	4 vespers	4	5 vespers	5	5 vespers	5	6 vespers	4 vespers
Confessions	4-6 7-on	usual	3:30-6 7-9	usual	usual	usual	usual	usual
Population	15,000	16,000	6,700	2,000	15,000	10,000	25,000	16,000
Baptisms	665	821	374	263	936	828	1,533	872
First Communions	270	350	204	246	289	575	436	405
Confirmations	798	358	221	520	377	400	739	591
Marriages	134	250	94	85	196	167	331	125
Deaths	115	95	43	36	164	97	193	117
Catechism Attendance	600 (Sunday)	400 (3 days)	250 (3 days)	300 (3 days)	650 (5 days)	550 (3 days)	600 (2 days)	500
Male Societies	3	3	2	3	2	3	9	2
Female Societies	5	3	4	4	3	3	4	4

Source: Archives Diocese of Brooklyn, *Reports of Churches for 1923.*

Thus, in their areas of service, the national parishes encompassed a large clientele: the regular and occasional church members; the poor people—most of the immigrants—who needed social and moral assitance and aid in emigration; legal and welfare cases; the people who had only the *feste* to relax and express their feelings of being together with their own kind. Many of the interpersonal relations of the immigrants became circumscribed within their ethnic group where their social needs were fulfilled by the organizational structures which had developed around the national church. This factor and the isolation from the existing institutions of the receiving society due to language and culture barriers brought about a high degree of institutional completeness and a consequent reduplication of institutions that added a new dimension to the process of pluralization of American society. For their part, the Italian immigrants turned to the Church for the sacraments and the exercises of their piety in rather large numbers.

At the turn of the century and well into the 1920's, the average urban Italian parish was a large parish. St. Joachim (Roosevelt Street, New York) had a population of about 20,000 Italians with a succursal chapel attached to it. It had an average of 1,000 baptisms, 300 marriages and 350 first communions a year, 9 societies, a kindergarten with 200 children

Table 4. *Pastors' Estimate of Percentage of People
Actually Attending Sunday Mass in Selected Italian Parishes,
New York Archdiocese, 1929-1930*

Parish	Estimate
St. Benedicta, Staten Island	60%
Our Lady of Loreto, Manhattan	50%
Our Lady of Peace, Manhattan	60%
Our Lady of Mt. Carmel, Manhattan	50-75%
St. Lucy, Manhattan	40%
The Most Holy Crucifix, Manhattan	15-20%
Our Lady of Mt. Carmel, East White Plains	40%
St. Vitus, Mamaroneck	50%
Our Lady of Mt. Carmel, Yonkers	75%
St. Ann, Staten Island	35-40%

Source: Status Animarum Reports, AANY—The reports are incomplete and the estimates of pastors can be taken only as indications. Reports could not be located for all Italian parishes.

Table 5. *Pastor's Report on Population and Church Participation*
Our Lady of Mt. Carmel Italian Parish (East 117th Street, Manhattan)
1926-1931

Year	1926	1927	1928	1929	1930	1931
1. No. of Families	2,000	1,800	1,800	1,800	1,800	1,800
Adults	5,000	4,500	4,500	5,000	5,000	5,000
Children	6,000	5,000	5,000	4,000	4,000	4,000
2. Baptisms	1,015	950	902	904	1,301	840
3. Confirmations	754	512	660	717	638	541
4. Marriages	305	274	310	270	264	176
5. Funerals	100	92	100	95	133	122
6. Average Attendance at all Sunday Masses	4,000	3,500	3,000	3,000	4,500	4,500
7. No. Attending Mass at Other Churches					many	many
8. No. of Parish Societies	12	13	12	13	14	10
9. Total Membership of Societies	3,035	2,970	2,325	2,175	2,725	1,520
10. No. of Children in Sunday School	310	310	310	360	445	295
11. No. of Children Attending Catechism During Week	310	310	310	360	445	295
12. No. of Parochial School Children	950	950	980	995	540	445

Source: Status Animarum Reports, AANY.

in daily attendance. Our Lady of Pompei (Bleecker Street, New York) had a population close to 25,000 people, an annual average of 1,300 baptisms, 450 marriages, 500 first communions, 7 societies and a kindergarten.[71]

St. Anthony's (Sullivan Street, New York) had in 1924 eight societies with a total membership of 4730 persons, 1,500 children freely attending the parochial school, a kindergarten, an annual average of 1,107 baptisms, 218 marriages and 268 confirmations. In the early 1920's the parish of Precious Blood (Baxter Street, New York) was already losing families of its congregation who were moving out. It still had about 10,000 Italians. In its period of greatest activity, 1890-1910, there were up to 50 baptisms and 20 marriages a week. St. Clare (36th Street in New York) had a population of over 12,000 with an annual average of 600 baptisms, 160 marriages, 25 thousand annual communions, a school

with twelve classrooms and several flourishing societies. Our Lady of
Solace (Madonna del Suffragio) parish had 16,000 Italians, 800 children
in the parochial school by 1924, an annual average of 900 baptisms, 175
marriages. Our Lady of Peace in Brooklyn had a population of about
18,000 Italians, an annual average of 1,050 baptisms, 180 marriages, 650
confirmations, 90,000 annual communions, 1,400 children in the
school, 6 active societies.[72] The other parishes in the Italian areas of
Brooklyn and Queens indicate large populations and significant
activities, as Table 3 on the spiritual reports of some Italian parishes of
Brooklyn shows. In the archdiocese of Newark, the parishes were
smaller with a population between 6,000 and 10,000 people, but with
proportionate religious and social activities.[73]

The ecclesiastical substructure that grew out of the Italian national
parishes network was strengthened by the ideological revival of

Table 6. *Pastor's Report on Population and Church Participation*
Holy Rosary Italian Parish (125th-117th St., E. River & 2nd Ave.)
1926-1931

Year	1926	1927	1928	1929	1930	1931
1.* No. of Families	2,500	2,320	1,709	973	1,383	1,523
Adults	5,550	5,640	4,728	3,892	4,624	4,506
Children	6,500	6,960	3,524	2,919	3,291	3,109
2. Baptisms	535	505	489	469	440	416
3. Confirmations	471	457	488	442	449	394
4. Marriages	150	137	139	119	105	125
5. Funerals	75	83	110	83	87	92
6. Average Attendance at all Sunday Masses	4,500	3,500	3,000	2,500	2,500	2,800
7. No. Attending Mass at Other Churches	1,000	600	300	300	200	350
8. No. of Parish Societies	14	13	14	13	13	13
9. Total Membership of Societies	2,511	2,982	3,136	3,163	2,459	2,401
10. No. of Children in Sunday School	1,010	1,150	—	—	1,065	1,241
11. No. of Children Attending Catechism During Week	715	715	2,050	1,255	1,065	1,241
12. No. of Parochial School Children	—	—	—	—	—	—

Source: Status Animarum Reports, AANY.

nationalism brought about by World War I and its immediate after-math. Yet the national parish managed to avoid schisms and total religious indifference by remaining within the existing diocesan struc-tures already accepted by American society. Gradually, the parishes let the processions and the feasts of Patron Saints die out. They replaced Italian with the English language in the church activities. The novenas became obsolete and the attendance at mass and the reception of sacraments more regular. The voluntary system of church support was accepted by the children of the immigrants.[74] In terms of the church, the experience of the Italian immigrants in the national parish was one of integration through separation, a pluralization that made the immigrant comfortable, strong enough to move into another socio-religious system more acceptable to society at large.

Table 7. *Pastor's Report on Population and Church Participation*
St. Joseph Italian Parish (5 Monroe Street, Manhattan)
1927-1932

Year	1926	1927	1928	1929	1930	1931	1932
1. No. of Families		750	600	600	600	500	460
Adults		5,500	2,400	2,400	1,800	1,600	1,500
Children		4,200	3,500	3,500	3,300	2,500	2,350
2. Baptisms		330	319	317	252	245	220
3. Confirmations		401	383	445	231	235	144
4. Marriages		70	75	90	75	67	64
5. Funerals		73	107	93	84	62	61
6. Average Attendance at all Sunday Masses		3,200	3,200	3,000	1,800	1,800	1,700
7. No. Attending Mass at Other Churhces		2,000	800	800	200 to 300	200 to 300	200 to 300
8. No. of Parish Societies		7	10	10	10	10	10
9. Total Membership of Societies		1,085	1,142	1,051	983	1,010	1,060
10. No. of Children in Sunday School		1,500	1,350	1,350	600	650	650
11. No. of Children Attending Catechism During Week		1,000	950	950	250		
12. No. of Parochial School Children		300	370	380	460	250	215
Source: *Status Animarum Reports*, AANY.							

Table 8. *Pastor's Report on Population and Church Participation*
St. Anthony Italian Parish (233rd St. to City Line, Bronx)
1926-1932

Year	1926	1927	1928	1929	1930	1931	1932
1. No. of Families	203	213	532	506	510	441	372
Adults	521	536	1,532	1,494	1,490	910	519
Children	230	246	1,106	1,031	1,039	861	422
2. Baptisms	37	49	57	80	76	72	78
3. Confirmations	—	126	94	—	144	103	65
4. Marriages	6	6	16	20	34	22	24
5. Funerals	4	5	5	7	14	17	22
6. Average Attendance at all Sunday Masses	500	550	750	850	900	700	700
7. No. Attending Mass at Other Churches	100	100	400	450	450	200	200
8. No. of Parish Societies	9	5	8	9	9	9	9
9. Total Membership of Societies	355	275	552	615	717	545	621
10. No. of Children in Sunday School	196	—	365	372	360	290	255
11. No. of Children Attending Catechism During Week	93	—	330	295	285	245	235
12. No. of Parochial School Children	—	—	—	—	—	—	—

Source: Status Animarum Reports, AANY.

Conflict and Cooperation.

On August 18, 1908, the *Bollettino della sera* of New York was distributed throughout the Little Italies of the city with a first page catchy headline: "Revolver shots against a priest" (*Rivoltellate contro un prete*). No priest had been murdered, however. The night of August 17 had been one of those hot and humid summer nights that keep New Yorkers up until late, restlessly awaiting the breeze of the ocean. Father Mariano of the church of Our Lady of Mt. Carmel in White Plains had been sitting on the porch of his house; he was suddenly disturbed in the late hour by three shots emptied into his bed through the window of his room. He had been at odds with his congregation. He had proposed to abolish the feast and procession of St. Rocco traditionally held around August 16 to use the money collected on the occasion for a new church.

Table 9. *Pastors' Reports of Italian Families in Selected Non-Italian Parishes of the Archdiocese of New York, 1929-1931*

Parish	No. of Families			No. of Italian Families			Cumulative % of Italian Families
	1929	1930	1931	1929	1930	1931	
1. St. Alphonsus, Manhattan	260	210	210	98	98	98	43.2
2. Immaculate Conception, Manhattan	2,769	—	—	1,500	—	—	54.1
3. St. Andrews, Manhattan	208	177	146	42	32	32	19.9
4. Our Lady of Lourdes, Manhattan	2,953	3,028	3,028	90	90	90	2.9
5. St. Matthew, Manhattan	1,079	1,136	786	375	300	250	30.8
6. The Resurrection, Rye, N.Y.	415	454	524	50	100	170	22.9
7. St. Mary, Marlborough	146	138	129	30	32	30	22.2
8. Assumption, Peekskill	639	545	598	100	90	167	20.0
9. St. Athanasius, Bronx		177	126		56	29	28.0
10. St. Peter's, Liberty	114	110	108	22	20	22	19.2

Source: Status Animarum Reports, AANY.

But, the newspaper wryly concludes, the feast was celebrated and thousands of persons took part in it.

Already in the 1880's Archbishop Corrigan had forbidden public processions of Italians, and Irish pastors had simply defined them a disgrace.[75] The Bishops of Brooklyn and Newark had followed the same course of action. In fact, a Father E. J. Donelly had given close attention for 9 years to the so-called religious parades of Italian societies claiming to be Catholic; as a result of his own investigations, and that of others who had given attention to the subject, on November 17, 1908, he prepared a circular letter in opposition to said parades. He had the letter signed by about 250 clergymen in charge of Catholic parishes in the Borough of Brooklyn.[76]

The Italian priests had found themselves at the boundary-lines of two worlds—with the risk of being shot by the *paesani* or of being excommunicated by the Bishops.

The Church officially accepted and considered herself a pluralistic society only as an unavoidable and temporary condition while working to shape Southern, Eastern Europeans and non-Latin rite Catholics into "true Americans." At least at the time of mass emigration from Italy, the Catholic hierarchy was struggling to reassure itself of being a "monocolor," monolithic group completely American.

The Catholic Church was caught in a contradiction. Although a pluralistic society, it perceived itself, officially, as an homogeneous group and it tried to implement this perception in political decisions and pastoral planning. To what extent conflict among ethnic groups stemmed from such a dilemma is still an open field of research. The ideological and political fights which emerged in the Church in the life-span of first generation Italian immigrants cannot be understood in isolation. The Italian ethnic group was not the only one marked by outbursts of open conflict with the surrounding ecclesiastical and civil societies. Neither is the period of mass immigration at the turn of the century, and well up to the 1930's, the only one in American history characterized by intergroup tensions.[77]

The Irish and the French Bishops had felt that the other nationalities had undue preponderance in Church management. Archbishop Marechal referred to the Celtic priests and people as "la canaille irlandaise." Fr. Taylor of New York's St. Patrick's Cathedral preached at the consecration of Bishop DuBois by Archbishop Marechal in Baltimore and tactlessly prophesied great trouble since the appointment of a Frenchman over a largely Irish flock could not but be hazardous. The Irish and Germans enjoyed a few decades of cross fire. Anti-German feeling was present at the First Plenary Council of Baltimore in 1852 and it grew to explosion with the Cahensly question in the 1880's[78]

The remedy proposed for the multiplicity of nationalities was a more intense, simplified version of the ideology of nationalism under the new name of Americanism. The question, however, remains open if it was the functional need of unity that prompted the campaign against French, German, Latin and Slavic groups or the "desire to eliminate the only significant resistance to the Irish American domination of the hierarchy," as Robert Cross puts it.[79] Power is rarely given away. The religious ideology of Church unity might have played the least objectionable and the most efficient role in the self-maintenance of the "elite-rulers" of the Church. In 1905 John Talbott Smith summed up well the official ecclesiastical view of the Italian immigrants. The Italians were seen as unorthodox in their religious practice, ignorant and accompanied by pastors who did not care for them. Some signs of better pastoral care given by Italian priests were detected, however, after 1902. As for political ideas, Smith wrote:

> Nothing more hateful to American Catholics could be named than the 20th of September, which the Italian colony celebrated as the consummation of national glory, the date of Victor Emmanuel's occupation of Rome and of the downfall of the temporal power. For very slight cause the Irish would at any moment have attacked the annual procession, eager to drive the Garibaldians off the face of the earth, as in the case of the Orangemen; and as for considering them Catholics and aiding them to keep their faith alive, that was out of the question.[80]

On December 1, 1884, the Council of Baltimore took into discussion Italians and Negroes. The printed minutes of the Council are sketchy, but revealing. J. L. Spalding of Peoria, the only liberal Bishop who had not opted for rapid Americanization of the immigrants and had clearly expressed his cultural pluralistic position, sounded the only optimistic note in the controversy over Italians. He suggested that they should be oriented out of the cities to agriculture. Bishop Chatard of Vincennes said many Italians kept their faith, and Bishop de Goesbriand emphasized the need for Italian priests. Corrigan of New York, however, carried the day. He summarized a report he had sent to Rome. There were about 50,000 Italians in New York and surroundings, but not more than 1200 attended Mass, even if it was easy for them to do so. Two or three hundred had been confirmed by a heretical Bishop. Of the 12 priests working for Italians, ten had been forced out of Italy for immorality. Southern Italians were hopelessly ignorant as if they had never been instructed in the faith. Northern Italians, fewer in number, were better. Bishops and priests in the New York area had tried every means, even Italian language sermons, but to no avail.[81] Bishop Mullen of Erie confirmed Corrigan's report for the Italians working on the railroads in his diocese. It is a curious observation to make, but the Irish Bishops at this session of the Council were totally negative on the Italians, while the French, German and English were much more optimistic. Besides, of the 31 provincials of religious orders who were present in Baltimore, five were Italians, while two other Italian provincials could not attend. Of the eighty-eight theologians at the Council, about eight were Italians and among them was Gennaro de Concilio, the author of the Baltimore Catechism.

The immigrants and the priests from Italy arriving in the United States in the last part of the nineteenth century were unaware of the ideological battle they were coming into. Nativism was reviving in the 1890's with exacerbated anti-Catholic feelings and racist stereotypes. Italians in particular were targets of anti-foreigners attacks. Categorized as *mafiosi*, impulsive, prone to assasinate in revenge for a fancied wrong, addicted to vendetta, they had the added burden of being Catholics, the swarthy army of the Pope for the domination of America.[82]

The Catholic Church as a whole, in fact, was under bitter attack by Protestant Churches, the National League for the Protection of American Institutions, and the American Protective Association. The Catholic Bishops were desperately seeking a way out of the dilemma they faced of leading an immigrant church, keeping the immigrants within the fold and, at the same time, of Americanizing the church by making it an acceptable and functional institution of the whole society.

The Germans, the Italians, and the Poles saw in the preservation of the national language and culture the way for the preservation of the faith. For Italians, even the opposite was considered valid. The Irish on the other hand, saw the future of the Church in its functional integration into American society. The Bishops became divided on this issue into conservatives and liberals, the latter opting for fast Americanization and the former giving a more significant play to the ethnic groups. On the high level of ideology the polarization of the Church was expressed in a concise way by Bishop Zardetti of St. Cloud, Minn., at the Buffalo Katholikentag of 1891. He said:

> We want no American Church; but a holy, Catholic Roman Church in America.

The following year, the *Christliche Woche* summed up Archbishop Ireland's fixed idea:

> Crush the parochial school; destroy national churches; coquet with the State—and the great Republic of the West will be Catholic.

The furor raised by the Cahensly petition focused the conflict in even sharper terms. The *Volksfreund* of Buffalo said:

> The principal error of Archbishop Ireland lies in his ideas of America, Americans, American Church. America is no nation, no race, no people, like France, Italy, or Germany. . . .[83]

The horns of the dilemma were pointing in the direction of two opposite temptations: sectarianism and nationalism; neither side could calmly accept the universality of Catholicism. Italian immigrants on the political level of daily living allied themselves with the conservative group headed by Corrigan of New York, who had become much more open toward the Italians in the 1890's and who accepted the founding of national parishes. In this way, immigrants and priests worked hard to build their Italian churches and parochial organizations, sometimes forcefully protesting to the local Bishops, sometime imploring with great submission. If conflict emerged, several Bishops who had studied in Rome could send out conciliatory letters in Italian or speak to the immigrant groups in their language. For example, Bishops Corrigan of New York, McDonnell of Brooklyn, Wigger of Newark, and Walsh of Trenton could handle the Italian language fairly well. Protests that Italian immigrants forwarded to the Apostolic Delegate in Washington or directly to the Pope in Rome against Irish pastors and bishops were normally sent back to the local Ordinary. The diplomatic notes accompanying these protests requesting further information for an adequate reply of the Apostolic Delegate to Propaganda, however, had certainly a significant function of control on the decisions and work of the Bishops for the immigrants.[84]

The Census of Religious Bodies of 1916 reported the figure of 476 churches using Italian alone or with English with a membership of 1,516,000. The Catholic Directory for 1918 reported 431 churches and 149 missions serving with the regular parishes an approximate Italian and Italian-American Catholic population of 3,082,000. The population of Italian descent in the States in 1920 was 3,461,200. Even accepting the 1916 figure of 53,000 Italian Protestants, Italian immigrants had arrived at the initial stage of structural integration into the Catholic Church in America without great losses and disruptions. This happened in spite of the excited polemics at the turn of the century and the official desperation of the Bishops in their comments on the Italians.[85]

If this is the case, several questions must be answered. Was the process of institutional integration so smooth that the socio-cultural differences of the Italian ethnic group cannot be taken as a significant variable of inter-ethnic conflict? Was the religiosity of the immigrants an artificial super-structure that at a moment of crisis left them indifferent? Or was it so deep that it made them indifferent to other interests? To what extent was the form of allegiance of the Italian ethnic group to the Church as an institution different from that of other ethnic groups? What was the relationship of this form of allegiance to the sacred cosmos and religious world's view of the immigrants and of these two variables to Christian and Catholic theology?

A crucial factor that changed the position of subordination of the Italian ethnic group, symbolized by worship in church basements, is the role of religious protesters and dissenters. Commenting on schisms and controversies that had troubled the Italian American church in years past, an elderly pastor in Brooklyn remarked: "Salutem ex inimicis nostris," (Salvation from our enemies). There has been no faster or more encouraging support given by the Bishops for ethnic parishes than when there was an incipient schism.[86]

The few cases of rebellion recorded in Italian-American church history seem to have a common pattern. Ideological principles of belief did not bring about dissent and separation. Rather, political decisions and administrative policies caused rebellion by their disregard of the cultural traditions and social organization of ethnic groups.

The determination of these groups to achieve equality with other groups vis-a-vis the American society was also significant in the situations of conflict.

In reviewing the case of the priests who wanted to remain Catholic, we can discover more effectively the motivation of those who became Protestants, thus giving up the fight for change from within the ecclesiastical structures.

Father Marcellino Moroni was laboring in 1887 in the poorest Italian ghetto of the Lower East Side of New York. In a letter to Archbishop Corrigan he summed up the frame of mind of his Irish pastor in the statement he had made that all Italian priests should be servants here.[87] A rumor was spreading from East Harlem that a tough Irish pastor was persecuting some poor Italian sisters.[88] Corrigan was reminded of this rumor from Rome and from the immigrants themselves, who protested to him in 1891 that Carmody, the pastor, was "a barbarous man, totally incapable of understanding them." In 1889 the Apostolic Delegation in Washington had received a complaint against Fr. Carr, the Rector of St. Mary's in Williamsburgh. He had announced that the sacrament of baptism would not be administered to a child unless the Godparents could speak English and "that he will not assist in the marriage of persons laboring under the same unfortunate ignorance," as the Delegate

Archbishop Martinelli wrote.[89] Archbishop Corrigan's answer can be taken as an example of the role played by the Apostolic Delegation in keeping an open eye on the problems of immigrants. He pointed out that Fr. Carr had referred some Italians to neighboring churches where there were Italian priests, since his Italian assistant was temporarily in Italy. He had not, however, refused to baptize. Fr. Joseph Dwrzak, the closest neighboring priest, spoke Italian well, since he had studied at the Polish College in Rome and was willing to take care of the Italians. All the students in the seminary were required to study Italian and his cathedral paid $17,000 annually for the education of Italian children.[90] Fr. Vincentini, Superior of the priests of Bishop Scalabrini, reminded the Archbishop of New York in 1893 that Italians could not take advantage of mixed churches, as the past experience had shown. Two reasons advised against Irish-Italian parishes: the idea of the Italians of being despised by the Irish; the preference given in mixed churches by American and Italian priests to the care of the Irish.[91]

Their extreme poverty prevented the Italians from paying their church debts promptly. This factor became one of the most disturbing reasons for resentment and conflict with diocesan administrations. In a long memorandum to the Pope, however, Fr. de Vincentiis did not hesitate to state, as Fr. Vicentini had written before him, that religion goes beyond buildings. In 1906 he wrote from New Jersey:

> The gigantic enterprises involving the most difficult manual labor to be found here are bathed in the blood of the Italians. Hundreds and hundreds are buried in tunnels, killed by trains, entombed in mines and falling embankments; they have lost their lives in work so dangerous that no other will engage in it. Under such conditions how can the poor Italians build churches and support priests, compelled as they are to struggle for their very existence? And yet, poor, calumniated, unfortunate, they do credit to their religion if not by building and maintaining churches, by their sobriety and domestic virtues.[92]

In this climate of psychological and administrative conflict a few priests and people did not take refuge in their personal holiness and ascetical life. They rather openly defied the hierarchy. As the autobiography of Fr. Gambera vividly testifies, the St. Marco's Society of Boston remained from 1885 to 1889 without priests and sacraments rather than yield to the Bishop's demands requesting the property of their church for the diocese and their return to worship in the original parish with the Irish.[93]

In 1911 the 'Independent Catholic Church of Italy and Among the Italians Abroad' tried to open a mission in America. Bishop Miraglia, a former Sicilian priest excommunicated by Bishop Scalagrini and the

Holy See, escaped jail in Italy by going abroad. He appealed to the simple people of the Italian neighborhood between Carroll and Clinton Streets in Brooklyn by presenting the need for a church that was Italian and himself as a fellow Sicilian, educated in Naples and in Rome, who was, above everything else, an Italian loving the fatherland as much as religion. Miraglia succeeded in establishing his own church in a store front, where he gave confirmation to 12 persons in May 1911. The Catholic newspaper *L'Italiano in America* denounced the independent Bishop in no uncertain terms. At the same time, the Pallotine priests carried out the education of the local people at the grass root level. Miraglia tried for better luck in Massachusetts, but failed there also. He returned to Corsica and was forgotten apparently on that island.[94]

Italian immigrants were less concerned with Bishops of their own nationality than with their local churches, since high Church politics were not within their world.

In 1889 Archbishop Corrigan of New York wrote to a fellow Bishop commenting on how the Germans protested for their own Bishops and how Canadian Americans followed in that trend. "The same spirit," he added, "also invaded the Italians of this neighborhood some months ago, but by prudence and persuasion the bad spirit seems to be exorcised." Exorcisms were not equally easy, however, when the local ethnic parish was involved.[95]

The church of Sant' Antonio di Padova in Hackensack, New Jersey, was the first attempt to set up an ecclesiastical structure parallel to that of the Catholic Church but independent of Irish Bishops. In 1913 the Italian colony of Hackensack had more than five thousand people in what was known as the First Ward. Italian groceries, bakeries, and meat markets were developed. The only church was St. Mary's, Irish and Polish, with Fr. Dolan as pastor, and it was more than a mile and a half from the Italian settlement. Bishop John O'Connor was repeatedly asked to send an Italian priest and to organize an Italian parish, but to no avail. A priest from Our Lady of Mt. Carmel in Newark, Antonio Giulio Lenza, used to visit his *paesani* in Hackensack. He went along with their request and incorporated a parish with the intention of forcing the Bishop's hand. The Bishop, however, suspended Lenza and dispatched another Italian priest to form a bona-fide Italian parish. A letter from the Apostolic Delegate was circulated to all the Italians admonishing them to be united with the Bishop and support the new church at St. Francis. But a tiny group of families remained with Lenza and declared a schism. A vicious polemic ensued between the two churches from the pulpit and the press. The two patron saints, St. Francis and St. Anthony, who had gone along so well on earth, were waging war in heaven. In 1916 Rome informed O'Connor he should ask for the resignation of Fr. Dolan of St. Mary's. Dolan hastily replied with his version of the schism. He wanted to build a mission for the Italians in the area of their residence, but he had been discouraged by the local Dean Father Cunneelly. Father Cunneelly needed the people for his church. He had to pay for the rectory he was building and had informed Father Dolan that Italians do not support the church. Then, the St. Anthony's Society of Mutuo Soccorso, not under church supervision and established on an insurance plan, had split in two factions because of internal quarrels. The banner of St. Anthony became the cause of polarization. The group allied to St. Mary's wanted the banner to remain there; the group based in the Italian colony wanted the banner for themselves. The pastor was threatened with murder and therefore he couldn't take sides. After the Civil Court decided the banner was the property of St. Mary's, the disappointed party immediately started to form an Independent Italian Catholic Church. Thus concluded Father Dolan. *Il Corriere della Domenica* and *La Voce di Sant'Antonio di Padova,* publications directed by the dissenting Italians, placed the focus of the conflict elsewhere. Lenza aimed at "making heard the voice of just resentment of the Italian priests maltreated as if they were Cain, sold by their own brothers in America." By 1919 Lenza had styled himself Vicar General of the Italian Diocese of St. Anthony of Padua with Francis Hodur of the Polish National Catholic Church, as Bishop Protector. Besides the church of St. Anthony in Hackensack, the church of St. Anthony in Passaic, New Jersey, erected in five months at the cost of $32,000.00, had joined in the schismatic movement. Bishop Hodur had blessed the latter church in Passaic and confirmed 1700 persons on that occasion. Father Bianchini, the pastor, had also bought a house for $4,000.00 for an orphanage. The dissenters picked up support. On September 14, the church of St. Mary Magdalene was begun in North Dakota and on September 20 the church of St. Ann in Marboro, Massachusetts was solemnly blessed. In 1922 the church of Our Lady of Miracles in Garfield also accepted the jurisdiction of Lenza. In the meantime, Lenza had not ceased to proclaim his Catholicity and his nationalism. He wrote:

> My church is Italian, because the buildings are property of the people that support them and cannot be administered but by an Italian priest.

He also was very eloquent on the universality of the Christian community.

> ... there is no difference between Samaritan and Galilean, Greek and Roman ... the Church must not make any distinction of tongue or color. ... Instead here in America Irish Bishops, only because their

tongue is similar to the American, cast out of Ireland, have usurped America; and theirs is an attitude of absolute masters, becoming unjust, ferocious, hostile and without charity toward Italian priests. Many priests born in Italy will say that this is false. Should I forget . . . several of them who up to not so long ago were barking like hungry dogs against the Bishops accusing them of every accusation. . . . Should I forget the cowardly insults of these priests in accusing the Apostolic Delegates . . . saying that they are doing nothing for the Italians so as not to displease the American Bishops that furnish money for the vaults of the Vatican? . . .[96]

The counterattack of the diocesan officials of Newark through able Italian priests voided Father Lenza's initiative as well as that of his few followers like Father Bianchini and Father Bocache of Garfield. In 1924 the primatial parish of St. Anthony in Hackensack was closed and reopened a few months later as an Episcopal chapel with a handful of Italians. The incident, however, was fruitful, along the lines of the Brooklyn pastor's motto: Salvation from our enemies. The Bishop was forced to be more careful in dealing with the ethnic traditions of the immigrants.[97]

Lenza's complaint was only an incident in a pattern of relationships existing long before and after him. In 1906 *L'Opinione* of Philadelphia described the humiliating life of the Italian priest:

Once they have arrived in New York, Pecorini wrote, (the Italian priests) present themselves to the Archbishop, expecting to be sent to a parish. But they realize they are received with sweet-sour words, always discouraging. They can obtain only a temporary permit to say Mass for sixty days. The most fortunate are recommended to some Irish pastor, who allows the poor 'dagoes' to meet in the basement of his church to say Mass on Sundays and the Poor Italian priest is obliged to find himself in contact with someone who almost always despises him, because he belongs to a nation that keeps the Pope prisoner. . . .[98]

Attempts to start Italian independent dioceses were made by some censured priests who in most cases ended their careers by either returning to the Catholic Church or by joining Protestant denominations.

In Corona, New York, Luigi Lops tried his luck in that large Italian colony in the 1920's, but without success. When in 1913 the Rev. Prof. Guadagnino proclaimed himself as the Bishop elected by the Italian people for the same area,[99] only a tiny immigrant flock remained with him for a long time.

Possibly the most notorious career of an Italian Independent Catholic Bishop started in 1914. Father Michael di Ielsi had arrived in the United States from Lucera in 1902 at the age of 26. He was a kind-hearted man, intelligent and hard working. As his fellow teachers at the Abraham

Lincoln High School in Brooklyn commented years later, he was a
scholar and a gentleman. He worked among Italians in the diocese of
Trenton, New Jersey, and established for them four churches at
Minitola-Landsville, West Berlin and Camden, where he also instituted
the first Italian school of the diocese. In 1911 he was finally incardinated
into the diocese. In 1914 he fell ill and in 1918 he was forced to marry at
gun-point a widow whose jealous father thought Di Ielsi had molested
her. He succeeded in obtaining a divorce from the woman with whom he
had had no relations. He approached Bishop Walsh of Trenton and then
of Newark for rehabilitation. He was, however, constantly ignored.
Bishop Kiely of Trenton accorded the same treatment, refusing to
answer letters and requests for a meeting. Abandoned to his destiny, di
Ielsi writes, he agreed in 1934 to be consecrated Bishop of the Old
Catholic Church. By 1935 he had in his care the Churches of the Holy
Trinity, of Assumption, of St. Frances of Assisi, and the Charity Church
of Christ. The congregations of those churches in Brooklyn and Queens
were varying between 60 and 100 people. In 1936 the Shrine of St.
Anthony was added to the list of independent churches. Associated with
the Bishop were some Italian censured priests. Di Ielsi himself administered 200 Confirmations, ordained two priests and an Auxiliary
Bishop, all Italians. Capitalizing on the ignorance of the immigrants
and their desire for their Italian language and traditional churches, a
beginning of ecclesiastical organization was emerging around Di Ielsi,
who now called himself Patriarch and Primate. Apparently ten or
twelve churches were formed by the end of 1936.[100] The ideology of
separation was formulated along the lines of a return to the primitive
Christian communities with the election of the Bishop from the people. The factual causes, however, were the expectations of the immigrants for ethnic churches and the rebel priests' frustration with
Irish and Irish allied clergy. Di Ielsi died in 1945 after due penance and
reconciliation with the Church. Yet Bishop Molloy of Brooklyn refused
him a funeral with religious ceremonies. On the other hand, Di Ielsi
had not spared the Irish Bishops in his letters to Italy. Writing to the
Bishop of Nusco he summarized his feelings by saying:

> . . . This cursed Irish race is the most immoral; they are stone-drunk, ig-
> norant, the ruin of the Catholic Religion in America. . . . My misfortune
> was to be persecuted by the Irish 'canaille' for pure jealousy.[101]

The immigrants in Di Ielsi's area of work reacted with a series of
letters to the Bishops of New York and Brooklyn asking for clarifications
about the Bishop they were seeing saying Mass. At the same time, they
took the occasion to press for their rights. The 7,000 Italians of
Sheepshead Bay wrote at that time to the Consul General of Italy:

In this area there doesn't exist any Italian Catholic Church. The closest is not less than three miles away and the only American church that exists here doesn't render us any service, since there has never been even a priest who could at least hear the confessions of our people. A former priest, excommunicated and in trouble with the police, knew enough to take advantage of this sad situation. He has opened here an Italian Independent Church several months ago and this is naturally frequented by not a few of our people who believe it a Catholic Church. The Bishop of Brooklyn, to whom we addressed ourselves repeatedly asking to open a parish here, never listened to us. Consequently we desire to address ourselves directly to His Holiness. . . .[102]

In fact, to remedy the schism, the Italian pastors had permission to start new mission chapels and intensify their activity so that in a few years the schismatic population was drawn back into the fold. This policy was also constantly re-enforced by the proselytizing efforts of the Protestants. In fact, the divergent cultural and social positions of the immigrants clashed with the established Catholic Church, brought about separatist tendencies and even formal rejection of Catholicism. No doubt, if many Italians converted to Protestant denominations they did so under pressure of economic advantages. But a few at least were convinced that true Americanism meant also Protestantism.[103]

The Protestant work among immigrants had three moments:

1) The experimental stage, that lasted from 1880 to 1900, a period of short-lived experiments conducted by individual ministers on the basis of their personal missionary inclinations.

2) *The stage of permanent work,* from the beginning of this century to about 1918, with erection of buildings for the social and religious needs of the immigrants, regular investments of money in the 'Little Italies,' formal training of Italian-American ministers for Italian congregations, organizing of the Italian-American ministers into a formal association.

3) *The intensive or consolidation stage,* a third stage beginning around 1918 and planned for the purpose of putting on a more efficient and secure basis for the already existing work. The years following 1918 saw the end of the Protestant missionary work among the new immigrants with the close of immigration, the vitality of the national churches, and the emergance of the immigrants out of the extreme poverty of the time of their arrival.

Two main reasons are given by Bisceglia for the failure of the Protestant work: first, because the various denominations' Boards became discouraged for lack of apparent results; secondly, because of insufficient qualified workers. But we must attempt an explanation of why the results, a change of values and behavior concerning religion, did not materialize.[104]

An exact statistical rundown concerning the Italian membership in the Protestant Churches seems at this point an impossible task, because of lack of records, duplication of figures, inclusion of non-Italians, returns to the Catholic Church, lack of figures on birth and death rates. Available are indications of trends, which seem to be general enough to guarantee a reliable picture of the volume and direction of conversions to Protestantism.

For the first stage of work among Italians (1880-1900) the following incomplete table describes the work of Presbyterians, who alone seem to account for more than half of the membership of Italians in all Protestant denominations.

To understand the significance of Table 10, it must be kept in mind that:

a) Other places where Presbyterian missionary activity was started by the turn of the century, but for which data are not available, were: New York State: New York City Mission, West Side Evangelical Church, Bethlehem Chapel, Thompson Street Mission, Westchester Mission, Schenectady, Auburn; Pennsylvania (where members were congregating in American Churches): Scranton, Hyde Park, Old Forge, Carbondale, Edgerton, Jessup, Pittston, Wilkesbarre; Louisiana: New Orleans; Illinois: Mission Chapel (Taylor & Jefferson Streets); Michigan: Detroit Mission; California: San Francisco Mission.

b) For the evaluation of the figures given, the case of the Montclair Italian Evangelical Missionary Society can be significant. There was a total membership of 67, of which 38 were active and 29 supporting members; two conversions in one year and 26 Italians out of an Italian population ranging from 1,200 to 1,500. cf. *First Annual Report* (1903).

c) The figures given as the membership for the turn of the century represent all the Italians received into the particular church up to that time, but we do not know if they remained there.

In 1900 the foreign-born Italians in the United States were 484,027. Among the total figure of Protestants were included the Waldensians who were already Protestants when they came from Italy. The volume of Italians converting to Protestantism, therefore, appears rather small.

For the second period of the Protestant work among Italians, data on the number of churches and their membership become a little more elaborate and reliable. From 1900 to 1918 c. there is a significant growth in the Italian missionary field throughout the United States and for all denominations, with the Presbyterians in the lead. In 1916-17 the Immigrant Work Committee of the Home Missions Council, representing the interests of thirteen evangelical denominations, engaged in a survey of the Italian communities to assess the religious needs and the work of

Table 10. *Presbyterian Churches and Mission
for Italian Immigrants, 1880-1900*

City	Beginning of Work	Date of Founding	Members of Foundation	Members at Turn of Cent.	Sunday School Members
Trenton, N.J.	1899			24 (1904)	
Newark, N.J.	1889	1891	28	260 (1901)	200
Westfield, N.J.	1895			28 (1901)	
Montclair, N.J.	1900c.	(mission)		26 (1903)	
Vineland, N.J.		1904			
Hammonton, N.J.					
New York City	1883	(Broome St.)		1,200 (1905)	600
				300	453 (1915c.)
Hazelton, Pa.	1891c.	1895		130 (1905)	
Philadelphia, Pa.	1896	1902		200	
Devon, Pa.	1904			1 fam. (5)	
Pittsburgh, Pa.	1899	1903c.		400	
				127 (1905)	
Roseto, Pa.	1895c.				
Chicago, Ill.	1889	1892	54	100 (1901c.)	145
Oakland, Cal.		1902			

Source: Rev. Chas. E. Edwards, "Our Latin and Slavonic Population," in *The Assembly Herald*, August, 1901, p. 300-302; Rev. G. P. Williams, "Italian Work in Chicago," Ibid., pp. 303; "Italian Work in and Near Newark, New Jersey," Ibid., pp. 306-307; this is a resume of the history of that church published on the tenth anniversary.

The Montclair Italian Evangelical Missionary Society. *First Annual Report*, combined with an address by Mr. Alberto Pecorini on the Italian Immigration Problems delivered at Annual Meeting, November 30, 1903, pp. 16.

Rev. William Wynkoop McNair, "The Evangelization of our Italians," *The Assembly Herald*, vol. XI, Aug. 1905, pp. 404-409.

Rev. Robert Bonner Jack, "Italians in Lehigh Presbytery," Ibid. pp. 413-414; Rev. Samuel McLanahan, "New Jersey and her Foreigners," Ibid., pp. 414-415.

the churches. Table 11 represents the statistics emerging from the survey conducted by A. Mangano of Colgate University. If it is taken into account that the foreign-born Italians in the United States in 1910 numbered 1,343,125 (even if the figures of the number of Italian church members and the number of Italian church school pupils are combined) only approximately 1.8 percent Italians converted to Protestantism.[105] But even the latter figure seems too high. In fact, in Mangano's own figures, at the time of his survey there were at least 3,500,000 Italian Americans, and this figure would reduce the total Italian Protestant population to much less than one percent. Although some Pentecostal

Table 11. *Statistics of Italian Work by Several Protestant Denominations in the United States, 1917**

Denominations	Number of Churches or Missions Doing Italian Work	Number of Italian Church Members	Number of Italian Church Schools with Ital. Pupils	Number of Italian Church School Pupils	Salaried Italian Workers engaged in Italian Work	Total Contributions of Italian Members for All Purposes	Total Expenditure of the Denomination for Italian Work
Baptist (Northern Convention)	82	2,750	n.a.	n.a.	60	$9,000	$69,030
Congregational	44	983	n.a.	1,000	19	961	13,279
Evangelical Association	3	n.a.	n.a.	n.a.	n.a.	n.a.	n.a.
Methodist Episcopal & Methodist Episcopal, South	60	5,241+	42	4,927	52	7,357#	45,000
Presbyterian in U.S.A.	107	4,800	n.a.	8,000	70	14,253	100,000
Protestant Episcopal	24	n.a.	n.a.	n.a.	n.a.	n.a.	n.a.
Reformed in U.S.A.	3	n.a.	n.a.	n.a.	n.a.	n.a.	n.a.
United Presbyterian	8	n.a.	n.a.	n.a.	n.a.	n.a.	n.a.
Total	326	13,774	42	13,927	201	$31,571	$227,309

n.a. = not available at the conclusion of Mangano's survey of 1916-17
+ = Of this number, 1,839 are probationers
\# = The sum reported by 46 churches
* = *Source:* A. Mangano: *Religious Work Among Italians in America*, 1917.

and Independent churches may not have been accounted for by Mangano, still his total figures can be considered inflated. In 1818, the Board of Home Missions of the Presbyterian Church stated, with a remarkable difference from Mangano's report (Table 11) for the same denomination:

> In 1904 the Board made a special feature of work among foreign-speaking people. This service has been developed especially under the later leadership of the Rev. W. P. Shriver until it now calls for an annual appropriation of $87,268.00. We have today 123 ministers and other workers employed among foreigners with 30 churches and a membership of 1,827. There are also 55 unorganized missions.[106]

A survey of Italian Protestant work in New York City in 1912 gives us a figure of about 1.5 percent Protestants for the Italian population of a little more than half a million.[107]

The conclusion for this second period of Protestant work among the Italians reveals a permanent inconsistency in the figures available. There is, however, a clear direction to the volume of converts which is very frustrating in terms of the money and personnel invested in the effort.

Finally, the third period of the Protestant work among Italian Americans may be summed up quickly in the statement of a very knowledgeable and reliable minister, Dr. Bisceglia:

> An Interdenominational National Conference of Ministers of Italian extraction was held in the Broome Street Tabernacle, New York City, during the first week of November, 1946. . . . At this meeting three hundred churches and missions were reported, with over twenty-five thousand communicants, as many as forty thousand Sunday School pupils, and many people's groups, which brought the aggregate number to over one hundred thousand. In this country and in Canada the Presbyterian Church is in the lead, followed closely by Methodists, Baptist, Lutherans, Episcopalians and many smaller groups.[108]

In the context of the demographic evolution of the Italian ethnic group in the United States and Canada, the figures reported by Bisceglia seem to remain below the 1 percent mark.[109] It is impossible to find out how many in this above figure are new converts. From the literature consulted, the real missionary work stopped around 1920 so that the natural increase of the people recruited to this date should account basically for the hundred thousand figure. Table 12, Italian Protestants in Brooklyn and Queens, New York 1935, confirms the general trend.

Further information is derived from the 1936 *Census of Religious Bodies*. The General Council of the Italian Pentecostal Assemblies of

Table 12. *Italian Protestants in Brooklyn and Queens,*
New York, 1935

Denominations	Brooklyn		Queens	
	Italian Churches	Italian Members	Italian Churches	Italian Members
Baptist Church	5	753	—	—
Congregational Ch.	1	30	—	—
Lutheran Church	1	40	—	—
Episcopal Methodist Church	—	—	2	926
Presbyterian Church	5	816	—	—
United Presbyterian	1	152	—	—
Protestant Episcopal	1	(closed)	—	—
7th Day Adventists	1	90	—	—
Church of the Brethren	1	85	—	—
Pentecostal	5	550	—	—

Source: ADB, Risposte speciali a domande proposte nella lettera del Delegato Apostolico No. 117-35 e ai suggerimenti fatti nella relazione inviata all'Ordinario di Brooklyn dalla Sacra Congregazione Concistoriale mediante la Delegazione Apostolica, 1938

N.B. 1) Brooklyn and Queens, total Italian population 814,725; of these 3,442 were Protestants.

2) 16 other Protestant denominations reported no Italian members.

God reported 16 churches and a membership of 1,547. The Unorganized Italian Christian Churches of North America reported 104 churches and a membership of 9,567.[110] The elaboration of these statistics confirms the prevalent urban character of the Italian Protestant population as well as the concentration in a few states: New York, New Jersey, Pennsylvania, Ohio, Illinois, California, in particular. While this could have been expected, since it follows the overall distribution of the Italian ethnic population, Protestant Italian groups in West Virginia, the District of Columbia, Michigan and Wisconsin, may be explained by the problem of isolation in almost completely Protestant surroundings and the lack of Catholic clergy. In any event, even adding these official Census figures, and even forgetting about the problems related to their gathering process, the overall picture of a relative lack of success of the Protestant work among Italian immigrants and their children is not changed.

Schismatic and Protestant dissenters expressed the immigrants' condition of uprootedness in a more dramatic way. Conflict, especially at the local level, was unavoidable. Ethnocentric orientations, in fact, were based not only on differing values and expectations but also on class. The immigrants were in the lowest position in the socio-economic structure of the American society. They were expected to subscribe to all the rules of that society, if they intended to share in the economic rewards for which they had come. The Catholic Church had chosen adaptation to American society. The Italian immigrants had implicitly opted for the same adaptation: it was the only path open to them to reach their objective of economic betterment. But they clashed with the Church and with society to the extent to which they thought they could obtain their goal and still preserve their village culture. The degree to which the conflict and alienation of the first generation is maintained in today's Italian ethnic community is probably related to the degree to which the communal outlook of the immigrants' culture is surviving in the individualistic outlook. The cultural and juridical conflict, stemming from the background and poverty of the immigrants, was largely resolved by adaptation. Where adaptation was completely rejected, the immigrant protesters became marginal and slowly disappeared into the American population and their story is not yet told.

Ethnic Church Leadership.

Religious leaders frequently become advocates and preachers of a national ideology, providing a *raison d'etre* for the ethnic community and a motivation for identification with it.[111] At first, the Italian priests, like the Bishops of the Third Council of Baltimore, were convinced a solution for the spiritual problems of the immigrants was in sending them into agriculture in Kansas, Arkansas and elsewhere. Father D. Monti, for example, writing from Mississippi in 1887 proposed the formation of a committee in Italy and one in the United States and with Italian capital set up agricultural colonies around an Italian church and school.[112] In 1896 Father Bandini moved to Sunny Side, Mississippi and then to Tontitown, Arkansas, to establish a rural Italian parish.[113] In 1899 Father Baccherini insisted with Scalabrini on encouraging Bishop Glennon of Kansas to carry out his idea of settling Italians in agriculture.

> It is the best thing we can do for our migrants: to send them to the countryside. 95% of them are peasants. But once they set foot in the city, they become so demoralized that they prefer to suffer famine, take up the vilest jobs, make themselves slaves to the *padroni*, crowd in fifty in a *catapecchia* (barn), lose every sense of morality and faith rather than return to the land.[114]

Since its beginning in 1909, *Italica Gens* aimed at directing the immigrants into agriculture to preserve them both as Italians and as

Catholics.[115] With the Italians, it was a reversal of a kind. While the Germans pointed out that German language and culture had to be preserved if the faith had to survive, the Italians, in response to an anti-clerical government, insisted that the Church had to be given to the Italians to preserve their faith in God and their land of origin.[116] Archbishop Ireland, quite embarrassed by the presence of Italian immigrants, was also favoring their settlement in agriculture in the Mid-West and in Cuba.[117] But no significant movement of Italians toward agriculture took place. The vast majority of the Italians remained in the city and the priests did the same. Serving in the basement of existing parishes brought about situations of conflict and resentment.[118] Southern Italian priests, accustomed to live at home and leave the administration of the finances of the church to laymen, were found by the American bishops to be inexperienced administrators and too much worried about their own families.[119]

The priests, whose families were not in the States, had nostalgia for their own land. As Father Fannizzi wrote after twenty years in New York: "I have nostaglia for Italy and have written to our Superior that I yearn always to be there." [120] On the personal level, the priests had several difficulties in securing the appropriate papers for emigration and for incardination, having to move from one Bishop to another in the hope of getting settled.[121] It took time for the people to trust their priests. In 1900, Father Vogel wrote to Bishop McDonnell of Brooklyn: "The character of the Italians is such a queer one, that they will not trust in a priest until they have known him for years. . . ." [122] Father Nisco, to keep the sheriff from closing down his church, since the Italians could not contribute much to the church, lived for four years in the rear of a barbershop; for three years he was his own cook, sexton, wash-woman and all, never taking one penny of salary.[123] Normally, for the first years of existence of churches, priests were taking no salaries. The Italian language press was often anti-clerical and was attacking the priests daily.[124] If the diocesan priests had difficulty in being incardinate, religious priests were not quite acceptable either. There was a fear of double jurisdiction on the part of Bishops, their own and that of the superiors of religious orders.[125] In 1911, Gambera wrote:

> . . . if all this is taken into serious consideration, everyone will understand that, if there is in America a hard mission, it is that of the Italian clergy. The Italian priests must fight against ideas and popular customs. They must defend themselves against unjust aversion, both political and religious. If this is kept in mind, it will be clear that up to the present the Italian priests have done for the emigrants all that was humanly possible." [126]

The priest in the ethnic community was carrying out several functions as adviser, counselor, notary public, employment agent, lawyer, intermediary with hospitals and orphanages. Even so, the immigrant would angrily disavow the priest if he could not meet the expectations for even the most desperate cases.[127] But the priests were embarrassed and occasionally openly humiliated because Italians were not contributing much and were not knowledgeable about religion. Addressing a memorandum to the Pope, Father Gideon de Vincentiis stated the American Bishops' opinion that it was much better to send missionaries to Italy from America than to America from Italy so that they may have a class of immigrants more instructed and more christian. He continued:

> Therefore, Your Holiness, we earnestly beg you to save us that shame which more than any other causes us Italian priests to blush. This terrible and glaring ignorance of our people makes us the butt of sarcasm and depreciation. It is our real cross in America.[128]

To increase their effectiveness and perhaps to reassert their position vis-a-vis the Bishops, Italian priests in the New York Metropolitan Area slowly tried to organize, at first, around *L'Italiano in America,* then, in presenting a united front against the evangelizing effort of the Protestant denominations.[129] By 1914 there was a Bulletin of the Unione del Clero Italo-Americano.[130] In 1917 the first general meeting of the Italian clergy in North America took place in New York. The Brooklyn and New York clergy were divided. The New York Diocesan Council for Italian Affairs, under the leadership of Gherardo Ferrente, who had been made Vicar General for Italians in 1915 and had been Archbishop Corrigan's secretary,[131] was resented by the priests of Brooklyn. Monsignor Alfonso Arcese, who was Bishop McConnell's trusted liaison with the Italian priests, was interested in a union within the Brooklyn Diocese.[132] The *Congresso,* as it was called, commended the attendance of 326 priests on December 5, 1917. The purpose of the Italian Clergy Convention was to study the best ways and means to preserve the faith among the immigrants through religious and social work among the people. The Apostolic Delegate had fully approved the meeting and was present to encourage the priests officially. Three proposals were formulated: 1) a union of the Italian clergy in North America; 2) an Italian Catholic Union of laymen to protect jobs, demand compensation in case of accident and sickness and care for orphans; 3) an Italian Catholic newspaper. The president-elect of the Unione, Monsignor Alfonso Arcese, spoke on the zeal of the Italian priests, unsurpassed by laymen and priests of other nationalities, in serving the immigrants in every form. He deplored the lack of unity among priests and among immigrants. He advocated unity in order to have the united Italian American Catholics as a civic, moral, and religious force of utmost power. The Apostolic Delegate stated that the Italian priest is the best suited to care for the immigrants. He added that in the United States, where everyone tries to organize to obtain his goals, the Italians should do the same for their religious and material welfare.[133] The movement for the union of the clergy started in 1914 with the formal beginning of the organization in the church of Our Lady of Pompei. After the meeting in New York, *L'Italiano in America* became for a while the newspaper advocated and supported by the Italian priests. In publication was also the *Bollettino* of the Unione del Clero Italiano. But after three or four years there is no more evidence of the persistence of either publication, and the national union of clergy or laity never came to much. The Brooklyn Diocese, however, moved on its own to strengthen the Italian Catholic Union of Brooklyn. This Union, aimed at celebrating Columbus Day and the XX September, was supported by the clergy who, by their presence, hoped to avoid open attacks on religion.[134]

The priests, like the immigrants, were never able to organize beyond a strictly parochial basis, where they were effective in socio-religious work of assistance and in bringing about an ideological service to the immigrant community, the acceptance of *"italianita"* without rejection of Catholicism.

In the celebration of the XX September, the policy of the priests was first one of opposition along the lines of the American Bishops; then, it became one of neutrality and defense of Italy.

> Coming to the United States, Zaboglio wrote, the Missionaries will do well, in my opinion,—in fact, I am deeply convinced of this—never to deal with questions regarding Italian politics either in public or in private, and leave alone Victor Emmanuel, Mazzini, Garibaldi and the others. Here the situation is explosive. By talking of these arguments, for sure, interests of far greater substance and importance will be hurt. . . .[135]

The patriotic attitudes of Italian priests were viewed as rebellion against the Papacy. A typical view of an Irish pastor is in a letter sent to Archbishop Corrigan in 1891:

> In reference to the conduct of the Piacenzan priests in this city on the occasion of the 20th of September. . . . The Piacenzan Fathers *never* spoke in defense of the rights of the Holy Father either in or out of the pulpit and made no allusion to the celebration on the previous Sunday. They thought it would be "bad policy" . . . and would estrange the people from them. Father Rampini gave an excellent discourse on the rights of the Holy Father on the Sunday before the 20th of September and several Italians came to him and told him he had a "hot head" on the subject and that he ought to be silent like the Piacenzan priest.[136]

In 1889, a complaint was sent to Rome charging that a priest sent by Scalabrini marched between two flags—the Italian and the American—which were borne in a procession in New York for the unveiling of the statue of Garibaldi.[137] Priests arriving from Italy were regarded as troublemakers and apostates, and the burden of proof was with them if they wanted to be considered differently.[138]

In the interest of the immigrants, the Italian priests never hesitated to call on Italian consular officials:

> Fatherland and Faith. . . . Yesterday we paid a visit to the Consul General of Italy; he received us kindly and he made us civil officers for marriages. . . .[139] We paid a visit to the consul . . . he received us very well. I explained to him our program and he praised it. Since he himself thinks of the founding of schools and a kindergarten, we agreed to unite our efforts.[140]

Count de Revel, consul in New York until 1885, was a practicing Catholic.[141] Diplomatic and consular authorities from Italy were often invited to and attended significant religious celebrations of the community at the request of the Italian pastors. In fact, Scalabrini's words to the Italians of New York asking him for a hospital in 1890 became the guidelines for most priests:

> On the field of charity every dissension should die, every initiative should have free way without exclusions or preferences, without regard to partisan positions, without distinctions of any sort.[142]

During Italy's war against Turkey in 1911, the Italian consul in Chicago, the Italian priests and the societies were together 'for the honor and greatness of Italy' and a celebration of 'religion and patria.'[143]

The Italian clergy of the New York Metropolitan Area organized special Masses for the soldiers fallen during the First World War. Special commemorations and collections were held to show allegiance and love for Italy.

A committee of Italian clergy was formed in New York to direct relief to the families of Italian soldiers. Monsignor Ferrante, Vicar General for the Italians, presided over the committee which had the cooperation of most Italian diocesan pastors, who personally contributed $50.00 each, of the religious clergy and of the *Italica Gens*. The wave of '*italianita*' that swept the Italian colonies found its expression in the parishes where sermons and prayers and money were sent to Italy to cooperate with its effort against the Central Powers.[144] For Italy's victory in 1918, an Italy Day was celebrated in the Italian Churches.[145] An altar, as a memorial to the victory against the Austria-Hungarian Empire on the river Piave, was erected in the parish of Our Lady Help of Christians in Manhattan.

By the 1920's the Italian churches were perceived as the true strongholds of *'italianita'* in America[146]

From the cautious, simple blessings of Italian flags for Italian fraternal societies at the turn of the centuries, the priests moved in to take the place of the disappearing Italian liberals and patriots who could not express their *'italianita'* without acrimonious attacks on the Church. Even the Italian leftists were gradually divided by their fights over the beginning of World War I. The immigrants did not know about Italian politics; most of them did not even care to. The feeling of *italianita'*, however, was the feeling of their identity and this the immigrant expressed by simply parading the flag of Italy their priests had not refused to bless. At the same time, the American bishops were made to understand by the Italian priests that there was no anti-religion in Italian national manifestations.

Defying prejudice, the language barrier, anticlericalism and poverty, the Italian priests seem to have rather successfully carried out their role of mediators between the established ecclesiastical structures and the immigrants attached to the cultural expressions of their peasant faith and their sentimental nationalism.

Writing to Scalabrini, Cardinal Simeoni, the Prefect of Propaganda Fide, had said that the priests in the United States should be advised:

> . . . to oppose rather than favor the public feasts of the Italians, which were in little harmony with the American customs or had political significance . . . to foment less among the immigrants the national spirit, that separates them from their new countrymen, and rather promote the Catholic spirit, not separating the Italians from the other faithful.[147]

For the Italian priests in the United States the issue was not separation and assimilation, but the strategy of bringing together all groups. Their experience had shown that the second-generation Italian children were Americanizing very rapidly.[148] Their concern was the preservation of ethnic identity, of religion and family stability by avoiding useless generational conflicts. In this way, the priests and the church structure they built responded to the same objectives the immigrants had.

The Italian priests were indeed aware of their mediating role between the immigrant community, the American Church and society at large. They also were seen in that light.

In Newark, the Italian priests formed the *Unione Sacerdotale S. Filippo Neri* in 1914.[149] In New York and Brooklyn they had formed the *Unione del Clero Italiano dell'America del Nord*.[150] Although the great effectiveness of the priests was at the local parish level, through their unions they developed some significant supra-parochial organizations that obliged them to keep in constant touch with the existing official ecclesiastical structures. Thus, the Diocesan Council on Italian Affairs in New York met monthly from about 1909 to at least 1926, and it gathered all Italian pastors and priests as well as non-Italian pastors of Italian parishes. The meetings were presided over by a Vicar General for Italians, Monsignor Lavelle and later Monsignor G. Ferrante. Discussions ranged from the issue of Protestant proselytizing to an Italian Christian Labor Union, from the Italian Catholic newspaper *L'Italiano in America,* to religious processions and parish boundaries.[151] Occasionally Italian priests were asked to carry out unpleasant tasks in the process of molding the immigrants into the expected diocesan assimilation model. In 1914 processions must have been numerous. A certain Father Francis J. Sullivan wrote to Monsignor Lavelle:

> I have seen the (Police) Commissioner in regards to the parades and he has promised me that the law will be carried out to the letter. I also told him some Captains overlooked it last year. It will not be overlooked this year.[152]

The Vicar General hurriedly sent his comments to Father A. Demo, a spokesman for the Union of the Italian Clergy:

> Herewith I am sending you a copy of the letter received from Father Sullivan this morning. I deem it important that you should know of it. However, it will be necessary that you keep your eyes open, and let me know any case of trangressions on the Law. Please also notify any of the Italian pastors with whom you come in contact. I do not like to send out a circular letter to them.[153]

The priests carried out the diocesan directives without generally antagonizing the immigrants. They, however, extended their mediating or linkage role beyond purely ecclesiastical structures. The organizing of *Italica Gens,* of the St. Raphael's Society for the Protection of Italian Immigrants and of its succeeding organization, the Italian Auxiliary in New York, of the Association of Italian Clergy for War Widows and Orphans—these were activities transcending liturgical functions. The following circular letter, written by Dr. Grivetti of *Italica Gens* to Father Demo on June 7, 1912, summarized the ideological commitments and aspirations of most Italian priests:

> . . . reverend and dear colleague in the priesthood, you know better than I do how necessary and urgent it is that we proceed united in mind, heart and hand in our undertaking on behalf of our people.
> The land that hosts us is the most evident example of the value of cooperation and unity. In the economic field as well as in the social one

there isn't a person who doesn't see the gigantic force that radiates on society and on individuals from the channeling of energies.

In the religious field as well it is the coordination of activities that has given so fast and so many fruits in this country. Unfortunately, however, in this contest of magnificent activities and fruitful work, we Italians are at the rear-guard of the other Catholic countries; and not because less zealous or less capable than others, but only and exclusively (it seems to us) because disunited (disgregati).

This observation is painful, but in our opinion it is the real truth.

Life in the colony is rickety. The Italian element, even the best, is in disrepute (not to say something worse) by all, clergy and laity of this country. The reason is that Italian people, while exploited by thousands of predators (succhioni) through all kinds of tricks and shady enterprises are still shattered in hundreds of little churches (chiesoule) and local (campanilistiche) societies, which, instead of educating them and elevating them, push them more and more to withdraw from the civic life of the country and let them exclusively vegetate under the form of numerous patronal feasts.

Here and there once in a while some initiatives have blossomed in the colony but they are isolated instances and too lay for the clergy to favor them. In any case, the more objective minds, even in the non-clerical field, have admitted that the only force of cohesion is and can be only the clergy.

It is time, therefore, that we of the clergy clasp each other's hand, close ranks in a compact phalanx and in the name of God, of our Church and of the fatherland enter the arena. Around us is a people with whom we have in common the faith and the language and who expect from their clergy some courageous, dynamic action.

There are dangers, traps, necessities, injustices and impudent favoritisms that hover threateningly over our people: how long will we be silent and let things go?

We better than the laymen see the evils that vex our colonies in the big cities and more than the laymen are obliged to educate, defend and save.

Let us unite them in a general action of protection and redemption of our people. Let us organize this work of ours on the example of other peoples. Let us not tolerate any longer that in the very works of Christian charity we be excelled by Jews and non-Catholics.

Vis unita fortior. And the only ground on which all secular and religious Italian priests can unite with the laity for a common moral and social action on behalf of our immigrant brothers seems to us to be indeed that of the *Italica Gens.* . . .

. . . In the hope to see soon united a powerful band of Italian clergy who, while they sanctify the souls, do not forget the new social problems that are emerging nor stand by passive before the life and struggles of their *gens.* I salute you. . . .[154]

In New York, *Il Progresso Italo-Americano,* the Italian language publication with largest circulation in America, constantly depicted the role of the Italian clergy as that of "sacerdoti di Dio e della Patria— priests of God and Country (Italy)."

We know by experience the great influence that, rightly so, the Italian priests exercise in our colony: they are here true apostles of charity and love, heralds of the religion of Christ and of the religion of the fatherland. . . .

. . . two things remain always impressed in the memory of the exile and are constantly present in his heart and memory: *Patria* where he was born and religion, in which his mother, the first teacher of life, educated him when a child. For this very reason the mission of the priest, especially in a foreign-land, is the most noble and beyond any praise. It keeps alive in our hearts the twofold flame that enkindles us with love toward God and love toward the *patria*.

And the splendid proof, that incontestably demonstrates how the priests answer to their highest mission here in the midst of the colonies, is in the work they have done. . . .[155]

Like the national parish, the Italian priests played a double role in relation to the church and in relation to society. While the national parish was more of an institution oriented toward the immigrant community, the priests, as a group, were more aware of the total surrounding society within which the immigrant community had to be inserted and made functional in a competitive pluralistic system.

Conclusion: The Role of Social Solidarity and Linkage of the Italian Ethnic Parish.

It was hypothesized that the ethnic parish had a relevant role as a social institution, both as a symbol and an agent of group solidarity and as a linkage system with the total society. The fierceness with which the Italian immigrants demanded churches of their own and an 'Italian religion' shows indeed how essential a catalyst the ethnic parish was in the social life of the ethnic community.

Organized life and collective entertainment were sectors of the immigrants society clearly identified with religious institutions and symbols. Schisms, protests, conversions and conflicts arose and developed as community movements in response to socio-religious situations of discrimination and abuse. The ethnic parish, by transcending a strictly religious role and by symbolizing the immigrants' "sacred cosmos" (Luckmann), favored integration. Integration, in fact, as the insertion of a new immigrant group in a sufficiently competitive and functioning capacity within a pluralistic society (Chapter I), would not be possible without group awareness and solidarity. While the ethnic parish became the visible symbol and, to a large degree, an agent of group awareness and solidarity, the ethnic church leadership, clerical and lay, worked as a linkage system of the ethnic group with the total society, starting with the established Catholic Church.

In her autobiographical study of the Sicilian village of Milocca, Charlotte Gower Chapman observes of the Sicilians:

"In America he will be an Italian to all members of other nationalities, a Sicilian to all Italians. In Sicily, he will be a Milocchese. In Milocca, he tends to remain a Piddizzuna (clan) who has moved." [156]

In a parallel way, the ethnic church brought about an internal process of universalization in the ethnic group by bringing all the saints together. In this way the clan, the village, the region and even the country of origin were progressively transcended to meet the expectation of a pluralistic, urban society in a new definition of the sacred cosmos.

NOTES

1. Thomas Luckmann, *The Invisible Religion. The Transformation of Symbols in Industrial Society.* New York: The MacMillan Co., 1967, p. 61 and passim.

2. Fr. Felix Morelli to Bishop Giovanni Battista Scalabrini, New York, August 10, 1888, ACSC-USA, Prov., 1888-98.

3. Michele Rapuzzi et al. to Frs. Ansanelli and Moroni, New York, January 24, 1888, ACSC-USA, Inizi, 1888.

4. Lorenzo Perona et al. to G. B. Scalabrini, New York, March 27, 1888, ACSC, USA, Inizi 1888.

5. Memorandum to Bishop Wigger, Hoboken, December 20, 1892, AAN.

6. Ch. IV, Note 127.

7. Letter dated November 30, 1915, Mario Terenzio to Cardinal Farley, AANY.

8. Francesco Paolo Riccardi et al. to Bishop C. E. McDonnell, Corona, February 14, 1914, ADB.

9. Fr. Antonine, O. M. Cap., to Bishop C. E. McDonnell, Brooklyn, November 26, 1912, ADB.

10. Vincenzo Fazzari et al. to the bishop of Newark, Fort Lee, January 23, 1924. AAN.

11. Pietro Saldini, President of the Committee and Secretary of the Confraternity, Arata Cesare, Prior of the Confraternity of St. Anthony of Padua, to Msgr. Corrigan, New York, April 26, 1875; see also, Fr. Oreste Alussi to bishop G. B. Scalabrini, New York, April 30, 1889, ACSC, USA, M.C., 1888-80.

12. G. De Concilio to G. B. Scalabrini, Jersey City, May 27, 1888, ACSC, USA, Sup. Prov., 1888.

13. C. Piccirillo to G. B. Scalabrini, Woodstock College, May 20, 1888, ACSC, USA, Prov., 1888.

14. G. De Concilio to G. B. Scalabrini, Op. cit.

15. Zaboglio to Scalabrini, Boston, January 1, 1889; December 8, 1888; New York, July 19, 1888; G. De Concilio to G. B. Scalabrini, Jersey City, June 28, 1888, ACSC, USA, Prov. 1888.

16. Zaboglio to Scalabrini, Boston, August 5, 1889. ACSC, USA, Prov. 1889.

17. Scalabrini to Corrigan, Piacenza, February 27, 1888, AANY, 1-39.

18. Corrigan to Scalabrini, April 13, 1888, ACSC. See also, M. Moroni to Corrigan, January 28, 1889, AANY, 1-39.

19. Chas. Ferina to Vicar General M. Lavelle, October 1, 1907, AANY, St. Rita's File.

20. Antonino Grasso et al. (a Committee of 25 families) to bishop Charles E. McDonnell, Brooklyn, November 10, 1910, ADB.

21. Morelli to Scalabrini, New York, August 16, 1888, ACSC, USA, Prov. 1888-89.

22. Ibid.

23. Cf. Zaboglio to Rolleri, Boston, October 12, 1889; Zaboglio to Scalabrini, Boston, April 13, 1889, ACSC, USA, Prov. 1888.

24. Letter dated August 10, 1892, Rev. Thomas F. Lynch to Archbishop M. A. Corrigan, AANY.

25. Letter dated November 30, 1915, Mario Terenzio to Cardinal Farley, AANY.

26. Cf. for example, Amos Vincenzo Astorri to G. B. Scalabrini, New York, October 10, 1888.

27. Cf. Alussi to Scalabrini, New York, December 13, 1898, ACSC, USA, M.C., 1898-1903.

28. Rev. A. Arcese to Fr. Coan, Brooklyn, September 23, 1909, ADB; Louis Lapetina et al. to bishop McDonnell, Brooklyn, April 5, 1914.

29. Pietro Pisani, *L'Emigrazione Italiana nell'America del Nord Note e Proposte*—Estratto della *Rivista Internazionale di scienze sociali e discipline ausiliarie*—November 1910—Roma, 1911, pp. 32.

30. Rev. Simonetti to bishop McDonnell, Brooklyn, October 10, 1910.

31. Societa' di San Gerardo to Cav. Salvatore D'Auria, Newark, N.J., July, 1926, AAN, St. Lucy's File.

32. G. Gambera, *Autobiografia*, op. cit. p. 27, ACSC.

33. Ibid., p. 62.

34. Cf. Francesco Paolo Cerase, *L'emigrazione diritorno; innovazione o reazione?* Rome: Istituto di Statistica e Ricerca Sociale "C. Gini," 1971. Pp. 302.

35. Pietro Bandini, "Il ritorno ai campi, per la salvezza dei nostri emigranti," *Italica Gens*, II, 6-7-June-July, 1911, pp. 266-267.

36. Oscar Handlin, *The Uprooted*. Boston: Little, Brown, & Co., 1951, p. 117.

37. Karl W. Deutsch, *Nationalism and Social Communication: An Inquiry into the Foundations of Nationality*. Cambridge, Mass.: The M.I.T. Press, 1953, p. 96; also, Joel B. Montague, Jr. *Class and Nationality: English and American Studies*. New Haven: College and University Press, 1963; Boyd C. Shafer, *Nationalism: Myth and Reality*. New York: Harcourt, Brace & World, 1955.

38. See chapter III, Italian responses to the experience of mass emigration.

39. Fr. Felix Morelli to G. B. Scalabrini, 1892, ACSC-USA, Prov. 188-98. Any anniversary history of local Italian parishes offers evidence of the role played by the Church in making groups from different Italian provinces work together in America.

40. Fr. Manlio Ciufoletti, "Importanza sociale delle parrocchie italiane in America," L'Emigrato Italiano, Anno XVIII, 4, (October-December, 1924), 1-6.

41. Ibid. p. 6.

42. Sac. dott. G. Capra, "I Padri Scalabriniani nell'America del Nord," *Italica Gens*, (January-June, 1916), 1-14.

43. ——. "Dagli Stati Uniti," *Italica Gens*, 7-12, 1916, pp. 230-250; P.P. "La parrocchia di San Francesco e la colonia italiana di Hoboken, N.J.," *Italica Gens*, II, 2, 1911, pp. 137-140; A. Sayno, "Buffalo e la sua colonia italiana," *Italica Gens*, VII, 1-6, 1916, pp. 82-86; Sac. Antonio Sartoris, "Fra gli Italiani emigrati nella Pennsylvania," *Italica Gens*, VI, 3-6, 1915, pp. 132-135; Ibid., "Una corrispondenza da Huston," pp. 35-37; *Il Carroccio*, Nov. 1915, n. 10, pp. 60-61 and pp. 23-31.

44. P. Pisani, "Asili infantili e orfanatrofi pei figli d'Italiani a New York," *Italica Gens*, I, n. 7-8, 1910, pp. 307-315.

45. Rev. J. B. Garbottini, s.m.m., to bishop McDonnell, Woodhaven, November 23, 1909, ADB.

46. ——. "Gli Italiani negli Stati Uniti," *Il Carroccio*, November 1915, n. 10, p. 60.

47. Pasquale Toscano et al. to G. B. Scalabrini, Brooklyn, August 16, 1901, ACSC-USA, Dir. Gen., 1901-02.

48. Fr. F. Morelli to bishop Scalabrini, various letters of 1888 and 1889, ACSC-USA, Prov.

49. Rev. John Vogel, p.s.m., to Bishop of Brooklyn, November 26, 1910, ADB.

50. ——. "Discussione della Camera dei Deputati dello Stato di previsione dell'entrata e della spesa del Fondo per l'emigrazione per l'esercizio finanziario 1904-1905," *Bollettino dell'Emigrazione*, n. 12, 1904, pp. 11-31.

51. Pastoral letter of Archbishop M.A. Corrigan to the Italian Pastors of New York, July 10, 1891, ACSC & AANY.

52. Rev. Peter Bandini. *First Annual Report of the St. Raphael's Italian Benevolent Society, July 1, 1891 to June 30, 1892*, New York: 1892, pp. 28.

53. F. Prat, "Gli Italiani negli Stati Uniti e specialmente nello Stato di New York," *Bollettino dell'Emigrazione*, Anno 1903, n. 4 pp. 14-41; Ibid., Anno 1903, n. 4, pp. 29-44; G. B. Volpe-Landi, "Sulla Associazione detta di San Raffaele per la protezione degli immigranti italiani negli Stati Uniti," 1903, 1, pp. 56-58; Ibid., 1904, n. 16, pp. 3-138.

54. Luigi Bodio. *Sulla Emigrazione Italiana e sul patronato degli emigranti*. Relazione al primo congresso geografico italiano (Genova, 1892). Genova: Tipografia del R. Istituto Sordo-Muti, 1894, pp. 44; Antonio Perotti, "La societa' italiana di fronte alle prime migrazioni di massa," *Studi Emigrazione*, Anno V, nn. 11-12, February-June, 1968, pp. 1-199.

55. Antonio Perotti, op. cit.; Bandini to Scalabrini, New York, April 6, 1891, ACSC-USA; Abbe A. Villeneuve to bishop Scalabrini, New York, October 1891, ACSC, B-IV, 1890-1939; Rev. De Nisco, p.s.m. to archbishop Corrigan, Brooklyn, November 30, 1891, AANY C-36.

56. Thomas Fitcher, Commissioner, to Corrigan, December 13, 1899, AANY, G-30. Also, Thomas Fitcher to Corrigan, New York, February 11, 1901, AANY, G-30; same, February 14, 1901. For some financial difficulties of the St. Raphael's Society, see, Bandini to Corrigan, New York, January 20, 1894; July 21, 1894, AANY, I-40. "Notizie circa le istituzioni di patronato, beneficienza, assitenza ospitaliera e previdenza a favore di immigrati italiani in Nuova York, Pittsburgh (Stati Uniti), Cordoba e Parana (Argentina)," *Bollettino dell'Emigrazione*, 1907, n. 13, pp. 87-124; —— "Per la tutela degli italiani negli Stati Uniti: Lettere dell'Ispettore Cav. Adolfo Rossi, scritte al Commissariato dell'Emigrazione nel corso di una sua missione negli Stati Uniti dell'America del Nord," *Bollettino dell'Emigrazione*, 1904, 16, pp. 58-68.

57. Bonaventure Piscopo, O.S.F., to archbishop Corrigan, Letter dated New York, May 1, 1899. AANY, I-34.

58. Ibid. "Statistics of the American Italian Protectorate."

59. ——. "*L'Italica Gens*. Federazione per l'assistenza degli emigranti italiani in paesi transoceanici," *Le Missioni Italiane*, XIII, 4 December, 1909, pp. 55-59.

60. cf. *Italica Gens*, I, 1910, n. 4.

61. ——. "All' Italica Gens dalle Americhe. Dal segretariato centrale di New York," *Italica Gens*, II, 8-9, 1911, pp. 314-337; —— "Da New York City—Segretariato dell' Italica Gens di Baxter St., 113," *Italica Gens*, II, 1911, pp. 452-53; dott. G. Grivetti, "L'Italica Gens negli Stati Uniti e Canada al 31 Dicembre 1910. Prima Relazione del Segretariato Generale di New York, 35 Broadway," *Italica Gens*, II, 4, 1911, pp. 145-169; —— "Dagli Stati Uniti del Nord America," *Italica Gens*, V, 3-4, 1914, pp. 152-163; —— "Dall'America del Nord," *Italica Gens*, VII, 1-6, 1916, pp. 92-113.

62. Msgr. Germano Formica, AANY, Deceased External Priests Files. Several letters, reports, memoranda and newspapers clippings on the Italian Auxiliary, Inc., are found in this file. See also *La Voce dell'Emigrato*, monthly review, official organ of the Italian Auxiliary, edited by Msgr. Formica.

63. Morelli to Scalabrini, New York, January 1, 1889, ACSC-USA, Prov. 1889.

64. Morelli to Scalabrini, New York, April 11, 1890; December 17, 1890, ACSC-USA, Inizi.

65. Sac. dott. Serafino de Santi to the Bishop of Brooklyn, Brooklyn, January 31, 1893, ADB.

66. Alessandro Caccia to Corrigan, New York, Dec., 10, 1900; February 19, 1900; July 9, 1901.

67. Sac. dott. Carlo Ferina to a priest, New York, 14 November 1899, ADB.

68. Sac. Ernesto Coppo to Bishop McDonnel, New York, December 1, 1900, ADB.

69. Rev. A. Arcese to Bishop McDonnell, Brooklyn, January 29, 1915, ADB.

70. Rev. A. Arcese to Bishop McDonnell, Brooklyn, December 1, 1918; January 7, 1919; January 23, 1919, when the circulation of the *Bollettino* had decreased to half its initial figure, ADB.

71. ——*Nel XXV anniversario dell'Istituto dei Missionari de San Carlo per gli italiani emigrati.* Rome, 1912, pp. 8-11.

72. —— *L'opera dei Francescani italiani a favore degli emigrati negli Stati Uniti d'America, MCCCCLV-MCMXXV.* Rome, 1925, pp. 96.

73. Archives Archdiocese of Newark, Reports of parishes for 1922 and 1923.

74. Nicholas J. Russo. "The Religious Acculturation of the Italians in New York City." Doctoral Thesis, Sociology, St. John's University, 1968. pp. 341.

75. See note 29 above.

76. Supreme Court, Kings County, In the Matter of the Application of the Mount Virgin Society for a peremptory writ of Mandamus against William F. Baker, as Police Commissioner of the City of New York, September 16, 1909. Copies in ADB.

77. Colman Barry, op. cit., describes the German-Irish conflict. For the Polish-Irish conflict, cf. Joseph John Parot, "The American Faith and the Persistance of Chicago Polonia, 1870-1920," Ph. D. Thesis, Department of History, Northern Illinois University, 1971. Pp. 370.

78. Will Herberg, *Protestant-Catholic-Jew*, op. cit., p. 139 and all chapter 6.

79. Robert D. Cross, *The Emergence of Liberal Catholicism in America.* Cambridge, Mass.: Harvard University Press, 1950.

80. John Talbot Smith, LL.D, *The Catholic Church in New York.* A History of the New York Diocese from its establishment in 1808 to the present time. New York: Hall and Locke, Co., 1905. Vol. 11, pp. 448-49.

81. Cf. Sacra Congregazione de Propaganda Fide, *Rapporto sull'emigrazione italiana con sommario.* Rome, 1887. Anno 1887, no. 30 Relazione d'udienza, f. 682 and following.

82. John Higham, *Strangers in the Land.* Patterns of American Nativism, 1860-1925. New York: Atheneum, 1963, pp. 181 and passim. Also, Richard Hofstadter. *The Age of Reform, From Bryan to F.D.R.* New York: Vintage Books, 1960. Ch. V, pp. 174-214.

83. George Zurcher, "American Ideas vs. Cahenslyism," *The Roycroft Quarterly*, Nov. 1896, n. 3, pp. 30 and following.

84. AAN, Letterbook, 1, 572-573, Wigger to Satolli, n.p., Sept. 5, 1893 (in Italian); Scalabrini to Cardinal Ledochowski, Piacenza, February 26, 1894 ACSC-USA, MC; Satolli to Scalabrini, Washington, D.C., October 16, 1893, ACSC-USA, Inizi; Satolli to Corrigan, Washington, D.C., April 28, 1893, AANY, where the Apostolic Delegate states that a problem with which the Delegation and Propaganda Fide were very much concerned, was that of Italian emigration and invites the Archbishop of New York to spend his energies in this direction. Martinelli to Corrigan, Washington, D.C., September 15, 1899, AANY I-41-C.

85. Aurelio Palmieri. *Il grave problema religioso degli Italiani.* op. cit. U.S. Department of Commerce. Bureau of the Census. *Census of Religious Bodies, 1936.* Bulletin No. 64: *Italian Bodies. Statistics, Denominational History and Organization.* Consolidated Report. Washington, 1940, pp. IV-9.

86. Interivew with Msgr. Santi Privitera, Pastor of St. Bernadette parish, Brooklyn, 1970.

87. Marcellino Moroni to Card. Simeoni, New York, May 16, 1888, ACSC, D.I. 2.

88. Antonio Petrucci et al. to Corrigan, New York, September 2, 1891, AANY I-40-A; Card. Simeoni to Corrigan, Rome, August 22, 1891, AANY, I-41-C, where the Prefect of Propaganda sends back to Corrigan a protest received from the Italians of East Harlem. On the behavior of Fr. Carmody, see Card. Simeoni to Corrigan, Rome June 25, 1892, AANY, I-41-C. Corrigan to Carmody, New York, June 26, 1891 and August 25, 1891, AANY, C-18.

89. Sebastian Martinelli, Apostolic Delegate, to Corrigan, Washington, D.C., September 15, 1899, AANY, I-41-C.

90. Archbishop Corrigan to Martinelli, New York, September 16, 1899, AANY, G-37.

91. Fr. D. Vicentini to Corrigan, New York, December 28, 1893, AANY, I-40.

92. Rev. Gideon de Vincentiis, *Memorial to the Pope*, 1903, (copy) AAN, pp. 1-2.

93. G. Gambera, *Autobiagrafia*, op. cit., pp. 38-41; cf. the archives of the custody of the Immaculate Conception of the Franciscan Fathers at St. Bonaventure University.

94. John Vogel to McDonnell, Brooklyn, May 21, 1911, ADB; "Vita e Miracoli di Don Paolo Miraglia." from *L'Italiano in America*, n.d.; "Revival of Religion in Italy by means of Catholic Reform," pp. 4 about 1909. This is Miraglia's statements on his activities, g. i. "Glorie Protestanti," *L'Italiano in America*, February 21, 1915. Also, *Il Progresso Italo-Americano*, August 2, 1910.

95. Corrigan to a Bishop, New York, March 29, 1889, AANY, C-39.

96. "Che cosa e' la Chiesa Cattolica Apostolica Romana Nazionale Italiana di S. Antonio di Padova," *La Voce di St. Antonio de Padova*, Anno 1, n. 1, October 5, 1919, pp. 2-9. Also the issues of May-June, 1920 (11, 6) and October, 1922 (III, 13).

Giovanni Bonzano, Apostolic Delegate, to Rev. J. F. Dolan, Washington, D.C., April 19, 1916, AAN; Rev. J. F. Dolan to Bishop O'Connor, Hackensack, February 9, 1917, AAN; Copy, Certificate of Incorporation of the Old Roman Catholic Church of Saint Antonio di Padova, dated November 6, 1915, received and recorded in the Office of the Clerk of the County of Bergen this 9th day of November 1915. Carles F. Thompson, Clerk, AAN. Joseph Anastasi, S.J.B., *The History of St. Anthony of Padua*, Hackensack, N.J., 1962, pp. 16.

97. Joseph Anastasi, op. cit., passim.

98. Alberto Pecorini, "L'attivita' religiosa degli italiani in America," *L'Opinione*, (Philadelphia) March 29, 1906, p. 1. Pecorini wrote on the sad conditions of exploitation and ignorance affecting the Italian immigrants in the United States also in his book: *Gli americani nella vita moderna osservati da un italiano*. Milano; Fratelli Treves Editori, 1909. He says: "It would be unfair, however, not to acknowledge the little efforts made so far by the few who more than money loved and felt a duty toward the oppressed. Many initiatives on behalf of the immigrants have been carried out under the direction of various religious sects. At present, there are in the United States more than two hundred Italian priests. Even though it is true that too many priests left their country under the burden of guilt, it is not less true that a considerable part is made up of good elements, who use their influence for the social mobility of the masses. They have not learned yet, it is true, that certain noisy *festeggiamenti* and some processions make our people to be considered as a superstitious and inferior race by the Americans, who have never seen Catholics of other countries do these things. But at least they speak our language and, more important, since in America do not exist the political difficulties of the Italian situation, they behave as good patriots. Almost all Protestant churches have some missionaries and ministers among the Italians, about ninety of them scattered among all the most important colonies. In many places special churches have been built for them. Since the main purpose of these sects is to Americanize the newcomers as soon as possible, evening English language schools are attached to the place of cult and reading rooms are opened there. Protestantism, however, does not make such progress among Italian immigrants as it could be expected in the case of other races, because the Italian immigrants lack that evolved individualistic conscience that Protestantism presupposes. It helps, however, to give to the Italian Catholic Church that spirit of initiative and that impetus that only in the United States she seems capable of having. . . ." pp. 399-400.

Luigi Villari, who spent several years in the Italian communities of the United States as a consular official for the Italian Government made similar comments on the Italian American religious scene in his book: *Gli Stati Uniti d'America e l'emigrazione italiana*. Milano: Fratelli Treves Editori, 1912, pp. 286-287.

99. "To the People of Corona—Important Protest," 1913, ADB Rev. J. L. O'Toole to McDonnell, Corona, May 9, 1913; John Whelan to McDonnell, Brooklyn, April 22, 1913, ADB.

100. Bishop T. E. Molloy to Cardinal D. Sbarretti, Brooklyn, May 18, 1938 (Bocache case). "Self-Syled 'Bishops' and Six Others Face Trial for Fraud." *Brooklyn Times Union,* October 12, 1936; *Daily News,* Brooklyn Section, October 14, 1936, pp. 15. *Memorandum del Rev. Michele Enrico Francesco di Ielsi,* to the Pope, ADB, 1937, *Historical and Doctrinal Sketches of the Old Roman Catholic Church.* Niagara Falls, N.Y., 1950, pp. 53.

101. Rev. M. Di Ielsi to Bishop P. Mores of Nusco, Italy, no date, copy, ADB, Di Ielsi File. S. Cafiero to Griffiths, Brooklyn, December 13, 1935; December 3, 1935, ADB.

102. Giovanni Errante to Foreign Ministry of Italy from Brooklyn (no date) (copy), ADB. Mario Giani to Msgr. Arcese, New York, September 10, 1936, ADB.

103. Gino Speranza, *Race or Nation: A Conflict of Divided Loyalties.* Indianapolis: The Bobbs-Merrill Co., 1925, pp. 278. Antonio Mangano: *Sons of Italy.* A Social and Religious Study of the Italians in America. New York: Missionary Education Movement of the United States and Canada, 1917, pp. 163-166. From a critical point of view, this book is ambivalent. Norman Thomas considered it accurate in describing the Protestant work with Italians, and the Author was a participant observer of this work. Yet the book is loaded with sweeping and biased statements against the Catholic Church. John Mariano in *Italian Contribution to American Democracy* (Boston: the Christopher Publishing House, 1921) points out some of the exaggerations concerning the number of converts to Protestantism. On the other hand, Thomas comments that there are some errors in the book, but these are not big; that what is said about ex-priests is not exact, since the Italian Ministers Association told him that 35 ex-priests do valuable work in the Protestant (all denominations) field.
cf. *Norman Thomas Papers,* New York Public Library, Division of Manuscripts, Box 3, Letters 1917.

104. John B. Bisceglia, Th.D., *Italian Evangelical Pioneers.* Kansas City, Mo.: Brown-White-Lowell Press, Inc. 1948, pp. 143. Cf. pp. 14-17.

105. Department of Commerce, Bureau of the Census, *Fourteenth Census of the United States, 1920.* Washington, D.C., 1922, II, pp. 685. The combined figures from Mangano would give little less than 28,000 persons associated with the Protestant Church.

106. John Dixon, D.D., Secretary, "Twenty Years in Home Missions: The Home Board's Progress," in *The Assembly Herald,* June 1918, pp. 273-275.

107. Rev. Howard V. Yergin, "Survey of Italian Work in New York City, 1912," in Antonio Mangano, *Religious Work Among Italians in America.* A Survey for the Home Missions Council. Philadelphia: The Board of Home Missions and Church Extension of the Methodist Episcopal Church, 1917 Appendix N. Yergin surveyed all denominations, including the independent Churches. The Total membership of the Churches was 5,584 and the total Italian population of the Sunday Schools was 4,741. Also emerging from this survey are the two facts: 65 paid workers for New York and 32 native Pastors.

108. John B. Bisceglia, Th.D., *Italian Evangelical Pioneers,* op. c. pp. 15. The seemingly negligable number of Italian Protestants, observes the A., gives fine leadership: La Guardia, Polletti, Pecora were Protestants.

109. Massimo Livi-Bacci: *L'Immigrazione e l'assimilazione degli Italiani negli Stati Uniti secondo le statistiche demografiche americane,* Milano: Giuffre', 1961.

110. U.S. Department of Commerce. Bureau of the Census. *Census of Religious Bodies, 1936.* Bulletin No. 64: *Italian Bodies.* Statistics, Denominational History, and Organization. Consolidated Report. Washington, 1940, pp. IV-9.

111. Raymond Breton, "Institutional Completeness of Ethnic Communities and the Personal Relations of Immigrants," AJS, LXX, 2, Sept. 1964, pp. 193-205.

112. Rev. Defendente Monti to Zaboglio, Valley Spring, Miss., September 16, 1887, ACSC-USA, Inzi, 1888.

113. Everybody Magazine, January 1910.

114. Rev. F. Beccherini to Scalabrini, Detroit, May 2, 1899, ACSC-USA, M.C.

115. *Italica Gens,* I, 1 (February 1910), pp. 7-8, R.V.P., "La colonizzazione e l'avvenire dell'emigrazione italiana in America," *Italica Gens,* 1, 3 (April 1910) pp. 106 f.; Ranieri Venerosi, "La coscienza nazionale fra gli emigranti italiani," *Italica Gens,* 11, 8-9 (Agosto-

September 1911) pp. 299-300; Soc. Giuseppe Capra, "La Italica Gens negli Stati Uniti," *Italica Gens*, VI, 10-12, 1915, pp. 255-261. "La colonizzazione agraria negli Stati Uniti e l' America." Ibid, pp. 221-237; Pietro Pisani, "Emigranti, alla terra." *Italica Gens*, 1, 5, 1910, pp. 212-224.

116. P. P. Bandini, "Il ritorno ai compi etc." Op. cit., pp. 265.

117. Ireland to Scalabrini, St. Paul, 25 April 1901, ACSC-USA.

118. Zaboglio to Scalabrini, Jersey City, June 28, 1888, ACSC-USA Prov. 1888.

119. Zaboglio to Scalabrini, Boston, April 13, 1899; Moroni to Scalabrini, New York, February 17, 1888, ACSC-USA Inizi; Corrigan to Scalabrini, New York 22 Nov. 1893, ACSC-USA-549; Corrigan to Ledochowski, New York April 3, 1894, pp. 18, AANY I-40.

120. Fannizzi to Rinaldi, New York, May 19, 1920, ACSC-USA, N.C.

121. A. Arcese to Bishop McDonnell, Brooklyn, December 13, 1916; Nasca to Mc-Donnell, January 30, 1891, ADB; Rev. V. Sorrentino to McDonnell, Dec. 6, 1913; Corrigan to Rev. B. Lupo, Nov. 4, 1888, AANY, C-39.

122. Vogel to McDonnell, Munichen, Germany, Aug. 12, 1900, ADB.

123. De Nisco, PSM to McDonnell, Brooklyn, January 3, 1893.

124. Rev. E. d'Aquila to the Bishop of Newark, Oct. 15, 1900, AAN, Our Lady of Mt. Carmel, Newark.

125. R. Gilmour to G. B. Scalabrini, Cleveland, June 27, 1889, ACSC-USA-M.C.

126. Rev. G. Gambera, "Our Italian Immigrants," *The New World*, Chicago, February 25, 1911, p. 2. Also, see Alberto Pecorini, "L'attivita' religiosa degli Italiani in America." *L'Opinione*, Anno I, n. 68, 29 Marzo 1906.

127. Giuseppe Capra, "I Padri Scalabriniani nell'America del Nord," *Italica Gens*, op. cit., pp. 5-6; Rev. G. Gambera, "Il Clero italiano in America e l'assistenza degli emigranti italiani," *Italica Gens*, II, 5, 1911, pp. 217-225.

128. Rev. Gideon de Vincentiis, A memorial to the Pope, 1903, pp. 7. This document of 19 typewritten pages describes the religious situation of Italians in New Jersey at the turn of the century, especially outside the large cities. Copy of the document is in the AAN, but there is no way to say if it ever reached Rome.

129. Minutes of meetings of December 17, 1902; January 22, 1903; March 31, 1903, AANY, I-6.

130. Rev. John Vogel to McDonnell, November 2, 1914, ADB.

131. *Il Carroccio*, December 1915 n. 11-12, pp. 76-77.

132. A. Arcese to McDonnell, Dec. 6, 1917, ADB.

133. *Atti del primo congresso cattolico italiano dell'America del Nord* tenuto nella Citta' di New York il 5 Dicembre 1917. New York: Polyglot Publishing House, 1918, pp. 84.

134. A. Arcese to McDonnell, October 18, 1919, ADB.

135. Zaboglio to Scalabrini, Boston, Oct. 18, 1888; P. Luigi Paroli to P. Rolleri, Providence, January 24, 1890. ACSC-USA, Prov.

136. Letter dated October 12, 1891, Rev. Thomas F. Lynch to Archbishop Corrigan, AANY.

137. Letter dated December 21, 1889, Giovanni Cardinal Simeoni to Archbishop M. A. Corrigan, AANY. Simeoni was Prefect of the S. Congregation for the Propagation of the Faith.

138. Letter dated August 24, 1917, R.E. Diffendorfer to Norman Thomas, NTP. In a statement Thomas prepared concerning the dispute that ensued from the publication of Mangano's book *Sons of Italy*, he recalls his six years of work with Italian newcomers in Harlem and expresses himself against creating divisions among them. Mangano's position against the use of ex-priests was reinforced by Pannunzio in an article, that was unchallenged, for *Zion's Herald* of Boston. See NTP, Letters 1917.

Howard R. Marraro, "Il problema religioso del Risorgimento italiano visto dagli Americani," *Rassegna storica del Risorgimento*, XLIII, 3, July-September 1956, pp. 463-472; Howard R. Marraro, "American Opinion on the Occupation of Rome in 1870." *The South Atlantic Quarterly*, LIV, 2, April 1955, pp. 221-242.

139. Morelli to Scalabrini, New York, August 10, 1888, ACSC-USA, Prov.

140. Morelli to a priest, New York, 1889, ACSC-USA, Prov.

141. De Cesnola, Director of the Metropolitan Museum of Arts, to Corrigan, New York, August 28, 1885, AANY.

142. Quoted in: *Il venticinquesimo della prima chiesa italiana sorta per Mons. Scalabrini su terra dell'Unione, 1888-1913.* New York, 1913, pp. 43; See also, Giovanni Petrarolo, "I missionari per gli Italiani emigranti, "Il Progresso-Italo-Americano, XXXI, n. 252, Novembre 2, 1910, pp. 1.

143. Rev. G. Gambera, *Discorso tenuto il 30 Novembre, 1911,* Chicago, 1911, pp. 16, ACSC.

144. "Il patriottismo delle colonie," *Il Carroccio,* Novembre 15, n. 10, 1917, pp. 51-59; "Solidarieta' nazionale," Ibid., November 1917, pp. 448; "Gli Italiani negli Stati Uniti," Ibid., December 1915, n. 11-12, pp. 106-108; Ibid. January 1916, n. 1, pp. 55-56; "Il patriottismo del clero italiano," *Il Carroccio,* January 11, 1916, n. 1, pp. 35, 55-60.

145. "Cronache dell'Italy Day," *Il Carroccio,* July 1918, pp. 92-94.

146. P. Giovanni Semeria, Che cosa fanno i nostri preti," *Il Carroccio,* X, 5, May 1924, pp. 560-562.

147. Cardinal Simeoni to Scalabrini, Rome, December 11, 1891, ACSC-B-IV.

148. Morelli to Scalabrini, New York, August 16, 1888, ACSC-USA, Prov.; Rev. M. Simonetti to McDonnell, Brooklyn, April 23, 1914; Msgr. A. Arcese to Bishop McDonnell, December 15, 1919, ADB; John F. Carr, "L americanizzazione degli Italiani, *Il Carroccio,* May 1915, pp. 8-9.

149. cf. *L'Italiano in America,* September 13, 1914. A letter of approval from bishop J. J. O'Connor of Newark is also reported. ACMS, clipping.

150. cf. *Constitution and By-Laws of the Association of the Italian Clergy of North America.* Pp. 33, n.d. and no publisher. The *Bollettino dell'Unione del Clero Italiano dell America del Nord* was published from 1914 to 1920 at least. ACMS.

151. cf. Letters of Michael J. Lavelle to A. Demo, January 17, 1922; Gh. Ferrante to Demo, 20 February, 1914; 26 February, 1914; Msgr. Michael J. Lavelle, V.G., to Fr. A. Demo, c.s., letter dated March 29, 1910. ACMS.

152. Francis J. Sullivan to M. J. Lavelle, letter from St. Aloysius Rectory (221 W. 132 d St, New York, June 25, 1915 ACMS.

153. M. J. Lavelle to A. Demo, New York, letter dated June 26, 1915. ACMS. Obviously, processions continued with candle-bearing girls dressed in white, statues, music and lights, taking over long city blocks in area of immigrants settlements. cf. *Il Progresso Italo-Americano,* July 18, 1915. Most of the processions, however, died out over the years, even because the priests discouraged them, as advised by the bishops.

154. Rev. G. Grivetti to Fr. A. Demo, letter dated June 7, 1912 (in Italian) ACMS. The Offices of the *Italica Gens* were at 35 Broadway, New York City.

155. "Per l'Album della Colonia al Principe di Udine pro vedove ed orfanelli dei morti in guerra." *Il Progresso Italo-Americano,* mercoledi,' 20 giugno 1917, p. 2. This interpretation of the work of the Italian priests was an editorial line of the newspaper maintained for many years.

156. Charlotte Gower Chapman, op. cit, p. 27.

CHAPTER VI

Pluralism in the Church

After the Third Council of Baltimore in 1884, the American Catholic Church emerged as a national force, recognized as a major religion of the country and efficiently organized. The debate of the Council's bishops regarding immigration, however, could not be concluded with a clear policy statement. The religious conditions of Italians and of other southern and eastern European Catholic immigrants had been dealt with by Cardinal Gibbons of Baltimore, by Archbishop Corrigan of New York, by Archbishop Elder of Cincinnati and by other bishops with the view of preparing possible decrees on the ways and means to assist the newcomers. But neither the issue of immigration nor the germane issue of the status of the German parishes vis-a-vis ecclesiastical discipline had a chance to reach the floor of the Council. As a consequence, the pastoral care of Italian immigrants and the canonical status of non-English language parishes became the occasion of partisan polemics throughout the following decade of American church history.[1]

Immigration and nationality parishes, in fact, were intrinsically connected issues. Their solution depended on the capacity of developing a formula acceptable to the bishops demanding 'Americanization' and to the immigrants intent upon preserving their language and tradition.[2]

While the two factions within the church, the Liberals and the Conservatives,[3] were defending their respective ideologies in regards to the church's relation to American society and the preservation of the immigrants' faith, the volume of Italian immigration was steadily growing to the point of becoming a major ethnic community of the United States. But national ecclesiastical disputes transcended the world of the *contadini* whose real concerns were summed up in the business of living: to settle, to find a job and save some money.

Italian immigrants found themselves at the very bottom of the social structure of the new country. In a detailed and carefully documented report of 1887, the Prefect of Propaganda Fide presented the Cardinals of that Vatican Congregation with a bleak picture of Italian immigration in the United States:

> . . . it is humiliating to acknowledge that, after the disappearance of the Indians from the United States and the emancipation of the Negroes, the Italian immigrants are those who in great number represent the *pariahs* of this great American Republic . . . very many, reduced by misfortune and vice to extreme misery (miseria), go begging. The vast majority of the poor Italians do not know any other language except their own native dialect. For this reason they find themselves isolated even when they are in large numbers. The Irish, the Germans, the French, even while learning English, preserve with their language their own nationality in the midst of the American people. They form colonies in the bosom of the great Republic, in which they participate with the natives in the economic and political life. But the poor Italians remain individuals lost in a multitude. . . .[4]

As individuals, the immigrants would have lost ethnic and religious identity in the pluralistic American society. Propaganda Fide, that considered the two variables of ethnicity and religion interdependent, had received enough documentary evidence to support a plan which could "paralyze the causes that bring about the dissolution of the Italian Catholic element." Contrary to the opinion of several American bishops, the low religious practice of the Italian immigrants was seen by Propaganda as a possible consequence, not a cause, of their condition of abandonment. If capable and zealous priests could be sent to America to receive the immigrants at the moment of arrival, to organize them against dispersion, to build churches, schools, hospitals and other social assistance structures, success could be expected in keeping the group within the fold of the faithful.[5]

The immigrants, on their part, had come to the same conclusion intuitively. They moved on to build their own churches as centers of ethnic identity and traditional religious and social manifestations, and they forced the American bishops to accept their choice, at least momentarily. The problem analyzed was indeed that of the role played by the Italian ethnic church taken as the outcome of a compromise among the principal factors: Propaganda Fide's preoccupation with the preservation of the faith of the immigrants, the American bishops' preoccupation with inserting the Church as a viable and influential force on the national scene, and the immigrants' preoccupation with safeguarding their social, peasant world, within which they felt human.

It would have been misleading to study the institutional development of the immigrant's religion in a perspective of assimilation which could not take into account the peculiar structure of the receiving society. As a nation of sub-societies, to recall Gordon's terminology, the United States has constantly maintained as a political priority the balance of its constituting groups. Assimilation, therefore, is seen as a process of pluralization of society determined by variables of times sequences and of social stratification, rather than a monolinear movement toward conformity to a pre-established model-group. The Italian immigrants, from a number of "individuals lost in a multitude," had to become a community, at least at the local level of the neighborhood. Although individuals had the alternative of moving up and out on their own, the immigrant group could compete in the pluralistic structure of American society only as a group. The theoretical framework adopted rejects the image of American society espoused by American liberalism, wherein the minority problem is defined in the narrow sense of providing adequate, if not equal, opportunity for members of minority groups to ascend as individuals into the mainstream culture.[6] It was within a theoretical paradigm of group assimilation that the answer was sought to the question of the role of the ethnic church in making the immigrants a group and in subsequently linking the group to society at large. As tools of research, all available historical data have been used for the area covered by the New York-Brooklyn-Newark dioceses.

It has not been the purpose of this research to prove the insitutional dispersion of the immigrants within the structures of the host-society as a measure of assimilation nor to study all the organizations of the immigrant community.

The first immigrant generation, as it arrived in the United States between the 1880's and 1920's, was selected in order to see the use it made of its own church for its own organizing.

The best suitable method for the research was that of historical sociology. Historical data document past social behavior and, as Charles Tilly remarks, "all archives are brimming with news on how men used to act, and how they are acting still."[7] Besides, the perspective of time gives a more adequate view of the patterns of social relations, of the growth of institutions and of the movements of the lower classes of society.

The historical case of the Italian ethnic church has been the occasion for a specific application of Durkeim's advice to marry history and sociology, to study trends in order to go behind events and to make orderly sense of them. The religious, social and assimilation functions, in fact, have been the three main units of analysis, even if some unavoidable overlapping may have occurred.[8]

In the hypotheses formulated on the conditions for assimilation in an ethnically pluralistic society like the United States, the Italian immigrants' church was proposed as portraying a new type of religious institution, defined as a quasi-sect. The ethnic church was also expected to act as a social institution for group solidarity and linkage with society at large, the latter function being a latent one, especially as far as the immigrants were concerned. First, then, the ethnic parish was proposed as a social institution created to bring about ethnic solidarity, i.e. to perform an internal function of strengthening the group by fulfilling its basic needs. Secondly, it was proposed as a critically significant institution in linking the immigrants with the larger national society because of its integration into a national religious system like the Catholic Church and its diocesan set-up that transcended the local allegiances of the immigrants.

In the latter aspect of inter-institutional communication the ethnic priest was perceived as mediator and a legitimizer, since he had to accept and serve the ethnic community of which he was a part and at the same time constantly challenge it to remain loyal to the demands of a universal religious system.[9]

The Italian immigrants and their priests were caught between an imposed religious organization (the system of duplex parishes where the immigrants had to worship in the basement of existing churches) and that of totally separate parishes, which some rebellious priests and immigrants advocated and established as, for example, Independent Roman Catholic Churches. The historical survey presents the general solution given to the dilemma: the religious function of the national church as a bridge between local and universal loyalties. From separate shrines in courtyards and street corners the Saints of many villages were housed in the same church, where old customs survived some of the more drastic antifolkloristic policies. Thus, the national church seen as a quasi-sect indicates, in terms of the sociology of religion literature, that the quality of deprivation of a social group is not as crucial as the fact of deprivation in evoking sectarian responses.

In the documentation it was shown also how the background of the immigrants led them to choose the parochial structure as a symbol of their solidarity. In particular, the role of the priests and the overall role of the ethnic church were analyzed and documented for their function in inserting the immigrant community in the inter-group play of American society. Immigrants from different provinces settled and began to unite around the Church. There also sprang up scores of voluntary organizations within which social interaction beyond the family clan and political action were often experienced for the first time. As Luigi Villari reported in 1912:

> The Catholic Church has an important role in the life of our colonies, since they are mostly made up of southern Italians of deep faith. In every place where there is a somewhat numerous colony there are Italian churches directed by priests from Italy, who exercise a great influence on their compatriots. The immigrants are generous with offerings. In the feast days, they are seen carrying around statues of the Madonna and Saints to whose vestments the faithful pin dollar bills. Thus are collected the funds for the building of churches both in the colonies and, sometimes, in the paesi of origin of the immigrants. Many of the priests are inspired by sentiments of true christian charity. They exercise their ministry on behalf of the community and not few of them are also good patriots. Unfortunately, there are other priests of much different character. They have come to America either because of some scandal of which they were the protagonists in Italy or simply to make money. Few are sent to America by their superiors for the purpose of governing a church, but these are the best. The others come on their own initiative 'looking for a mass,' as a doctor comes looking for clients. They settle in some central place where there are many Italians. They start by renting a place. Then, with their savings, they put enough money aside to build a new church. The influence of the American enviornment is such that they consider their mission too much as a simple business. Besides, some of them lead a not very edifying private life. The faithful seem much less scandalized, however, than they would be in Italy. Also the bishops take little care in punishing the culprits.
>
> All the Italian priests have the merit of keeping alive the sentiment of 'italianita.' Some do this for true patriotism; others, because they know that the americanized Italians either lose their faith completely or end up by going only to the American Catholic churches. It is beyond doubt that the Italian clergy exercises a more useful influence on our immigrants than the Irish American clergy, who are more fanatic and ferociously anti-Italian.

Two words on Protestant proselytising. The various reformed
churches seek to convert the Italian immigrants, even by the means of
pastors of their nationality. In general, however, this work does not take
roots. Many of the converts did not become such except to enjoy the financial benefits that conversion entails and they abandon Protestantism
when the need ceases. It happens also that a family, which has become
Protestant, as soon as a child becomes sick sees in it a proof of divine
wrath and comes back into the bosom of the Catholic Church.[10]

Italian immigrants seem to have organized mostly on a parochial level
to preserve their way of understanding the world and to obtain the
economic goals to which they had been pre-socialized. It would seem
futile to try to measure the degree of prevalence of the variables of ethnic
identity or of the class position of the immigrant group in the social
structure of the receiving society. The interplay between ethnicity and
class is not only complex, but it is—in the experience of the Italian
immigrants—the essential component for a definition of an ethnic subgroup in the American society. In the early 1880's when the immigrants
were working for survival at all kinds of 'dirty' jobs, they were the least
aware of their ethnicity. They were Colabrians, Sicilians and not yet an
Italian American community. As they moved from stage one to stage
three of social assimilation (see Figure I), their group identity became
clearer, as it was revealed in their response to Italy's entry into World
War I.

They arrived from Italy with a sense of ethnic identity confined to
their villages. But the situation of conflict the immigrants had to face
vis-a-vis the previously settled ethnic groups and the official policy of
American society—that expected all newcomers to make it on their
own—led the immigrants to accept the receiving society's definition of
themselves as all Italians and a new American group. Thus, they began
to respond to many of their problems in a collective way.

As one of the crucial primary institutions of the ethnic community,
the ethnic parish has operated as an intermediate institution between the
time of the immigrants arrival and the time of their assimilation, and
between the value system and communitarian patterns of the country of
origin and the value system and the associational pattern of the urban
environment of the host country. Because linked to the more general
social system of the larger society, through the diocese, the parish could
not avoid being a communication channel of this society's values.

The network of Italian parishes developed within the established
diocesan structure. The Italian priests not only continued to serve their
ethnic congregations, but slowly began to move into forms of ministry
not specifically identifiable as Italian American, thus strengthening the
acceptance of their mediating role and the positive function of an

autonomous base like the national parish for the adjustment of immigrants. (Table 1)

As new national parishes were erected, independent or schimastic parishes and Protestant proselytizing withered away. Through its function as a strong agent of social control and carrier of the weltanschauung of the community, the ethnic church gave the community the identity and the power required to make its systematic linkage effective. Vlachos and Zubrzychi also have called attention to the dysfunctional role of the ethnic church when the role of boundary maintanence becomes overemphasised in such a way that the ethnic parish becomes a mobility trap.[11] It is possible that the change of values may not bring about a corresponding institutional change, so that institutional forms remain standing as residual subsystems, as may be the case of the ethnic parishes after assimilation has taken place. It is also possible that a system closes the channels of communication with the larger society to the point of no longer being a subsystem, but a self-isolated group.

Between the extremes of schismatic isolationsim and overnight Americanization, the national parish functioned as an ideal and new solution for the immigrants in the period of their assimilation. The research, then, leads to a new interpretation of Italian emigration where the behavior of the immigrants, rather than ideological premises, is the key variable for understanding their social experience.

Table 1. *Distribution of Italian American Priests*
in the Dioceses of New York, Newark and Brooklyn in 1950

Italian American Priests*	New York	Newark	Brooklyn	Total
in officially-designated Italian parishes**	127	68	43	238
in other parishes	63	10	52	125
in diocesan-wide ministry (Chancery offices, etc.)	6	3	10	19
Total	196	81	105	382

Source: The Official Catholic Directory. New York: P. J. Kenedy & Sons, 1950.
*Priests were identified by last name; retired priests were not counted.
**By 1950 several Italian parishes were no longer officially listed as Italian. At this date there were in the three dioceses of New York, Newark and Brooklyn 74 parishes listed as Italian. But there were Italian priests working in 79 parishes not listed as Italian.

As Fitzpatrick observes, one integrates from a position of strength, not from a position of weakness.[12] The national parish played the role of strengthening the immigrant community by sanctioning the validity of extended primary groups, by re-enacting the ritual world of the old country, by becoming the focus of several formal and informal associations extending throughout the immigrant community.

The experience of the Italian ethnic parish is probably similar to that of other Southern and Eastern European immigrant groups in the United States. A comparative study of ethnic churches would certainly further enlighten the dynamics of conflict and cooperation that human relations reveal in modern pluralistic societies as well as the role of religious institutions in the assimilation process. This experience points out also the positive function ethnicity can play in complex societies like the United States where the various subgroups compete and maintain social equilibrium on the base of their internal solidarity.

Thus, the traditional theory of individual social mobility and assimilation is replaced for one of group behavior and political sociology. The implications of this new theoretical perspective extend to the concrete possibilities of intervening in the social process in order to affect the forces that strengthen or weaken an ethnic group. The future policy of Church administrators, therefore, should not be passive tolerance of ethnic adjustment to ecclesiastical structures. In the contemporary urban scene, newcomers would be competing for already scarce resources. As new immigrant groups enter American society, successful assimilation may very well depend on the degree of internal capacity and external support they will find in being free to make their own choices in the total political context of the receiving society.

Churches should give the immigrants an autonomous base so that their social expression of religion may become an integral part of their group solidarity. In turn, the new community can better adjust to an increasingly pluralistic world, because of the acceptance of pluralism within the Church.

NOTES

1. Colman Barry, op. cit. *Acta et Decreta Concilii Plenarii Tertii.* A.D. MDCCCLXXX-IV. Baltimore: John Murphy, 1886, pp. 130-132.

2. Sacra Congregatio de Propaganda Fide, *Relazione con sommario e voto intorno all'erezione di quasi parrocchie distinte per nazionalita' negli Stati Unit d'America.* Vol. 257, f. 215 and following. Rome, 1887, This is the most important policy statement of the American Bishops and the Holy See on National parishes.

3. Colman J. Barry, *The Catholic Church and German Americans.* Milwaukee: The Bruce Publishing Compnay, 1953. Pp. 348. op. cit. ch. 5.

4. Sacra Congregazione de Propaganda Fide. *Rapporto sull'emigrazione italiana con sommario.* Rome, 1887. Anno 1887, no. 30. Relazione d'udienza, f. 682 and following. Also, Ida van Etten, "Shocking Plight of Italian Poor in New York City," *New York Herald,* Sunday, September 18, 1892, p. 44.

5. Sacra Congregazione de Propaganda Fide, op. cit. f. 686-687.

6. Cf. for a recent review of literature as applies particularly to the race problem, C. Paul Metzger, "American Sociology and Black Assimilation: Conflicting Perspectives," *American Journal of Sociology,* 76(4):627-647 (January, 1971). Cf. also the entire issue of *Dissent,* Vol. XIX, 1 (Winter, 1972).

7. Charles Tilly, *The Vendee. A sociological analysis of the Counter-revolution of 1783.* New York: John Wiley & Sons, Inc., 1964, pp. 342.

8. Emile Durkheim, "Prefaces to L'Anee Sociologique," in Emile Durkheim et al. *Essays on Sociology and Philosophy.* New York: Harper & Row, 1960, p. 341.

9. C. Wright Mills, *The Sociological Imagination.* New York: Grove Press, Inc., 1959. Pp. 234. op. cit., pp. 143-164, passim.

10. Luigi Villari, *Gli Stati Uniti d'America e l'emigrazione italiana,* op. it., pp. 287-288.

11. Jerzy Zubrzychi, *Settlers of the Latrobe Valley.* Canberra: The Australian National University Press, 1964. Pp. 167 f.

12. Joseph P. Fitzpatrick, "The Integration of Puerto Ricans," *Thought,* XXX (Autumn, 1955), pp. 402-20. Also, Joseph P. Fitzpatrick, "Puerto Ricans in Perspective: The Meaning of Migration to the Mainland," *The International Migration Review,* Vol. II, n. 2 (Spring, 1968), pp. 7-19.

BIBLIOGRAPHY

This research is primarily based on archival sources (cf. ch. I, note 1). Published literature, however, in the English and Italian languages was extensively utilized to gather as much information as possible. A forthcoming volume, *Italian Americans and Religion: An Annotated Bibliography* (New York: Center for Migration Studies, 1975), compiled by S. M. Tomasi and Edward E. Stibili provides the most exhaustive bibliography on this subject. The following books, pamphlets, articles, and unpublished dissertations together with the references cited in the footnotes, offer a sufficiently comprehensive documentation.

BOOKS

1. Adamic, Louis, *Nation of Nations*. New York: Harper & Brothers, 1914. Pp. 19-36.

2. Adams, Graham, Jr., *Age of Industrial Violence: 1910-15*. The Activities and Findings of the United States Commission on Industrial Relations. New York: Columbia University Press, 1966. Pp. 316.

3. Allport, Gordon W., *The Use of Personal Documents in Psychological Research*. New York: Social Science Research Council, 1942.

4. A.M.G.SS.C.J., *In Memoria della Rev. ma Madre Francesca Saverio Cabrini Fondatrice e Superiora Generale delle Missionarie del S. Cuore di Gesu, volata al Cielo in Chicago il 22 Dicembre 1917*. New York: A. Bernasconi, 1918. Pp. 462.

5. Amico, Salvatore, *Gli italiani e l'Internazionale dei sarti da donna; racolta di storie e memorie contemporanee*. Mamaroneck, New York, 1944. Pp. 190.

6. Antonini, Luigi, *Dynamic Democracy*. New York: Eloquent Press, 1944. Pp. XX + 463.

7. Aquilano, Baldo, *Ordine Figli d'Italia in America*. New York: Unione Tipografico Italiano, 1925.

8. Banfield, Edward, *The Moral Basis of a Backward Society*. Glencoe: Illinois: The Free Press, 1958.

9. Basso, Ralph, *History of Roseto, Pennsylvania*. Easton, Pa.: Tanzella Printing, 1952. Pp. 67.

10. Baudier, Roger, *The Catholic Church in Louisiana*. New Orleans: A. W. Hyatt, 1939.

11. Bernardy, Amy A., *Italia Randagia. Attraverso gli Stati Uniti*. Torino: Fratelli Bocca, 1913. Pp. 350.

12. Bonomelli, Geremia, *Questioni Religiose, Morali e Sociale del Giorno*. Rome: Desclee, Lafebvre E C., Editori Pontifici, 1903. Vol. 11. Pp. 422-466.

13. Brooks, Charles A., *Christian Americanization: A Task for the Churches*. New York: Council of Women for Home Missions and the Missionary Movement of the United States and Canada, 1919. Pp. 162.

14. Brooks, Philip C., *Research in Archives. The Use of Unpublished Primary Sources*. Chicago: The University of Chicago Press, 1969. Pp. 127.

15. Brandenburgh, Broughton, *Imported Americans. The Story of the Experiences of a Disguised American and His Wife Studying the Immigration Question*. New York: Frederick A. Stokes Co., 1903. Pp. 303.

16. Bynington, Margaret, *Homestead: The Household of Milltown*. New York: Charities Publication Committee, 1910.

17. Cabrini, Frances Xavier, *Travels of Mother Frances Xavier Cabrini, Foundress of the Missionary Sisters of the Sacred Heart of Jesus*. With a biographical sketch by the Most Rev. Amleto Giovanni Cicognani, D.D., Apostolic Delegate to the United States. Chicago: The Missionary Sisters of the Sacred Heart of Jesus, 1944. Pp. 277.

18. Capello, Amelia, *Notizie storiche e discrittive delle Missioni della Provincia Torinese della C. di G. nell'America del Nord*. Torino, 1898.

19. Capozzi, F. C., *Protestantism and the Latin Soul*. Philadelphia: J. C. Winston Co., 1918.

20. Cassigoli, B.R. and H. Chiariglione, *Il Libro d'oro*. Pueblo, Colo., 1904.

21. Child, Irvin L., *Italian or American? The Second Generation in Conflict*. New Haven: Yale University Press, 1943.

22. Ciesluk, Joseph E., *National Parishes in the United States*. Washington: Catholic University of America Press, 1944.

23. Ciufoletti, Manlio, C. S., *John Baptist Scalabrini, Bishop of Piacenza, Apostle of the Italian Immigrants*. New York: Congregation of St. Charles Borromeo, 1937. Pp. 72.

24. Clark, Francis E., *Our Italian Fellow Citizens*. Boston: Small, Maynard & Company, 1919.

25. Conte, Gaetano, *Dieci anni in America, Impressioni e Ricordi*. Palermo: G. Spinato, 1903.

26. Cordasco, Francesco & Salvatore LaGumina, *Italians in the United States. A Bibliography of Reports, Texts, Critical Studies and Related Materials*. New York: Oriole Editions, 1972. Pp. 137.

27. Cordasco, Francesco & Eugene Bucchioni, *The Italians. Social Backgrounds of an American Group*. Clifton, N.J.: Augustus M. Kelley Publishers, 1974. Pp. 598.

28. Covello, Leonard, *The Social Background of the Italo-American School Child*. Leiden: E. J. Brill, 1967. Pp. 488.

29. Coser, Lewis A., *Continuities in the Study of Social Conflict*. New York: Free Press, 1967.

30. Daniels, John, *America via the Neighborhood*. New York: Harper & Brothers, 1920. Pp. 462.

31. Di Donato, Pietro, *Immigrant Saint. The Life of Mother Cabrini*. New York: McGraw Hill Co., 1960.

32. Des Planches, E. Mayor, *Attraverso gli Stati Uniti. Per l'emigrazione Italiana*. Torino: Edicrice Torinese, 1913. Pp. 321.

33. Dohen, Dorothy, *Nationalism and American Catholicism*. New York: Sheed & Ward, 1967. Pp. 210.

34. Dragoni, Fr. Ladislao, O.F.M., *Visioni Serafiche*. New York: Catholic Polyglot Publishing House, 1926. Pp. 178.

35. Eisenstadt, Samuel N., *The Absorption of Immigrants*. Glencoe, Ill.: Free Press of Glencoe, 1955.

36. Fairchild, Henry Pratt, *The Melting Pot Mistake*. Boston: Little Brown & Company, 1926.

37. Fairchild, Henry Pratt, *Race and Nationality as Factors in American Life*. New York: Ronald Press Company, 1947.

38. Federal Writers Project, *Gli Italiani di New York*. Versione Italians riveduta ed ampliata da Alberto Cupelli. New York: Labor Press, 1939. Pp. 242.

39. Federal Writers Project, *The Italians of New York*. New York: Random House, 1938.

40. Ferrari, Robert, *Days Pleasant and Unpleasant in the Order Sons of Italy. The Problem of Races and Racial Societies in the United States. Assimilation or Isolation?* New York: Mandy Press, Inc., 1926.

41. Fitzpatrick, Joseph P., *Puerto Rican Americans*. Englewood Cliffs, N.J.: Prentice-Hall, 1971. Pp. 192.

42. Flynn, Joseph M., *The Catholic Church in New Jersey*. Norristown, N.J.: (Published by the author), 1904.

43. Flynn, Paul V., *History of St. John's Church*. Newark: Press of the New Jersey Trade Review, 1908. Pp. 217.

44. Foerster, Robert F., *The Italian Emigrant of Our Time*. Cambridge: Harvard University Press, 1919.

45. Fox, Paul, *The Polish National Catholic Church*. Scranton: School of Christian Living, 1957.

46. Fumagalli, Giuseppe, *La stampa periodica Italiana all'estero*. Esposizione Internazionale di Milano 1906. Milano, 1906. Pp. 155 + XCIV.

47. Gallagher, John, Scranton, *Industry and Politics*. Ann Arbor: University Microfilm, 1964.

48. Gans, Herbert J., *The Urban Villagers: Group and Class in the Life of Italian Americans*. New York: The Free Press of Glencoe, 1962.

49. Gittler, Joseph B., *Understanding Minority Groups*. New York: John Wiley & Sons, Inc., 1956.

50. Glazer, Nathan & Daniel Moynihan, *Beyond the Melting Pot*. Cambridge: Harvard University Press, 1964.

51. Gordon, Milton M., *Assimilation in American Life: The Role of Race, Religion and National Origins*. New York: Oxford University Press, 1964.

52. Gottscholk, L. C., Kluckhohn & Robert Angell, *The Use of Personal Documents in History, Anthropology and Sociology*. New York: S.S. R.C., 1945.

53. Grasso, Pier Giovanni, *Personalita' Giovanile in transizione*. Zurich: Pas Verlag, 1964. Pp. 489.

54. Greco, Emilio, *Il Padre degli Emigrati Italiani in America e l'Apostalo dei suoi Missionari*. New York: Polyglot Publishing House, 1916. Pp. 24.

55. Gregori, Francesco, *La Vita e l'Opera di un Grande Vescovo: Mons. Giovanni Battista Scalabrini (1839-1905)*. Torino: L.I.C.E., Roberto Berruti & Co., 1934. Pp. 615.

56. Grieco, Rose, *The Listening Heart. The Life of John Baptist Scalabrini Father to the Immigrants*. New York: Society of St. Charles, 1965. Pp. 95.

57. Grose, Howard B., *Aliens or Americans?* New York: Congregational Home Missionary Society, 1906. Pp. 337.

58. Guetti, Lorenzo, *Statistica dell'Emigrazione American avvenuta nel Trentino dal 1870 in poi*. Trento: 1888.

59. Guilday, Peter, *A History of the Councils of Baltimore (1791-1884)*. New York: Macmillan, 1932.

60. Hammon, Walter, O.F.M., *The First Bonaventure Men. The Early History of St. Bonaventure University and the Allegany Franciscans*. St. Bonaventure: St. Bonaventure University, 1958. Pp. 249.

61. Handlin, Oscar, *The Americans*. Boston: Little Brown & Co., 1963.

62. Handlin, Oscar, *Immigration As a Factor in American History*. New Jersey: Prentice-Hall, 1959.

63. Handlin, Oscar, *The Newcomers*. New York: Doubleday & Co., 1962.

64. Handlin, Oscar, *Race and Nationality in American Life*. Boston: Little Brown & Co., 1948.

65. Handlin, Oscar, *The Uprooted*. New York: Grosset & Dunlap, 1951.

66. Hansen, Marcus Lee, *The Immigrant in American History*. Cambridge: Harvard University Press, 1948.

67. Harkness, Georgia E., *The Church and the Immigrant*. New York: George H. Doran Co., 1921. Pp. 110.

68. Hawley, Willis D. & Frederick M. Wirt, eds., *The Search for Community Power*. Englewood Cliffs, N.J.: Prentice Hall, 1968. Pp. 379.

69. Higham, John, *Strangers in the Land*. New Brunswick: Rutgers University Press, 1955.

70. Hobsbawn, E. J., *Primitive Rebels. Studies in Archaic Forms of Social Movement in the 19th and 20th Centuries*. Manchester: Manchester University Press, 1959.

71. *Inchiesta Parlamentare sulle condizioni dei contadini nelle provincie meridionali e sulla Sicilia*. Roma: G. Bertero, 1910 (V).

72. Iorizzo, Luciano J. & Salvatore Mondello, *The Italian-Americans*. New York: Twayne Publishers, Inc., 1971. Pp. 273.

73. Jenks, J. W. & W. J. Lauck, *The Immigration Problem*. New York: Funk & Wagnalls, 1926.

74. Kenneally, Finbar, ed., *United States Documents in the Propaganda Fide Archives: A Calendar*. Washington: Academy of American Franciscan History, 1966.

75. Lalli, Franco, *La Prima Santa d'America*. Brooklyn: Casa Editrice Fortuna Publishing Co., 1944. Pp. 140.

76. Landolfi, Amalio, *La mia strenua propaganda all'Estero, (1925-1926)*. Pegola: Avellino, Premiate Tipografia, 1926. Pp. 139.

77. Larson, Calvin J., and Philo C. Wasburn, *Power, Participation and Ideology. Readings in the Sociology of American Political Life*. 1969. Pp. 544.

78. Lee, Robert, and Martin E. Marty, *Religion and Social Conflict*. New York: Oxford University Press, 1965.

79. Leveroni, Francesco, et al., *Venticinque Anni di Missione fra gli Italiani Immigrati di Boston, Mass*. Milano: Tipografia Santa Laga Eucaristica, 1913. Pp. 359.

80. Lord, Eliot, *The Italian in America*. New York: B. F. Buck & Co., 1906.

81. Maffei, Gioacchino, *L'Italia nell'America del Nord. Rilievi e suggerimenti per la grandezza e l'onore d'Italia*. Valle di Pompei: Tipografia di Francesco Sicignano & F., 1924. Pp. 164.

82. Mangano, Antonio, *Sons of Italy: A Social and Religious Study of the Italians in America*. Missionary Education Movement of the United States and Canada, 1917. Pp. xii + 234.

83. Mariano, T. H., *Italians Contribution to American Democracy or The Second Generation of Italians in New York City*. Boston: The Christopher Publishing House, 1921.

84. Martignoni, Angela, *Madre Cabrini, la Santa della Americhe. La vita, i viaggi, le opere*. New York: Vatican City Religious Book Co., Inc., 1945. Pp. 249.

85. Martellone, Anna Maria, *Una Little Italy nell'Atene d'America. La communita' italiana di Boston dal 1880 al 1920*. Napoli: Guida Editori, 1973. Pp. 597.

86. Mastrogiovanni, Salv., *Le prime societa' di patronato per gli emigranti nelgi Stati Uniti ed in Italia*. Venezia: Tip. dell'Istituto Industriali, 1906. Pp. 31.

87. McAvoy, Thomas T., *The Great Crisis in American Catholic History: 1895-1900*. Chicago: Henry Regney Co., 1957.

88. McLanahan, Samuel, *Our People of Foreign Speech. A Handbook Distinguishing and Describing Those in the United States Whose Native Tongue if Other than English. With Particular Reference to Religious Work Among Them*. New York: Fleming H. Revell Co., 1904. Pp. 105.

89. Moberg, David O., *The Church As a Social Institution. The Sociology of American Religion*. Englewood Cliffs, N.J.: Prentice-Hall, Inc., 1962. Pp. 569.

90. Ministero degli Affari Esteri. Commissariato Generale dell'Emigrazione, *L'Emigrazione Italiana del 1910 al 1923*. Relazione Presentata al Ministro degli Affari Esteri, 1926. Vol. I. Pp. 937.

91. Niebuhr, H. Richard, *The Social Sources of Denominationalism*. New York: Meridian Books, Inc., 1959.

92. Noce, Angelo, *Columbus Day in Colorado*. Denver: Angelo Noce Printer, 1910. Pp. 120.

93. Park, Robert E. & Herbert A. Miller, *Old World Traits Transplanted*. New York: Harper & Brothers, 1921.

94. Parsons, Anne, *Belief, Magic and Anomie. Essays in Psychological Anthropology*. The Free Press, 1969. Pp. 392.

95. Pellegrini, Angelo, *Americans by Choice*. New York: Macmillan, 1956.

96. Pisani, Lawrence F., *The Italian in America*. New York: Exposition Press, 1957.

97. Preziosi, Giovanni, *Gl' Italiani negli Stati Uniti del Nord*. Milano, 1909.

98. Protestant Episcopal Church in the U.S.A. Domestic and Foreign Missionary Society. *Neighbors, Studies in Immigration From the Standpoint of the Episcopal Church*. New York, 1920. Pp. 246.

99. Riis, Jacob, *How the Other Half Lives*. New York: Sagamore Press, Inc., 1957.

100. Riis, Jacob, *The Battle in the Slum*. New York: The Macmillan Co., 1912.

101. Rizzato, Remo, *L'Apostolo degli Emigrati, Mons. Giovanni Battista Scalabrini*. Providence: Service-Plus Press, 1946. Pp. 128.

102. Rizzato, Remo, *Figure di Missionari Scalabrini*. New York: D'Aleri's Press, 1948. Pp. 122.

103. Rolle, Andrew F., *The Immigrant Upraised. Italian Adventures and Colonists in an Expanding America*. Norman, Okla.: Oklahoma University Press, 1968. Pp. 350.

104. Rose, Philip M., *The Italians in America*. New York: George H. Doran & Co., 1922. Pp. 155.

105. *Sadliers' Catholic Directory, Almanac and Ordo for the Year of Our Lord 1870 with a Full Report of the Various Dioceses in the United and British North America and a List of the Archbishops, Bishops and Priests in Ireland*. New York: D. & J. Sadlier & Co., 1870. No. 31.

106. Sartorio, Enrico C., *Social and Religious Life of Italians in America*. Boston: Christopher Publishing House, 1918. Pp. 149.

107. Sassi, Constantino, *Parrocchia della Madonna di Pompei in New York. Notizie storiche dei primi cinquanti anni dalla sua fondazione: 1892-1942*. Rome: Tip. Santa Lucia, 1946. Pp. 102.

108. *Schema Decretorum Concilii Plenarii Baltimorensis Tertii*. Baltimore: 1884. Pp. 250.

109. Schiavo, Giovanni, *Italian-American History, Vol. II: The Italian Contribution to the Catholic Church in America*. New York: Vigo Press, 1949. Pp. 1056, with 44 illustrations.

110. Sharp, John K., *History of the Diocese of Brooklyn, 1853-1953. Vol. II*. New York: Fordham University Press, 1954.

111. Smith, James Ward and Jamison, A. Leland, *Religion in American Life. Vol. 4*. Princeton, N.J.: Princeton University Press, 1961.

112. Sofia, Giovanni, *Missioni Scalabriniane in America. Monografia*. Roma: Tip. Poliglotta "C. do M.," 1939. Pp. 223.

113. Sorrentino, Giuseppe M., *Dalle Montagne Rocciose al Rio Bravo. Brevi appunti storici circa la Missione gesuitica del Nuovo Messico e Colorado negli Stati Uniti d'America*. Napoli: Federico e Ardia, 1948. Pp. 307.

114. Stark, Werner, *The Sociology of Religion. Vol. 5*. New York: Fordham University Press, 1966-72.

115. Steiner, Edward A., *The Making of a Great Race, Racial and Religious Cross-currents in the United States*. New York: F. H. Revell Co., 1929. Pp. 192.

116. Stella, Antonio, *Some Aspects of Italian Immigration to the United States*. New York, 1924.

117. Sterlocchi, Lorenzo, *Cenni Biografici di Monsignor Giovanni Battista Scalabrini, Vescovo di Piacenza*. 2a Edizione riveduta e corretta con appendice sulle Opere di Don Luigi Guanella ed il suo viaggio in America. 18 illustrazioni. Como: Scuola Tip. Casa Divina Provvidenza, 1913. Pp. 127.

118. Sullivan, James S., *One Hundred Years of Progress. A Graphic, Historical and Pictorial Account of the Catholic Church of New England. Archdiocese of Boston*. Boston: Illustrated Publishing Co., 1895.

119. Tait, Joseph W., *Some Aspects of the Dominant American Culture Upon Children of Italian Born Parents*. Clifton, N.J.: Augustus M. Kelley, 1972. Pp. 74.

120. Tomasi, S. M. & M. H. Engel, eds., *The Italian Experience in the United States*. New York: Center for Migration Studies of N.Y., Inc., 1970. Pp. 239.

121. Tomasi, Lydio F., *The Italian in America: The Progressive View, 1891-1914*. New York: Center for Migration Studies of N.Y., Inc., 1972. Pp. XII + 221.

122. Tourn, N., *I Valdesi in America*. Torino: Unione Tipografia Editrice Torinese, 1906.

123. Traverso, Edmund, *Immigration: A Study in American Values*. Boston: D. C. Heath & Co., 1964.

124. Troeltsch, Ernst, *The Social Teaching of the Christian Churches*. New York: MacMillan, 1931. 2 Vol.

125. United States Bureau of the Census, *Religious Bodies: 1926*. Washington: U.S. Government Printing Office, 1930. 2 Vol.

126. United States Bureau of the Census, *Religious Bodies: 1916*. Washington: U.S. Government Printing Office, 1919. 2 Vol.

127. Velikonja, Joseph, *Italians in the United States*. (Bibliography) Carbondale, Ill.: Southern Illinois University, 1963.

128. Villari, Luigi, *Gli Stati Uniti d'America e L'Emigrazione Italiana*. Milano: Fratelli Treves Editori, 1912.

129. Ware, Caroline F., *Greenwich Village, 1920-30*. Boston: Houghton Mifflin Company, 1935.

130. Weinberg, Abraham, *Migration and Belonging*. The Hague: Martinus Nijhoff, 1961.

131. Willcox, Walter F., ed., and Imre Ferenczi (Introd. & Notes) *International Migrations*. Vol. 1 Statistics. New York: National Bureau of Economic Research, Inc., 1929.

132. Williams, Phyllis H., *South Italian Folkways in Europe and America*. New Haven: Yale University Press, 1938.

133. Whyte, William F., *Street Corner Society*. Chicago: University of Chicago Press, 1943.

PAMPHLETS

1. Andreis, Giuseppe L., *Immigrazione e Colonizzazione Italiana negli Stati Uniti d'America*. Torino: Tipografia Solesiana, 1894. Pp. 16.

2. *Atti del primo congresso cattolico italiano dell'America del Nord tenuto nella Citta' di New York il 5 dicembre 1917*. New York: Polyglot Publishing House, 1918. Pp. 84.

3. Beccherini, Francesco, *Il Fenomeno dell'Emigrazione negli Stati Uniti d'America*. 1904. Pp. 35.

4. Bianchi, Enrico, *Guida per gli Stati Uniti. Norme e Consigli*. Genova: Tippografia C. Mascarello, 1926. Pp. 255.

5. Bove, Antonio, *Controversia circa il Proselitismo fra i Cattolici Italiani di Providence, R.I., praticato dai Protestanti Battisti*. Roma: Tip. del "Roma e Provincia," 1911. Pp. 33.

6. Bove, Antonio, *L'Ordine Figli d'Italia di Fronte alla Coscienza Cattolica. Lettera aperta alle Associazioni Italiane negli Stati Uniti*. Providence: Joseph M. Tally, 1918. Pp. 18.

7. Buonocore, O., *L'Emigrazione*. Napoli: Tip. Protosalvo, 1923. Pp. 40.

8. *Capita praecipua quae emi cardinales S.C. de Propaganda Fide censuerunt a rmis archiepiscopis et episcopis Foederatorum Statum A.S. Romae congregatis praeparanda esse pro futuro concilio*. Rome, 1883.

9. Carnaggia Medici, Luigi, *Un Profilo di Mons. Scalabrini Vescovo di Piacenza*. Estratto da *Rassegna Romana*, Quaderno 6, 1930. Pp. 17.

10. Ciaburri, Alfred, *The Story of a Parish. Our Lady of Assumption R.C. Church*. Bayonne, N.J., 1953. Pp. 78 + Illustrations.

11. Clot, Alberto, *Guida e consigli per gli emigranti negli Stati Uniti e nel Canada*. New York: American Waldersian Aid Society, 1913. Pp. 64.

12. Committee of the Golden Jubilee. *Santa Maria Addolorata Parish: 50th Anniversary 1903-1953*. Chicago, 1953.

13. Committee for the 50th Anniversary of St. Bartholomew's Parish. *Golden Jubilee. 50th Anniversary 1907-1957*. Providence: St. Bartholomew's Parish. Pp. 206.

14. Cosenza, Michael A., *Our Lady of Pompei in Greenwich Village. History of the Parish, 1892-1967 and St. Frances Xavier Cabrini's Story*. New York: Church of O.L. of Pompei, 25 Carmine Street, 1967. Pp. 34.

15. Criscuolo, Luigi, *Fifth Columnists and Their Friends in and out of Congress, with my particular respect to Emanuel Celler, M.C., Distinguished member of the New York Bar: an open letter to the members of the 77th Congress*. New York, 1942. n.p.

16. De Concilio, Gennaro, *Sullo Stato Religioso degli Italiani negli Stati Uniti d'America*. New York: Tipografia J.H. Carbone, 1888. Pp. 32.

17. Desmond, H. J., *The Neglected Italians. A Memorial to the Italian Hierarchy*. Milwaukee: The Milwaukee Citizen, 1900. Pp. 11.

18. Di Cenzo, George, *St. Anthony's Church 50th Anniversary 1904-1954*. New Haven, 1954.

19. *Eco delle feste giubilari pel XXV° Anniversario della Missione Italiana del S. Cuore in Boston, Mass., 25-26-27 Gennaio 1914*. Firenze: Tipografia Barbera, Alfani & Venturi Proprietari, 1914. Pp. 78.

20. Gillis, James M., *Common Sense of Immigration*. New York: The Palist, 1924. Pp. 23.

21. Hall, Prescott, F., *The Future of American Ideals*. New York: Publications of the Immigration Restriction League No. 58 (reprinted from The North American Review, January, 1912). Pp. 77.

22. Holy Rosary Parish. *Golden Jubilee 1913-1963*. Washington, D.C.: Holy Rosary Church, 1963.

23. Holy Rosary Parish. *Golden Jubilee, 1942*. Kansas City, Mo., 1942.

24. Lega Nazionale "Pro Emigrante"—Segretariato per gli emigranti transoceanics Dell'Italia Meridionale—Napoli. *Relazione e Dati Statistici, Anno 1912-1921*. Napoli: Stab. Tip. Gennaro Cozzolino, 1922. Pp. 39.

25. Lemke, W. J., ed., *The Story of Tontitown, Arkansas*. Fayetteville, Arkansas, Washington County Historical Society, 1963. Pp. 36.

26. Leonhard, Theo., "DeWitt Memorial Church. German Branch," in New York City Mission and Tract Society. *Work in New York*. 72nd Annual Report, 1899.

27. Levin, Jordan, *Our Lady of Pompei Parish*. Chicago: Department of Urban Renewal, 1963. Pp. 8 (mimeographed).

28. Maffi, Pietro, *La Madre Francesca S. Cabrini. Commenorazione.* Torino: Libreria Editrice Internazionale, 1919. Pp. 20.

29. *Minutes of the IV Annual Conference of the Most Rev. Archbishops of the United States. Chicago, Sept. 12, 1893.*

30. Nasalli, Giovanni Battista, Vescovo di Gubbio. *Commemorazione di Mons. Giovanni Battista Scalabrini.* Piacenza: Tip. F. Solari di G. Tononi, 1909. Pp. 27.

31. *Note di Cranaca sull'origine e progroesso della Chiesa di S. Antonio, 151 Sullivan St., New York.* Napoli: Tip. Pontificia N. D'Auria, 1925.

32. *Our Lady of Pompeii Church, Golden Jubilee, 1911-1961.* Chicago: Our Lady of Pompeii, 1961.

33. Palmieri, Aurelio, *Il grave problema religioso italiano negli Stati Uniti.* Firenze: Editrice Fiorentina, 1921.

34. Parolin, Pio, *Ricordo del venticinquesimo Anno della Fondazione della Chiesa di San Pietro in Syracuse, N.Y.* Syracuse: Fulco Publishing Co., 1920. Pp. 58.

35. Pisani, Lawrence and Paul Falcigno, "St. Michael's of New Haven: A History of a National Parish," in *75th Anniversary.* New Haven, 1965.

36. Pisani, Pietro, *L'Emigrazione, Avvertimenti, Consigli agli Emigranti.* Firenze: Ufficio Centrale dell'Unione Popolare fre i Cattolici d' Italia, 1907. Pp. 82.

37. Pizzoglio, William, *Fourtieth Anniversary 1927-1967. St. Anthony's Church of Everett.* Everett, Mass., 1967. Pp. 30.

38. Pizzoglio, William, *St. Mary of Mt. Carmel Church, Utica, N.Y., 1896-1936.* Pp. 64.

39. Protestant Episcopal Church in the U.S.A.—Province of New England: Committee on the Various Races. *Report.* Boston, 1915. Pp. 14.

40. *Publications of the Immigration Restriction League. No. 18.* (March-July 1897).

41. St. Joachim's Church. *May God Bless Your Jubilee: 1905-1930.* New York: St. Joachim's Church, 1930. Pp. 36.

42. St. Tarcisius Church. *50th Anniversary 1907-1957.* Framingham, Mass., 1957.

43. Shriver, William P., *At Work with the Italians.* New York: Missionary Education Movement of the United States and Canada, 1917. Pp. 37.

44. *La Societa' San Raffaele per la protezione degli immigrati Italiani in Boston. Monografia per l'esposizione di Milano in occasione del'apertura del Sempione.* New York: Tip. V. Ciocia, 1906. Pp. 96.

45. Societa' Dei Missionari di Emigrazione di Sant' Antonio di Padova. *Relazione dell'Operato dalla Societa' Dei Missionari di S. Antonio di Padova nell'Anno 1914.* Presentata al Regio Commissariato dell'Emigrazione. Roma: Fava, 1915. Pp. 25.

46. *Souvenir History of Transfiguration Parish—Mott Street, New York, 1827-1897.* 1897. Pp. 44.

47. Trione, Stefano, *L'emigrazione e l'Opera di Don Bosco nelle Americhe.* San Benigno Canavese: Scuola Tipografia Don Bosco, 1914. Pp. 24.

48. *Tu es Petrus—Dedication of Saint Peter's Church—September 18, 1955.* Syracuse, 1955. Pp. 74.

49. Turchi, Ottavio, *Parole di Elogio Nelle Funebri Onoranze Solenni di Trigesima rese dalle Missionarie del S. Cuore di Gesu' alla loro Amatissima Fondatrice e Superiora Generale M. Francesca Saverio Cabrini il 24 Gennaio 1918.* Roma: Scuole Tipografica Salesiana, 1918. Pp. 18.

50. Vicentini, Domenico, *L'Apostolo degli Italiani emigrati nelle Americhe ossia Mons. Scalabrini e l'Istituto dei Suoi Missionari.* Piacenza: Tipografia Editrice A. Del Maino, 1909. Pp. 80.

51. Villeneuve, A., *Les Estats—Unis d'Amerique et l'emigration. Extrait du XXme Siecle,* Juillet—Aout 1891. Pp. VI, 53.

52. Zarrilli, Rev. J., D.D., Ph.D., *A Prayerful Appeal to the American Hierarchy in Behalf of the Italian Catholic Cause in the United States.* Two Harbors, Minn., 1924. Pp. 26.

ARTICLES

1. Adams, Charlotte, "Italians Life in New York," *Harper's Magazine*, 62 (April, 1881), 676-84.

2. "America's Interest in the Education of Italian Children," *Review of Reviews*, 36 (1907), 375-376.

3. Aydelotte, William O., "Quantification in History," *American Historial Review*, 71 (1966), 803-25.

4. Bandini, Albert R., "Concerning the Italian Problem," *Ecclesiastical Review*, 62 (1920), 278-285.

5. Bandini, Pietro, "Origine della Colonia Italiana di Tontitown nell'Arkansas," *Bollettino dell'Emigrazione*, 1 (1903), 61-62.

6. Bennett, Alice, "The Italian as a Farmer," *Charities and the Commons*, (Oct. 3, 1908), 57-60.

7. Bennett, Alice, "Italians as Farmers and Fruit-growers," *Outlook*, 90 (Sept. 12, 1908), 87-88.

8. Bennett, Alice, "Italian-American Farmers," *The Survey*, XXII, (May, 1909), 172-175.

9. Betts, Lillian, "The Italian in New York," *University Settlement Studies*, 1 (1905-06), 90-105.

10. Boutet, Federigo, "Gli Istituti di Patronato dell'emigrazione italiana negli Stati Uniti," *L'Italia Coloniale*, Anno 4, 1 (June 1903), 574-580.

11. Breton, Raymond, "Institutional Completeness of Ethnic Communities and the Personal Relations of Immigrants," *The American Journal of Sociology*, 70, 2, (1964), 193-205.

12. Brissenden, Paul, *The I.W.W., A Study of American Syndacalism*, 43 (New York 1957).

13. Broom, Leonard and John Kitsuse, "The Validation of Acculturation: A Condition of Ethnic Assimilation," *American Anthropologist*, LVII, (1955), 44-48.

14. Broom, Leonard, et al., "Acculturation: An Explanatory Formulation," *American Anthropologist*, LVI (1954), 937-1002.

15. Browne, Henry J., "The 'Italian Problem' In the Catholic Church of the United States 1880-1900," *Historical Records & Studies, U.S. Catholic History Society*, XXXV (1946) 46-73.

16. Budenz, Louis, "A survey of Conditions in 'Dago Hill,' St. Louis," *Central Blatt and Social Justice*, 8 (1915) 126-128.

17. Campisi, Peter A., "Ethnic Family Patterns: The Italian Family in the United States," *American Sociological Review*, XXIII (May, 1948), 367-73.

18. Capra, Giuseppe, "L'opera dei Padri Francescani negli Stati Uniti d'America," *Italica Gens*, VII, 1-6 (Gen.-Giugno, 1916), 39-56.

19. Capra, Giuseppe, "I Padri Scalabriniani nell'America del Nord," *Italica Gens*, (Gennaio-Febbrario, 1916), 1-14.

20. Capra, Giuseppe, "Le scuole in America," *Italica Gens*, VII, (1916), 117-133.

21. Carr, John F., "The Coming of the Italians," *Outlook*, 82 (Feb. 1906), 419-31.

22. Carr, John F., "The Italians in the U.S.," *World's Work*, (1904), 5393-5404.

23. "Catholic Italian Losses," *Literary Digest*, 47, (October 11, 1913), 636.

24. Ciuffoletti, Manlio, "Importanza sociale delle parrocchie italiane in America," *L'Emigrato Italiano*, XVIII, 4 (Ott.-Dic., 1924), 1-6.

25. "La colonizzazione italiana negli Stati Uniti," *L'Italia Coloniale*, 5, 2 (Aug.-Sept., 1904), 146-149.

26. Conry, J. P., "Social Organization of Italian Catholics," *Catholic World*, CXIV (Oct., 1921), 35.

27. Cornelio, A. M., "L'Emigrazione Italiana e l'abate Villeneuve," *La Rassegna Nazionale*, LXVII (16 Sett., 1892), 241-258.

28. Corsi, Edward, "Italian Immigrants and Their Children," *Annals of American Academy of Political and Social Science*, 233 (Sept., 1942), 100-106.

29. Covello, Leonard, "Cultural Assimilation and the Church," *Religious Education Magazine*, 39 (July-August, 1944).

30. Creel, George, "Poisoners of Public Opinion," *Harper's Weekly*, LIX (Nov. 14, 1914), 465.

31. Criscuolo, Luigi, "*Il Mondo* and the Mercenaries of Karl Marx & Co.; Complimentary supplement for the readers of *Il Mondo* for Febr. 1942; a reply to the leading article in that issue entitled: "Luigi Criscuolo, a fascist in citizen's disguise," (New York, 1942) n.p. Clipping, ACMS.

32. Cunningham, George R., "The Italian, a Hindrance to White Solidarity in Louisiana, 1890-1898," *Journal of Negro History*, L (January, 1965), 22-35.

33. DeBiasi, Agostino, "The Artificial Change of Nationality," *Il Carroccio* 4, (April, 1916), 220-21.

34. DeBiasi, Agostino, "Le relazioni degli Italiani verso la terra d'origine e verso quella d'emigrazione," *Il Carroccio*, 1, (January, 1916), 1-15.

35. DeBiasi, Agostino, "Il Sacerdote dell'Italianita: Roberto Biasotti," *Il Carroccio*, XII, 1 (Luglio, 1926), 66-67.

36. DeBiasi, Agostino, "Dio e Patria," *Il Carroccio*, XXIX, 1, (January, 1929), 118-120.

37. De Ciampis, Mario, "Note sul movimento socialista tra gli emigrati italiani negli U.S.A. (1890-1921)," *Cronache Meridionali* (Napoli), 6, 4 (April, 1959), 255-273.

38. Depres, Leo A., "Anthropological Theory, cultural pluralism, and the study of complex societies," *Current Anthropology*, 9, 1, 3-26.

39. Des Planches, E. Mayor, "Gli Italiani in California," *Bollettino di Emigrazione*, (Febraio, 1904).

40. Di Domenica, A., "The Sons of Italy in America," *Missionary Review of the World*, 41 (March, 1918), 189-195.

41. Di Giura, G. Favoino, "La Difesa della nostra nazionalita.' Il Vescovo Walsh e le suole di Trenton," *Il Carroccio*, IX, 10 (Ottobre, 1923), 394-397.

42. Di Palma di Castiglione, G. E., "Dove possono andare gli Italiani immigranti negli Stati Uniti," *Bollettino Dell'Emigrazione*, 18 (1909), 1933-1956.

43. Di Palma di Castiglione, G. E., "Italian Immigration to the United States 1901-04," *American Journal of Sociology*, 11 (Sept., 1905), 183-206.

44. Dubofsky, Melvyn, "Organized Labor and the Immigrant in New York City, 1900-1918," *Labor History*, (Spring, 1961), 182-201.

45. Dubofsky, Melvyn, "Success and Failure of Socialism in New York City, 1900-1918: A Case Study," *Labor History*, 9, 3 (Fall, 1968), 361-375.

46. Durland, Kellog & Louis Sessa, "The Italian Invasion of the Ghetto," *University Settlement Studies Quarterly*, 1 (October, 1905 - January, 1906), 106-107.

47. Ellis, J. T., "A Guide to the Baltimore Cathedral Archives," *Catholic Historical Review*, XXXII (Oct., 1946), 34-1360.

48. Farrell, John T., "Archbishop Ireland and Manifest Destiny," *Catholic Historical Review*, XXXIII (Oct., 1947), 269-301.

49. Fava, Saverio, "Le Colonie Agricole Italiane Nell'Americana Del Nord," *Nuova Antologia*, 197 (Oct. 16, 1904), 462-468.

50. "Fede e Patria," *Il Progresso Italo-Americano*, XXV, 167 (13 Luglio, 1904), 7.

51. Fenton, Edwin, "Italians in the Labor Movement," *Pennsylvania History*, 26, 2 (April, 1959), 133-148.

52. Ferrante, G., "Chiese e Scuole Parrocchiali Italiane," *Gli Italiani negli Stati Unite d'America*, New York: Italiana American Directory Co., 1906. Pp. 89-94.

53. Ferraris, Luigi Vittorio, "L'assassinio di Umberto I e gli Anarchici di Paterson," *Rassegna Storica del Risorgimento*, 50 (March, 1968), 47-64.

54. Foerster, Robert F., "A Statistical Survey of Italian Immigration," *Quarterly Journal of Economics, 23 (November, 1908), 66-103.*

55. Franklin, Lawrence, "The Italian in America: What He Has Been, What He Shall Be," *Catholic World*, 71 (April, 1900), 67-80.

56. Freschi, John J., "The Loyalty of the Citizens of Italian Origin," *Il Carroccio*, 3, (March, 1916), 150-4.

57. Frost, (Dr. Gustavo Tosti), "Il problema Italiano negli Stati Uniti," *Tribuna*, (19 Ottobre, 1908).

58. Fusco, Nicola, "A Catholic Priest's Work," *Il Carroccio*, X, 9 (Settembre, 1924), 281-284.

59. Gambera, G., "Il Clero italiano in America e l'assistenza degli emigrati italiani," *Italica Gens*, 11, 5, (1911), 217-225.

60. Gertrude, M. Agnes, "Italian Immigration into Philadelphia," *American Catholic Historical Society of Philadelphia Records*, 58 (1947), 133-143, 189-208, 256-267.

61. Gilkey, George R., "The United States and Italy: Migration and Repatriation," *The Journal of Developing Areas* (1967).

62. "La guida del Clero Italiano di New York," *Il Carroccio*, 11, (Dicembre, 1915), 76-77.

63. Halpern, B., "Ethnic and Religious Minorities: Subcultures and Sub-Communities," *Jewish Social Studies*, XXVII (January, 1965), 37-44.

64. Hamilton, C. V., "Conflict, Race and System Transformation in the United States," *Journal of International Affairs*, 1, (1969), 106-118.

65. Hang, Marie R., "Social and Cultural Pluralism as a Concept in Social System Analysis," *The American Journal of Sociology*, 73, 294-304.

66. Hill, Howard C., "The Americanization Movement," *American Journal of Sociology*, XXIV, (1919), 609-42.

67. Hodges, Leroy, "The Church and the Immigrants: A Record of Failure and the Remedy," *The Missionary Review of the World*, XXV (1912), 167-72.

68. Howerth, I. W., "Are the Italians a Dangerous Class," *The Charities Review*, IV (Nov., 1894), 17-40.

69. "Italian Festivals in New York," *The Chautauqua*, 34 (Dec., 1901).

70. "Italian Immigration," *America*, 11 (1910), n. 24 (March 26, 1910) and following.

71. "Italians Killed in New Orleans" *Nation*, 52 (April 9, 1891), 291.

72. Jones, Frank E., "A Sociological Perspective on Immigrant Adjustment," *Social Forces*, 35, 1 (Oct., 1956), 39-47.

73. Jotodai, T. T., "Migrant Status and Church Attendance," *Social Forces*, XLII, (Dicembre, 1964), 241-248.

74. Lee, Everett S., "A Theory of Migration," *Demography*, III, (1966), 47-57.

75. Lee, O. J., "Religion Among Ethnic and Racial Minorities," *The Annals of the American Political and Social Science Academy*. 332, (1960), 113-114.

76. Leinenweber, Charles, "The American Socialist Party and the 'New' Immigrants," *Science and Society*, XXXII (Winter, 1968), 1-25.

77. Mack, Raymond W. and Richard C. Snyder, "The Analysis of Social Conflict: Toward an Overview and Synthesis," *The Journal of Conflict Resolution*, 1 (1957), 212-248.

78. "The Mafia Lynching," *New Review*, (May, 1891).

79. Marcson, Simon, "The Control of Ethnic Conflict," *Social Forces*, 24, 152.

80. Marraro, Howard R., "The Closing of the American Diplomatic Mission to the Vatican and the Efforts to Revive it, 1868-1870," *Catholic Historical Review*, 33 (1948), 423-447.

81. Marraro, Howard R., "Italians in New York in the Eighteen-fifties," *New York History*, 30 (1949), 181-203, 276-303.

82. Marraro, Howard R., "Rome and the Catholic Church in the Eighteen Century Magazines," *Catholic Historical Review*, 32 (1946), 157-189.

83. Meng, John J., "Cahenslyism: The First Stage, 1883-1891," *Catholic Historical Review*, XXXI, (January, 1946), 389-413.

84. Meng, John J., "Cahenslyism: The Second Chapter, 1891-1910," *Catholic Historical Review*, XXXII, (October, 1946), 302-340.

85. Merlino, S., "Italian Immigrants and their Enslavement," *Forum*, 15 (April, 1893), 183-190.

86. "Milizia di Dio e della Patria," *Il Carroccio*, XXXV, 2 (April, 1932), 130-132; 3 (July, 1932), 231-234; 4 (December, 1932), 310-14.

87. "Le Missionarie del S. Cuore in America," *Italica Gens*, 1, 3, (1910), 119-124.

88. Moseley, Daisy H., "The Catholic Social Worker in an Italian District," *Catholic World*, 114 (February, 1922), 618-628.

89. Moss, Leonard and Stephen C. Cappannari, "Patterns of Kinship, Comparaggio and Community in a South Italian Village," *Anthropology Quarterly*, XXXIII (Jan. 1960), 24-32. "The South Italian Family: Literature & Observation," *Human Organization*, XVIII (Sept. 1959), 35-41.

90. "La Mostra degli Italiani all'estero, all'Esposizione internazionale di Milano del 1906 (Relazione del Professore B. Frescura, Segretario Generale della Giuria," *Bollettino dell'Emigrazione*, 18 (1907), 129.

91. Murray, Nicholas Russell, "Independence Marks a Feast Day," *Morning Advocate* (March 22, 1953).

92. Myles, Muredach, "An Experiment in City Home Missions," *Extension Magazine* (April, 1923) 35-45 and 62.

93. Noa, T. L., "Religion and Good Citizenship" *Vital Speeches*, 19 (October 15, 1952), 29-32.

94. Pacia, Iacobus, S.A.C., "De Celebrationibus apud Sanctuarium B.M.V. de Monte Carmelo in New York," *Acta Societatis Apostalatus Catholici*, 11, 12 (19 Octobris, 1954), 548-550.

95. Palmieri, Aurelio, P., "Il Clero italiano negli Stati Uniti," *La Vita Italiana*, VIII, 36 (February, 1920), 113-127.

96. Palmieri, F. Aurelio., "Italian Protestantism in the United States," *Catholic World*, v. 107, 638 (May, 1918), 177-189.

97. Parisi, L. and others "Le colonie italiane negli Stati Uniti" *L'Italia coloniale*, anno 3 v. 2 (July, 1902), 53-60; (Aug. 1902), 184-195; (Sept. 1902), 286-304; (Nov. 1902), 500-509; (Dec. 1902), 645-656; anno 4 v. 1 (Feb. 1903), 194-198; (March, 1903), 302-309. Anno 3 v. 1 (Jan-Feb. 1902), 48-58.

98. "Parrocchia del Sacro Cuore in Denver," *Lettere Edificanti Provincia Napolitana*, ser. 8, n. 1 (1899), pp. 55-58.

99. Parsons, Talcott, "Racial and Religious Differences as Factors in Group Tensions," in Bryson, Finkelstein and McIver, eds., *Approaches to National Unity: Fifth Symposium of the Conference on Science, Philosophy and Religion*. New York: Harper & Brothers, 1945.

100. Pasteris, Emiliano, "Le scuole italiane agli Stati Uniti e al Canada," *Pro Emigrante*, Anno III, 1909, 21-22.

101. Pecorini, Alberto, "The Italians in the United States," *The Forum*, XLV (Jan., 1911), 15-29.

102. Peterson, W., "A General Typology of Migration," *American Sociological Review*, XXIII (1958), 256-66.

103. Un Piemontese, "L'avvenire degli Italiani negli Stati Uniti d'America," *La Rassegna Nazionale*, CXLIII, (1 Giugno, 1905), 464-488.

104. Pisani, P., "Asili infantili e orfanatrofi pei figli di Italiani a New York," *Italica Gens* 1, 7-8, 1910, 307-15.

105. Pisani, Lawrence F., "Oldest Italian Church in Connecticut, St. Michael's Marks 75th Anniversary," *New Haven Register* (May 16, 1965), 5.

106. Popper, S. H., "New Tensions in Old Newark," *Proceedings of the New Jersey Historical Society*, 70 (April, 1952), 122.

107. Porcelli, P. Clemente, "I Francescani Italiani negli Stati Uniti i gli Emigrati," *Il Carroccio*, XXI, 3 (Marzo, 1925), 432-434.

108. Prat, F., "Gli Italiani negli Stati Uniti e specialmente nello Stato di New York," *Bollettino dell'Emigrazione*, 2, 1902, 14-41.

109. Preziosi, "Le scuole italiane negli Stati Unite del Nord e la scuola parrocchiale del Buon Consiglio di Philadelphia," *Rivista Internazionale* (Settembre, 1906).

110. Przudzik, Joseph, "Schism in America," *Homiletic and Pastoral Review*, 1947, 896-900; 982-988.

111. Ravaioli, A., "La Colonizzazione Agricola Negli Stati Uniti," *Bollettino dell'Emigrazione*, Anno 1904, n. 4, 3-49.

112. "Religion of Lucky Pieces, Witches and the Evil Eye," *World Outlook*, v. 3 (October, 1917), 24-25.

113. Reynolds, Minnie J., "The Italian and His Church at Home," *Missionary Review of the World*, N.S. XX (August, 1907), 607-610.

114. "Rivoltellate contro un prete," *Bolletino della Sera*, XI, 3197 (New York, Martedi 18, Agosto 1908), 1.

115. Roselli, Bruno, "Our Italian Immigrants; Their Racial Backgrounds" p. 96-121 in H. P. Fairchild (ed.,) *Immigrant Backgrounds.* New York: Wiley & Sons, 1927.

116. Rossi, Adolfo, "Per La Tutela Degli Italiani Negli Stati Uniti," *Bollettino dell'Emigrazione*, anno 1904, no. 16, 82-87.

117. Rossi, Adolfo, "Italian Farmers in the South," *Survey*, XV (Dec. 2, 1905).

118. Russo, N., "The Origin and Progress of Our Italian Mission in New York." Letter dated, Jan. 29, 1896, *Woodstock Letters*, v. 25 (1896), pp. 135-143.

119. Santini, Luigi, "Alessandro Gavazzi e l'emigrazione politico-religiosa in Inghilterra e negli Stati Uniti nel decennio 1849-1859," *Rassegna Storica del Risorgimento* (Apr.-Sept., 1954).

120. Schriver, William Payne, "Evangelical Movement Among Italians," *Missionary Review*, 58 (Jan., 1935), 5.

121. Sheridan, Frank Joseph, "Italian, Slavic and Hungarian unskilled Immigrant Laborers in the U.S.," *U.S. Bureau of Labor Bulletin*, 15 (Sept., 1907), 403-486.

122. Shipman, Andrew J., "Our Italian Greek Catholics. A Remnant of the Oriental Church in Italy and America," *The Messenger* (February, 1906), 152-168.

123. Smith, T. L., "New Approaches to the History of Immigration in Twentieth-Century America," *American Historical Review*, LXXI, 4 (June, 1966), 1265-1279.

124. Smith, L. M., "The Clergy: Authority Structure, Ideology, Migration," *American Sociological Review*, XVIII, 3 (June, 1953), 242-48.

125. "La Societa' di San Raffaele Tedesca e l'Opera di Mons. Scalabrini per l'emigrazione italiana in America," *Italica Gens*, 1, 2, (1910), 59-65.

126. Speranza, Gino C., "The Italian Forman as a Social Agent," *Charities*, XI (July 4, 1903), 26-28.

127. Speranza, Gino C., "Political Representation of Italo-American colonies in the Italian Parliament," *Charities*, 15 (1906), 521-522.

128. Syrius, "Fede e Patria: L'opera di P. Alfonso da Serino," *Il Carroccio*, Anno XIII, 6 (Giugno, 1927), 633-634.

129. Tolino, John V., "Solving the Italian Problem," *American Ecclesiastical Review* (Sept., 1938; Jan., 1939; Sept., 1939).

130. Tosti, Gustavo, "The Agricultural Possibilities of Italian Immigration," *Charities*, 12, (May 7, 1904), 472-476.

131. Tosti, Gustavo, "Italy's Attitude Toward Her Emigrants," *North American Review*, 180 (May, 1905) 720-726.

132. van den Berghe, Pierre L., "Dialectic and Functionalisms: Toward a Theoretical Synthesis," *American Journal of Sociology*, 28, 695-705.

133. "Il Vaticano e la Patria," *Il Carroccio*, 1, 3 (Aprile, 1915), 53-54.

134. Vecoli, Rudolph J., "Prelate and Peasants. Italian Immigrants and the Catholic Church," *Journal of Social History* (Spring, 1969), 217-268. ["Contadini in Chicago: A Critique of the Uprooted," *Journal of American History*, LIV (1964), 404-17.]

135. Vidussi, M., "Cenni storici sulle origini della Chiesa del Carmine in New York," *Regina degli Apostoli*, VII (1927), 122-124.

136. Villari, Luigi, "L'Emigrazione Italiana Negli Stati Uniti d'America," *Nuova Antologia*, 226 (Sept. 16, 1909), 294-311.

137. Villari, Luigi, "Gli Italiani nell Distretto Consolare di New Orleans (Stati Uniti d'America)," *Bollettino Dell' Emigrazione*, 20, (1907), 3-42.

138. Villari, Luigi, "L'Opinione Pubblica Americana i Nostri Emigrati" *Nuova Antologia*, 148 (Aug. 1, 1910), 497-517.

139. Volpe Landi, Giovanni Battista, "Sulla Associazione detta di San Raffaele per la protezione degli immigrati italiani negli Stati Uniti," *Bollettino del'Emigrazione*, 1, (1903), 56-58.

140. Walsh, James J., "An Apostle of the Italians," *Catholic World*, 107, n. 637, (April, 1918), 64-71.

141. Walsh, James J., "The Irish and the Italians," *Il Carroccio*, Anno XIV, 1, (Gennaio, 1928) 114-116.

142. Whyte, William Foote, "Sicilian peasant society," *American Anthropologist*, n. 5, 46: 65-74.

143. Wickham, John E., "A Missionary Band of Diocesan Priests," *American Ecclesiastical Review*, LXVI (Jan., 1922) 1.

144. Willcox, W. F., "The Distribution of Immigrants in the U.S.," *Quarterly Journal of Economics*, 20: 523 1906.

145. Williams, Robin M., Jr., "Religion, Value Orientations, and Intergroup Conflict," in Eleanor E. Maccoby, Theodore M. Newcomb & Eugene L. Hartley, eds., *Readings in Social Psychology*. New York: Holt, Rinehart & Winston, 1958, pp. 647-53.

146. Wright, Frederick H., "The Italian in America," *The Missionary Review of the World*, XXX, 3 (old Series) (March, 1907), 196-198.

UNPUBLISHED DISSERTATIONS

1. Berman, Hyman, "Education for Work and Labor Solidarity: The Immigrant Miners and Radicalism on the Mesabi Range." Unpublished manuscript, Minnesota Historical Society.

2. Brenner, M. Rebecca, "Church Going Among Our Italian Immigrants." Unpublished M.A. Thesis, University of Notre Dame, 1944.

3. Fenton, Edwin, "Immigrants and Unions. A Case Study: Italians and American Labor, 1870-1920." Unpublished Ph.D. dissertation, Harvard University, 1957.

4. Galus, Walter J., "History of the Catholic Italians in Saint Louis." Unpublished M.A. thesis. Saint Louis University, 1936.

5. Giannotta, Rosario, "Contribution of Italians to the Development of American Culture in the Eighteenth Century." Unpublished M.A. thesis, St. John's University, New York, 1942.

6. Hinrichsen, Carl Derivaux, "The History of the Diocese of Newark, 1873-1901." Unpublished Ph.D. dissertation for the Catholic University of America, 1962.

7. Femminella, Francis X., "Ethnicity and Ego Identity." Unpublished Ph.D. dissertation, New York University, 1968.

8. Hoffman, George Joseph, "Catholic Immigrant Aid Societies in New York City From 1880 to 1920." Unpublished Ph.D. dissertation, St. John's University, 1947.

9. Mondello, Salvatore, "The Italian Immigrant in Urban America, 1880-1920: As reported in Contemporary Periodical Press." Unpublished Ph.D. dissertation, New York University, 1960.

10. Murphy, John F., "An Analysis of the Attitudes of American Catholics Toward the Immigrants and the Negro 1825-1928." Unpublished Ph.D. dissertation, Catholic University, 1940.

11. O'Leary, Humphrey M., C.SS.R., "The Missionary of Emigrants." Unpublished Ph.D. dissertation, Pontifical Athenaeum Angelicum, Rome.

12. Iorizzo, Luciano J., "Italian Immigration and the Impact of the Padrone System." Unpublished Ph.D. dissertation, Syracuse University, 1966.

13. Perrotta, Christofer, "Catholic Care of the Italian Immigrant in the United States." Unpublished M.A. thesis, Catholic University, 1925.

14. Poblete, Renato, "Puerto Rican Sectarianism and the Quest for Community." Unpublished M.A. thesis, Fordham University, New York, 1959.

15. Powell, Frank Evans, Jr., "The Italian as a Substitute for the Negro on the Southern Cotton Plantation." Unpublished M.A. thesis Tulane University, 1903.

16. Russo, Nicholas J., "The Religious Acculturation of the Italians in New York City." Unpublished Ph.D. dissertation, St. John's University, New York, 1968.

17. Sirvaitis, O.P., "Religious Folkways in Lithuania and Their Conservation Among the Lithuanian Immigrants in the U.S." Unpublished Ph.D. dissertation, Catholic University, 1952.

18. Sullivan, Edwin V., "An Annotated Copy of the Diary of Bishop James Roosevelt Bayley, First Bishop of Newark, New Jersey, 1853-1872." Unpublished Ph.D. dissertation, University of Ottawa, 1956.

19. Vecoli, Rudolph J., "Chicago's Italians Prior to World War I: A Study of Their Social and Economic Adjustment." Unpublished Ph.D. dissertation, University of Wisconsin, 1963.